DON'T FORGET TO WRITE

826 Valencia is extremely grateful to the many people who helped us with this book, especially to our tireless tutors and to the contributing authors who were so generous with their time and ideas. Thanks, also, to: Karen Koch, J. Robert Lennon, Jonathan Lethem, Paul Madonna, Naomi Shihab Nye, Gabriel Roth, Anhinga Press, Doubleday/Random House, the International Reading Association, the National Council of Teachers of English, and—in hopes that they will adopt us—Washington Mutual.

Extra-special thanks go to our teacher brain trust of Lisa Morehouse, Bita Nazarian, and Maureen Sullivan who made time in their incredibly busy schedules to pore over the manuscript and show us how to make it better. We sure are grateful.

Thanks!

Published October 2005 by 826 Valencia.

Copyright © 2005 826 Valencia.

Edited by Jenny Traig.

Special editorial attention was provided by Lisa Amick, Veronica Dakota, Eric Magnuson, Martin Nouvell, and Rebecca Winterer.

Illustrations on front cover, on pages 5, 31, 41, 85, 91, 116, 135, 155, 172, and appearing throughout as the Superteacher icon by Tony Millionaire.

Front cover illustration colored by George Slavik.

Illustrations on pages 26 and 27 by Todd Pound.

Illustrations on pages 114 and 115 by Erika Lopez.

Book design by Alvaro Villanueva.

"One Train" by Kenneth Koch, published by Alfred A. Knopf, 1994. Copyright © 1994 by Kenneth Koch. Reprinted with permission.

"Mint Snowball" by Naomi Shihab Nye, copyright © 2001 by Naomi Shihab Ney. Used by permission of Anhinga Press.

Motherless Brooklyn by Jonathan Lethem, copyright 1999 by Jonathan Lethem. Used by permission of Doubleday, a division of Random House, Inc.

Standards for the English Language Arts, by the International Reading Association and the National Council of Teachers of English, copyright 1996 by the International Reading Association and the National Council of Teachers of English. Reprinted with permission.

ISBN: 0-9770844-3-4

Printed in Canada by WestCan P.G.

DON'T FORGET TO WRITE

54 ENTHRALLING AND EFFECTIVE WRITING LESSONS FOR STUDENTS 6–18

Edited by Jenny Traig

Lesson Plans by
Steve Almond, Jonathan Ames, Christina Amini,
Julianne Balmain, Aimee Bender, Brenna Burns,
Meghan Daum, Dave Eggers, Stephen Elliott, Sophie Fels,
Daphne Gottlieb, Emily Katz, Ryan Harty, Noah Hawley,
Angela Hernandez, Abigail Jacobs, Taylor Jacobson,
Erin Jourdan, Bob Jury, Dan Kennedy, Susie Kramer,
Victoria Q. Legg, Hilary Liftin, Erika Lopez, Margaret Mason,
Molly Meng, Tom Molanphy, Erin Neeley, Amie Nenninger,
Risa Nye, Mark O'Donnell, Alvin Orloff, Julie Orringer,
Kate Pavao, Chris Perdue, Micah Pilkington, Neal Pollack,
Todd Pound, Melissa Price, Kazz Regelman, Jason Roberts,
Matthue Roth, Bonnie Schiff-Glenn, Laura Scholes,
Jon Scieszka, Sam Silverstein, J. Ryan Stradal,
Andrew Strickman, Jenny Traig, Jason Turbow,
Vendela Vida, Sarah Vowell, Doug Wilkins,
& Marcy Zipke

826
NATIONAL

CONTENTS

Middle School

High School

Appendix

AN INTRODUCTION

The first indication that this isn't the normal writing workshop is the pirate shop students have to pass through to get to the classroom. They troop by our fish theater and our tub of lard, our vat of treasures, our large selection of fake mustaches and peg legs and multicolored eye patches. They see shelves of student-authored books, 'zines, and newspapers. Then they arrive in the classroom, plop down on big velvet pillows, and look around. This doesn't look like a classroom, either. The ceiling is supported by tree trunks. There are chandeliers, colorful Persian rugs, big mahogany tables, and a cozy fabric tent whose couches beg you to curl up and read on them. The teacher appears to be wearing a wig and a feather boa. Just what is going on here?

It's just how we do things at 826 Valencia. From the beginning, our emphasis has been on fun, and there's been plenty of that. But something else happened: we helped students produce some great writing. Then we did it again. Students returned over and over and told their friends. Before long our workshops had long waiting lists.

We'd come up with a formula that worked. Teachers wrote, called, and came in, asking for ideas for their own classrooms. We got so many requests we decided it was time to put all our best ideas in one place. We compiled lesson plans from our very best workshops and our favorite authors, and you're holding the result in your hands. We hope it will help you recreate the 826 experience in your own classroom.

What makes 826 workshops special? Well, first of all, they are often completely nuts. We think play is paramount, so we use lots of props, costumes, and drama. Our tutors are invited to teach courses on anything related to writing. Sometimes it's very practical, like a workshop on writing the perfect college application essay. Sometimes it's just silly, like Writing for Pets.

Whatever the topic, it's taught by a professional working in the field. Our after-school newspaper club is advised by editors from *Salon*, *Time*, and *The San Francisco Chronicle*. Our sportswriting class is taught by real sportswriters who secure press passes that get our students into the Giants' locker room. At 826LA, the first workshop was taught by filmmaker Spike Jonze. In San Francisco, when Mi-

chael Chabon told his colleague Stephen King that he was using a piece of King's work in his Horror and Dark Fantasy class, Stephen offered to come teach the lesson himself.

We would love to be able to dispatch pros like these to your classroom too. Instead, we've done the next best thing: we asked them to write lesson plans for you. A professional screenwriter supplied our screenwriting lesson. A professional cartoonist wrote our lesson for comic book writing. Our favorite authors pitched in, too. We think the end result is like having Aimee Bender stop by to teach a class on magic realism or Sarah Vowell lead a workshop on revisions.

The whole enterprise is the classroom equivalent of hiding the good-for-you vegetables under the potato chips in the secretly nutritious casserole. We've based our activities on proven pedagogy. The students think they're having fun, and goodness knows they are, but they're also engaged in very academic endeavors. They are organizing their ideas, crafting arguments, revising their work, stating their points of view, peer editing for friends, and generally learning an awful lot about the hard work and craft of writing. They're playing, but they're also getting real experience. For two hours, they're food critics, reporters, or mad scientists, getting an idea of what it's really like to do this for a living.

And they leave with concrete proof. All of our workshops are project-based. Everyone likes to have something to show for their time, so we strive to produce something in every class, be it a chapbook, a play, or a newspaper. We know that the process of making that product is the important part, but having something to hold on to at the end is the perfect punctuation to work well done. Also, making them is incredibly satisfying and enjoyable.

We hope you'll enjoy the process, too. Supporting teachers is our first priority, and we've tried to create a book that will make your job just a little bit easier. We know that teachers are pressed for time trying to ensure content and skill requirements are met. To this end, we've made sure the lessons in this book meet the standards of the National Council of Teachers of English. We created a chart to show you (see page 196–201). Hope it helps.

If you're nearby, come pay us a visit (see page 206 for a listing of all our centers). Workshops are only a part of what we do at 826. You can learn more about our programs at www.826valencia.org. We also offer free drop-in tutoring, free writing field trips, and free in-school support. We'd love for you to come see all the excitement for yourself.

We hope you have as much fun as we have.

—*Ninive Calegari, Dave Eggers, and Jenny Traig*

HOW TO USE THIS BOOK

1. Come on in. Have a look around. We suggest you fix yourself a nice snack, then check out the table of contents to see if anything catches your eye. Bear in mind that most of the lesson plans can be adapted for other grade levels, so don't feel obligated to stick strictly to yours.

2. All of our workshops are different, so all of our lesson plans are too. Generally, they consist of an outline of the lesson for you, a handout for the students, and sometimes an example of our own students' work. We've tried to make them as user-friendly as possible.

3. To help you plan your class, we've headed each lesson plan with a time estimate. This is how long the class generally runs. In your classroom it might go slower or faster, but we've tried to ballpark it for you.

4. As much as we've tried to make things fun, we've also tried to keep things simple. A three-ring writing circus with actual trained animals and cotton candy machines would be great fun for your students, but a great big headache for you, so we've tried to keep the supplies and prep to a minimum. We've headed each lesson plan with the list of materials it requires. Most of the time this will consist of things you already have on hand. Fancier fixings are optional.

5. We encourage you to adapt these lessons to suit you and your students. These lessons were taught in an after-school environment, with students who were there by choice, so we expect they'll need some tweaking to work for you. Make them yours.

6. Sometimes you might have extra time and want to do something really, really special. When you do, look for the Superteacher bonus activity icon. Superteacher bonus activities are optional additions to the lesson plan that require a little more effort, but are guaranteed to dazzle your students.

7. In the Appendix you'll find some other tools we hope will make your life easier. Evaluation rubrics to guide grading are on pages 187–189. Student self-assessment checklists follow on pages 190–194. The National Council of Teachers of English's "Standards for the English Language Arts" is on page 195, and the chart on pages 196–201 will show you which ones each lesson plan meets.

8. Just for fun, we've included marked-up pages from authors' manuscripts on pages 181–186. These are a great way to demonstrate to your students that no one produces a perfect first draft.

9. We'd love to hear how it goes. We invite you to send us the tear-out sheet on page 207 and tell us what you think. Any suggestions? Comments? Send us your own favorite lesson plan, or samples of your students' fabulous work. We'd love to see it. Our second edition will incorporate your feedback and lessons—so send them on in! If we use your lesson, we'll send you a free book.

ELEMENTARY
LESSON PLANS

WRITING FOR PETS

by JENNY TRAIG

1 hour
Materials: One pet

This class started as a lark but quickly became one of our favorites for two good reasons: (1) anything involving pets is going to be fun; and (2) it's actually proven pedagogy. It turns out that reading to a non-judgmental audience, like a dog, is a great way to boost students' confidence and skill.

This class couldn't be simpler. We learn about writing for animals, then we do it, then we bring a pet in to listen to what we've written. The students really get into it. And, my gosh, watching a six-year-old solemnly read his story to a terrier is just about the cutest thing you'll ever see.

Because we keep getting interrupted by students who want to tell us what their dog did this one time—and because we want to hear—the discussion part takes about forty minutes.

Class begins with a brief discussion about animals and language. We explain that pets know more English than you'd think. They probably already know these words: *No. Down. Heel. Walk. Treat. Good girl/boy. Bad girl/boy.* They certainly know their names. They may even know whole sentences, like these:

"Go for a walk?"

"Who's a good girl?"

"If I told you once, I told you a thousand times: *don't drink out of the toilet.*"

We go on to say that you could build a pretty great story from any of this stuff. Drinking out of the toilet alone is subject matter enough for a whole novel.

Next, we explain that you need to be a little careful because pets don't understand abstract representation. When we say "walk," we're talking about the *idea* of a walk. But for a dog, *walk* means "We're going for a walk right now." So if you write a story about a walk, and use the world *walk* eighty times, you are going to have a very excited dog on your hands. This is sort of funny, but also sort of mean, unless you really are going to take the dog for a walk. So we advise the students to choose their words carefully.

Next we explain that pets do understand tone. In fact, they pay more attention to tone than to the actual words. If you shout *"Good kitty!"* in a scary tone, your cat will shirk and hiss. If you croon *"Stupid, stupid kitty!"* in a loving tone, she'll purr and do her I'm-a-special-girl dance. "Oh, what a stupid kitty.

Ha ha." Again, funny but kind of mean. The point is that tone matters most when you read to your pet, so we suggest students think about writing and reading in a tone that suits the material best.

Then we talk about writing for different species. Here is what we tell them. We are not sure if any of this is true, but it definitely inspires great writing:

Cats: Cats like literature more than any other species, and they enjoy it on several levels. Mostly, they enjoy napping on it. But they also enjoy being read to, especially if they can sit in your lap. They're sophisticated listeners who understand irony and dark humor. Lemony Snicket–type stories are ideal. They also like fanciful tales and stories about dictators. Most of all, cats like reading about themselves. Nothing will make your cat happier than an essay on her best qualities. Cats also enjoy writing. Put your cat on the keyboard and just see what she produces!

Dogs: Dogs generally like to read about dogs, and they like a lot of action. They do not understand metaphors or plays on words. They don't necessarily need a plot or a conclusion. A dog likes a story that's all *Go!*, all action and Frisbee chases. Dog stories are the most fun and the easiest to write. Odd as it may seem, dogs aren't too fond of shaggy dog stories—too long.

Birds: Birds only like one thing, and that's a good snack. If you want to hold a bird's interest, write about potato chips or hazelnuts. They especially enjoy hearing recipes. Whatever you write, it has to be true. You can't fool a bird. Lie all you like to a fish, but a bird knows the facts. They can see everything from their eagle-eye view. Even birds that aren't allowed out are very well-informed, because their cages are lined with newspapers.

Fish: Fish couldn't possibly be any more bored than they already are, so any story is a welcome diversion. But they especially like stories about the outside world. Since they've never been anywhere, you can make stuff up—they'll never know. Write a story about Bolivia or Sweden or Alaska. Write a fictional history of chewing gum or bicycles. Tell them what goes on, or what you wish went on, at your school. The only problem is getting them to hear what you write. But fish are expert lip-readers, so just get right in front of the glass, and don't cover your mouth while you read.

Vermin and Pests: Rats, fleas, spiders, and cockroaches may be smart and strong, but they are evil. The point of writing for vermin and pests is not to entertain but to scare them off. Write them morality tales to show them the error of their ways. All stories for these creatures should end with them getting their wagons fixed but good.

Pet Mice, Hamsters, and Guinea Pigs: Small household rodents enjoy fables, because they so often star in them. A country mouse/city mouse

tale is sure to be a hit.

For the Allergic: Allergic to animals but love writing for pets? You can write for stuffed animals instead. They're not quite as responsive as real animals, but they have much longer attention spans. Write your stuffed animal an epic story of a thousand adventures.

Finally, we distribute the handout (page 5) and go over it. Then we break for twenty minutes or so and let the students write a fabulous story for a pet. By this point our pet audience has arrived, and we spend the last thirty minutes bringing the students over one by one to read their stories. Usually, the audience consists of a borrowed dog. Cats bore easily. Guinea pigs will do in a pinch, but once one lost control of his bowels *on a student's story*, and since then we've been gun-shy.

TEN GREAT PET STORY IDEAS TO GET YOU STARTED

1. Write an extremely flattering poem about your cat. Describe her gorgeous coat, her glittering eyes, her many talents. Oh, she is a star, yes she is. She is a queen.

2. Write a heroic story featuring your dog. It could be made up (he saves a busload of kindergartners!) or true (he gets a flea shot and is very, very brave).

3. Write a movie for your pet to star in. Cats like historical dramas. Dogs like buddy pics.

4. Write your bird a research paper on the history of the doughnut.

5. Write a fairy tale in which your pet mouse/hamster/guinea pig is not the cute sidekick but the hero.

6. Scare off the bugs and rats with a tragic story of their downfall. Perhaps they meet their ruin at the hands of a vacuum cleaner or a skateboard.

7. Write a whole newspaper just for your fish. She's probably dying for some current events. She won't know if you're lying, so you can just make stuff up.

8. Write a mystery that your pet gets to solve, like "The Mystery of the Missing Treat." At the end of the story, you can help your pet find the treat, based on the clues.

9. Write a science fiction story about a future world that is run by whatever species your pet is. This is a favorite fantasy of cats.

10. If you have several pets, write a play with parts for all of them, then dress them up and try to get them to act it out.

DOES YOUR PET THINK HE'S PEOPLE?

1. Does your pet prefer people food? Even vegetables? Does he try to eat your nachos?

2. Does your pet seem embarrassed when he does something kind of dumb, like walking into the sliding glass door?

3. Does your pet enjoy wearing hats, bandanas, and little sweaters?

4. When your pet meows or barks, does it sound like a word? Like he's trying to talk?

If you answered "Yes!" to four or more questions, your pet thinks he's people! Be sure to include lots of people in your stories, because that's what your pet will relate to.

Student Work

THE MOUSE PLAY

EDELWEISS: Food! Food! Food! All you think about! Food!

EDELVERSA: Good! I like food! You should eat more!

EDELWEISS: Treats! Treats, too! All you think about! Treats!

EDELVERSA: Good! I like treats! You should eat more!

EDELWEISS: You like treats! You like food! Why not give away food? Why not give away treats?

EDELVERSA: Treats and food for me! All for me!

EDELWEISS: You leave some treats and food for me!

EDELVERSA: Hand gives much food and treats. I will save some food and treats to give away.

(*Later*)

EDELWEISS: See? Everyone's happy because you give away treats and food.

EDELVERSA: But no treats or food left for me!

EDELWEISS (*as food in hand comes through*): Here comes more!

THE END

—*Henry Cordes, 9*

HOW TO BE A DETECTIVE

by AMIE NENNINGER

2 hours

*Materials: A strange costume (and a person to wear it),
one copy of the handout packet (pages 8–11) for each student*

As a founding member of the Bluebird Detective Agency at age eight, I am well aware of the fascination kids have with mysteries. This lesson provides a fun way to introduce the necessary elements, or "usual suspects," of the mystery genre. The students practice both roles—mystery reader and writer—and learn to strike the right balance to create a fair but highly intriguing story.

Each Junior Detective receives a top-secret notebook (pages 8–11), and this provides materials for discussion and a number of activities for the kids to complete. The class begins with a general discussion about beloved mysteries and detectives. Trixie Belden, Harriet the Spy, Encyclopedia Brown, Nate the Great, and Nancy Drew always top the list. These characters all appear in engaging, clever stories, and the students are excited to hear that they are about to learn how to write an equally excellent mystery.

To warm up the detective side of the brain, the class incorporates a number of games that require an eagle eye for detail. This begins without the students' knowledge. As they enter the room, the instructor or an assistant greets them. This person is dressed oddly: skirt over pants, lots of layers, mismatched shoes, multiple watches, Band-Aid on the cheek, two pairs of glasses, a suspicious nametag (Jeremiah Fishmonger on a woman, FiFi Plendergrass on a man), and has unusual items tucked in his or her pockets. This person might also squeak or sneeze a lot, only walk backwards, or speak in an odd voice. After the class settles, that person disappears and removes all of the odd details. Then the kids take turns testing their powers of observation. What did they notice? Their notes are listed on the board.

Then the class takes turns reading aloud the story "Is the Principal Calling?" on page 9. The story ends abruptly, before the mystery is solved. We discuss what type of story we read. How can you tell that this is a mystery and not a romance novel or a science book? We also make predictions about the story and who the prank caller might be. Finally, it is time to pass out the ending. We discuss it. Were the clues in the story good? Too hard? Too easy?

We take a break to play Investigator. One child (the Investigator) leaves the area, and a Guilty Suspect is selected to start a hand pattern (clap, clap, snap). The rest of the group begins the pattern and the Investigator returns. The Guilty Suspect changes the hand pattern every thirty seconds or so (shoulder tap, finger clap) and everyone else attempts to shift seamlessly to the new pattern. The Investigator has three chances to guess the Guilty Suspect. Then the Guilty Suspect becomes the Investigator and the game continues.

After this, we turn to the "Usual Suspects of a Mystery" page in the notebook. We discuss what the terms mean and give examples from the story, "Is the Principal Calling?" Now that everyone is familiar with the important elements of a mystery, the kids generate possible settings, suspects, and motives in their notebooks.

For younger students, you may want to do a simpler activity. You could show the class a picture of a *Cat in the Hat*–style mess (a broken fishbowl, a guilty-looking cat, a cunning bird) and ask the class to solve what they think happened from the clues in the picture. Who's the suspect? What was the motive?

For the last activity, you have two choices: you can either have each student write his or her own mystery, or you can write a mystery as a class, ending abruptly at a good point for a cliff-hanger, and have each student write his or her own solution. Remind them to include the same characters, continue the story, and add one last fantastic clue that tips the scale to the guilty suspect. When everyone is finished, each child shares his or her own stunning revelation!

TOP SECRET

CASE #091804

**THIS TOP-SECRET NOTEBOOK
BELONGS TO: _____ , P.I.**

PART 1

CASE FILE #1:
IS THE PRINCIPAL CALLING?

Sam looked out the kitchen window at the new snow on the ground. He was thinking about going out to build a snow fort when the phone rang.

"May I speak with Sam Fredrickson?" the voice on the phone asked.

"This is Sam," answered Sam.

"Please hold for Principal Simmons."

Sam looked at the phone. Why was the principal calling? If Sam was in trouble, wouldn't the principal want to talk to his parents? Maybe Principal Simmons wanted to congratulate him, although Sam couldn't think of why.

Sam thought about all of the good and bad things he had done lately as he waited ... and waited ... and waited. Finally he realized the truth. Someone had played a trick on him, and it probably wasn't his principal.

Sam decided he probably knew the prank caller. But who could it be? Jenny was always goofing around. Maybe she called and pretended to be Principal Simmons. Sam dialed her number. It was busy.

"I'm going to get to the bottom of this!" he said, as he bundled up and headed out into the crunchy white snow.

Sam was walking over to Jenny's house, when he spotted someone building a snowman. It was his friend Emma.

"Hey Sam, I'm glad you walked by. I wanted to know if you could play this afternoon. I was going to call you, but my mom just grounded me from using the phone."

Sam explained that he would be back to play later, and headed over to Jenny's house.

It had been snowing all morning, and when Sam reached Jenny's house, a blanket of snow covered the lawn and the sidewalk. He walked up to the front door, making footsteps in the spotless snow. Sam rang the doorbell.

"Hi Sam," Jenny said as she opened the door.

"Hey Jenny, the oddest thing happened this morning. Principal Simmons called me. But I don't think it was really her. Did you call me this morning?"

"No Sam," Jenny replied. "It sounds like someone played a trick on you, but it wasn't me! I walked over to the library this morning to work on my report, and I just got home. I wonder who tricked you?"

"I think I have a pretty good idea who called," said Sam.

Did the principal really call Sam?

PART 2

[*Read after class has discussed suspects and evidence.*]

"**I** know who called," said Sam. "And I also know that you weren't at the library this morning."

Jenny smiled. "All right, maybe it wasn't Principal Simmons, but how did you know it was me?"

"Well, I was the first person to walk in the snow on your porch. No one's come in or out of your house yet today. You were definitely at home!"

Jenny giggled, "I can't trick you!" Sam and Jenny headed outside to help Emma build her snow fort.

WRITE YOUR OWN!

The Usual Suspects in a Mystery:

Crime: The *bad/sad/exciting mysterious thing that happens*

The crime in my mystery is: _____

Detective: *The smart and curious character who solves the crime*

The detective in my mystery is: _____

Setting: *An interesting environment where the story takes place*

The setting in my mystery is: _____

Suspects with motives: *Characters with good reasons to commit a crime*

The suspects in my mystery are: _____

Suspect #1
Name: _____ Motives: _____

Suspect #2
Name: _____ Motives: _____

Suspect #3
Name: _____ Motives: _____

Your Mystery Will Also Need:

Clues: *Evidence, pieces of the puzzle*

_____

_____

_____

_____

_____

_____

_____

_____

Red herrings: *A fake or distracting clue. Can you find any red herrings in "Is the Principal Calling?"*

_____

_____

_____

_____

_____

_____

_____

_____

Solution: *Solving the mystery, putting the pieces together*

_____

_____

_____

_____

_____

_____

_____

_____

Student Work

[*One class collaborated to write the following mystery. The students supplied their own endings.*]

THE CASE OF THE STOLEN GOLD

Young Judy Waider really enjoyed living in Washington, D.C., the most patriotic place around. Everything was always decorated in red, white and blue—but Judy always wore black.

Sora was Judy's classmate. He was an orphan who rode the ferry into D.C. every morning from his house on an island in the Atlantic.

Both students were excited for the school trip to the Arizona desert. Their school was always cold. The heat didn't work, and there were never any lightbulbs. Principal Al knew the school needed help, but decided to spend the last of the budget on this big trip. Judy's reading teacher, Mrs. Lila Lier, planned the field trip with Ms. Wanda's room across the hall. They were supposed to be studying pharaohs, but Judy and Sora had done their homework and knew that the very same Arizona desert had an abandoned gold mine. There was a rumor that piles of gold were left in the mine, however there was also supposed to be a zombie miner guarding the gold.

The class took the train to Arizona, although Ms. Wanda really wanted to travel by limo. They were met at the train station in the desert by Mr. Tree, their tour guide. He seemed nice enough, but deep down he was looking for a change. Twenty-five years talking about the famous tombs and pyramids in Arizona was really getting to him.

Later that night, Sora and Judy snuck out of their cabins. Sora had to be very quiet sneaking out because his best friend Riku was on the bottom bunk.

The two friends were frightened to explore the abandoned mine haunted by a zombie ghost. However, they were armed with bright flashlights and bravely traveled to the back of the deep mine shaft. Along the way, the students noticed a lot of litter. Judy found a crumpled brochure for limo rides to Las Vegas. Sora found a police uniform and a list of really good books. The most unusual thing was a set of blueprints for a new school in Washington, D.C.!

An hour later, with their arms full of evidence, they reached the end of the mine. Instead of a pile of gold, they were shocked to discover...

MESSAGE IN A BOTTLE

by BRENNA BURNS & MOLLY MENG

3 hours
Materials: Show-and-tell message bottles,
secret messages to hide around the room,
one blank, stamped postcard for each student

For years, desert island poets have sent their deepest thoughts out to sea in bottles. In this workshop we offer students a modern-day way to carry on the tradition by creating their own stack of original postcards to be sent out into a "sea" of unknown readers. We also explore fantastical and mischievous ways to send messages. (How about commissioning a whale to sing your message? Or maybe skywriting?) It doesn't take much to get the kids channeling the castaways of yore. By the end of our first class they were stashing secret notes around the writing center, devising their own codes and writing riddles and stories for their postcards.

Session One

This workshop is very theatrical, and props go a long way toward getting everyone's imaginations revved up. Of course we have the classic—a scroll in a bottle encrusted with genuine sea salt and sand (yes, we get some raised eyebrows when we take our pet bottle out walking on a leash in the surf...). But we also arrange "secret messages" around the room for the students to discover. A theater ticket bearing a distress message from a bored spectator is hidden in a red polka-dotted opera glove; an ancient calling card is tucked between

the pages of a book; a gumball-machine capsule contains a note from the trinket that has escaped; even Molly's T-shirt has a message ironed on. The kids have a great time finding and reading the messages, and this leads us right into brainstorming sessions on "Ways to Send a Message." (Save this list—the students might want to write it on the front of their postcard in the next session).

SUPERTEACHER BONUS ACTIVITY:
Before the lesson starts, hide a message for each student to find at his or her desk. It should say something cryptic like "The adventure begins ..." or "I need your help!" You could make little scrolls and tie them with ribbon, or sneak little notes inside the wrapper of a miniature candy bar. Superteachers who are pressed for time could simply leave a fortune cookie at each student's desk; they're like little messages in edible bottles.

Next we introduce the postcards to them. It really helps the students to see a concrete example of what they will soon be working on themselves. (See the examples on page 15—these are cards that somebody found and mailed back to 826 Valencia with a reply.)

After showing the students a postcard and giving

A BRIEF EXPLANATION OF THE POSTCARDS

- Students make their own postcard with a written message on the back and a drawing of a fantastical message delivery system on the front

- Cards are identified as "1 in a series of 15 modern-day messages in bottles released by students of _____."

- Cards have the school's mailing address on them. People who find them are invited to reply.

- The front of each card can list "Ways to Send a Message," taken from the brainstorming session.

- Students receive a copy of their own card to distribute as they wish. If you're feeling ambitious you can also give each student a complete set of everyone's photocopied postcards.

- Show students where replies will be kept—they'll want to come check them out.

them a brief explanation of how this part of the project will work (see box on page 13), we distribute pencils and scratch paper and the students spend half an hour composing a draft of their message. We circulate and help them with their writing.

There are a few potential pitfalls to look out for right about now. For example, one politically active young chap addressed his postcard to a notorious head of state, with a teensy bit of a threatening statement. (Though unforeseen, it did give us the opportunity to discuss both the "open letter" as a powerful tool and the prickly topic of sending threats via post!) In the end, our student rewrote his card with a peaceful appeal; everyone was really happy about the outcome. But the moral of the anecdote is that it's important to set down a few rules before the kids start writing: no threats; no violence; and no identifying information about yourself, your school, or your after-school activities.

At the end of the first session, we tell the students we will give them time in the next class to finish any ideas they havn't gotten down on paper. In fact, most of the kids have finished their messages and read them aloud to the rest of us. Some even get so carried away about putting their thoughts out into the world, they ask if they can do more than one. We keep it to one postcard per student to keep focused on the task at hand. To wrap up the first session, we go over their drafts and ask the students to think about the images they'd like to add to their cards for the next class. We tell them what materials we will provide and ask them to let their imaginations run wild in the meantime.

Session Two

We open the second class by asking the students to go around and each tell us about a secret message they noticed during the week. The results are so exciting! Their little antennae have been finely tuned to the world's messages all week, and what's more they seem to have photographic memories—one student recited the entire text of a long and very touching bit of bathroom graffiti; another told us, "I was walking along the sidewalk and I saw a secret message written in the cement, but it was filled in with dirt so I ran and got a stick and scratched out the dirt, and it said, 'WPA.'" Everyone oohs and aahs and offers ideas about what that might stand for ... Wild Penguin Acrobats, anyone?

Then comes the moment they've all been waiting for: passing out the postcards. The students decorate the front with the list of "Ways to Send a Message" from the last session. Next to that they draw a picture of their own imaginary message delivery system. They spend the next twenty minutes drawing talking parrots, trained mythical beasts, smoke signals, flying laptops, etc.

We like to make a copy of the cards before we send them out to the world, so we photocopy them and return them to the students

Now we're ready to dispatch our messages. The students leave with their postcards and an assignment: hide it somewhere for someone to find and send back. We ask them to share their best ideas. One student planned to hide hers in the library shelves at school. You could hide it in a tree, send it on a breeze, nestle it on a supermarket shelf—there are lots of places to leave a secret message.

Obviously, the more cards they have to distribute, the higher the likelihood of receiving a good return response. The response can also be boosted by adult involvement: we've given some cards to our friends and families and asked them to spread the word. However, the real joy in this project lies in the energetic interactions during class, the atmosphere of suspended disbelief (which the students take to like fish to water), the heightened awareness of all the messages floating out in our "sea," and the invitation to create benign, poetic mischief—like the student who told us she'd been inspired to hide a secret note for her parents in their underwear drawer. The postcards are just a good way to facilitate all of that happening!

Student Work

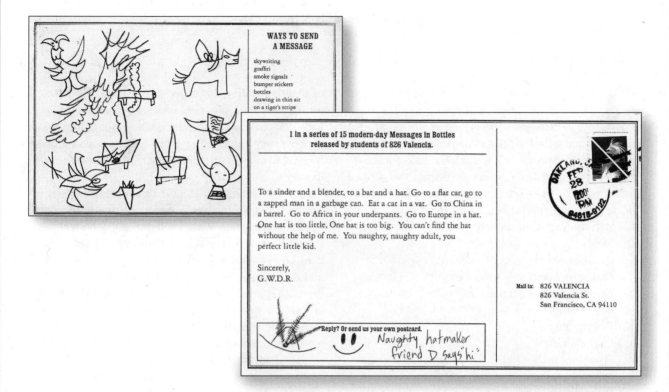

WAYS TO SEND A MESSAGE

skywriting
graffiti
smoke signals
bumper stickers
bottles
drawing in thin air
on a tiger's stripe

1 in a series of 15 modern-day Messages in Bottles released by students of 826 Valencia.

To a sinder and a blender, to a bat and a hat. Go to a flat car, go to a zapped man in a garbage can. Eat a cat in a vat. Go to China in a barrel. Go to Africa in your underpants. Go to Europe in a hat. One hat is too little, One hat is too big. You can't find the hat without the help of me. You naughty, naughty adult, you perfect little kid.

Sincerely,
G.W.D.R.

Reply? Or send us your own postcard.

Naughty hatmaker friend D says "hi"

Mail to: 826 VALENCIA
826 Valencia St.
San Francisco, CA 94110

—Guard Robinson, 9

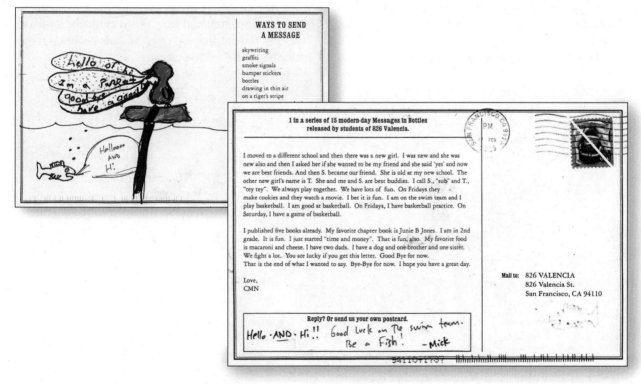

WAYS TO SEND A MESSAGE

skywriting
graffiti
smoke signals
bumper stickers
bottles
drawing in thin air
on a tiger's stripe

hello of i. I'm a Parret good bye have a again

Hellooo AND Hi.

1 in a series of 15 modern-day Messages in Bottles released by students of 826 Valencia.

I moved to a different school and then there was a new girl. I was new and she was new also and then I asked her if she wanted to be my friend and she said 'yes' and now we are best friends. And then S. became our friend. She is old at my new school. The other new girl's name is T. She and me and S. are best buddies. I call S., "sub" and T., "tey tey". We always play together. We have lots of fun. On Fridays they make cookies and they watch a movie. I bet it is fun. I am on the swim team and I play basketball. I am good at basketball. On Fridays, I have basketball practice. On Saturday, I have a game of basketball.

I published five books already. My favorite chapter book is Junie B Jones. I am in 2nd grade. It is fun. I just started "time and money". That is fun, also. My favorite food is macaroni and cheese. I have two dads. I have a dog and one brother and one sister. We fight a lot. You are lucky if you get this letter. Good Bye for now. That is the end of what I wanted to say. Bye-Bye for now. I hope you have a great day.

Love,
CMN

Reply? Or send us your own postcard.

Hello · AND · Hi !! Good Luck on The swim team. Be a Fish! —Mick

Mail to: 826 VALENCIA
826 Valencia St.
San Francisco, CA 94110

—Chelsea Marigliano-Nardella, 9

BEST IMAGINARY VACATION EVER!

by MICAH PILKINGTON

2 hours

This workshop has a simple but urgent goal: to combat the threat of dull summer vacations. Once everyone is seated, we go around the room and talk about some fun places for imaginary vacations: the woods, the lake, Grandma's house. We point out that, while fun, every single place we named had gravity. We know we can do better. Before jumping into a fantasy vacation plan, we list the vacation activities that we do not recommend on the board:

Getting bitten by angry spiders
Eating tuna and Jell-O sundaes
Being chased by a mob of any sort
Bee taming
Bear taming
Sock darning
Mosquito ranch hand
Downhill skiing without snow
Piano repair camp
Hair mowing

We ask the class to add to our list of bad vacation ideas. Cleaning your room, math, and yard work are often mentioned.

The instructor then gives the class a brief example of an ultimate dream vacation. In one class, the instructor used her cat's itinerary, which involved snorkeling, lots of accordion music, and a whole roast turkey for dinner every night. Other ideas have included a two-week stay in a candy store and a trip to the waterslide factory.

Now it's time for students to gather their own vacation ideas, so we go to the handout (page 17) and get started on specifics. Where will they go? Who will they bring? How will they spend their days? This section goes quickly; the instructor merely pushes for details and discourages conventional ideas about the laws of time and space. This is a good time to emphasize fiction and fantasy and to encourage the students to be as creative as they can. We agree that every vacation must end with a party, so we throw in some ideas for that, too.

The final step is to use all the ideas we've worked on to write a story about a typical day in the best vacation ever. If they're stuck, we encourage students to look at their notes for inspiration. The class ends with students sharing their awesome plans. Ice cream and flying figured largely in one vacation story; in another, Madonna appeared and gave everyone dance lessons. If there's time at the end of class, kids decorate their handouts with vacation pictures.

WRITE YOUR DREAM VACATION ITINERARY!

Where I will go:

What I will bring (supplies, clothes, toys, dodgeballs and so on. Be as detailed as possible. Is it a red dodgeball, or is it a red glitter light-up dodgeball with a jet pack?):

Who I will bring (family members? pets? friends? Why would they be good travel companions?):

What I will do for a job (ice cream taster? professional hoverbiker? Tell us all about it.):

What I will do for fun:

Transportation to and from vacation spot (surely nothing so boring as a car— get creative):

Things I will not have to do, not even once, because you can't make me:

Here's what my end-of-vacation blowout party will be like:

A THOUSAND WORDS: WRITING ABOUT ART

by ABIGAIL JACOBS & TAYLOR JACOBSON

6 hours
Materials: Artwork for inspiration
(small paintings, sculptures, photos, etc. Even postcards are fine)

Our thesis: art is everywhere! On the first day of class, when we ask our students if they saw any art today, they inevitably say no. It's so fun to see their excitement when they realize that art is an enormous category and doesn't just include things they see in a museum but stuff they see every day—things like graffiti, comic books, movies, and their own creative works. It's those types of art that they inevitably want to write about.

Session One

We start by bringing out a piece of art. It can be a painting, a collage, a sculpture. We give the students ten minutes to write about it. Then we share what we have written. We talk about the ways that we write about the art, how we describe its colors, its shapes, the way it makes us feel, what we think about the artist, if we can tell how it is made (the medium), whether it looks like anything we can identify and if so, if that makes us feel or think a certain way about the work. We talk about the artist and whether, just by looking at it, we can place the art in a certain category ("modern art" or "abstract" are popular category suggestions) or time period. Then we talk about where we might see a piece of art like this, why it might have been made, what its purpose is—if it even has a purpose. When they're done, we like to have the students share their work aloud.

SUPERTEACHER BONUS ACTIVITY: *For a really cool art-writing lesson your class will never forget, turn your classroom into a museum. Set up six pieces of art around the room. They can be fairly straightforward pieces, like a painting or a sculpture, or they can be weird installations like a crumpled juice box. Each piece should be identified by a card, like in a museum: "Title: Still Life with Gum Wrapper. Artist: Daphne de la Bazooka. Mixed Media, 2005." Give the students some time to go around the room and examine the art, and then ask them to write a student-friendly museum guidebook.*

Once they're warmed up we spend some time discussing art. We start by asking: What is art? (Painting, sculpture, collage, photograph, play, movie, book, graffiti, jewelry, stained glass, comics, industrial design, food, architecture, fashion, etc.). We write these on the board so that we can review them throughout the class.

Then we ask: Why do people write about art? (To share it, to review/critique it, to explain it, to compare it, because it evokes emotion.) To reinforce this discussion, we print out articles from the newspaper, magazines, and web about art. We may read through some of these or just talk about the different types of writing. We define "creative" art writing (e.g. poems inspired by paintings) and "analytic" art writing (e.g. reviews) and read examples of both.

For our next exercise, we ask the students to draw for ten minutes with no guidelines and without worrying or commenting on whether the drawing is good or bad. When they are done, they pass their drawings to the person on their left and write about the drawing that was passed to them. Again, we ask them to think about all the ways we wrote about art in the last exercise. We share the responses with the group. The students love to hear what someone has written about their drawing.

The homework assignment at the end of the first class is for everyone to look around for art and think about the art they see every day. Also, to find a piece of writing about art—maybe from a newspaper or magazine—and bring it to class with them.

Session Two

We begin by reading our homework. Then, we go around the room and talk about a piece of art that everyone saw over the last week. We remind them to refer to the topics and ways of thinking about art that we discussed in the last class. Sometimes it's helpful to write those on the board again.

We talk again about all the different things that can be classified as art and we show the students a table full of items we have brought with us, including paintings, photographs, a stapler, a piece of stained glass, a screen-printed t-shirt, a necklace, a magazine cover, a piece of wrapping paper, a CD case/cover, and a book. We ask them to pick one item and write about it for ten minutes, and then we share what everyone has written.

After that, we spend twenty minutes cutting up magazines and making collages. Again, there are no guidelines and no limitations. We pass these and write about what we see. We share what we wrote.

Homework is to find a piece of art and write about it: just describe how it looks, how it makes you feel, what you think of it. We suggest that a full page of writing would be amazing.

Session Three

First, we read our homework aloud and talk about any art they saw over the week. By this class, they are so excited to share the art they have seen and thought about over the past week.

In this session, we talk a little bit about the difference between writing *analytically* about art and writing *inspired* by art. (You may want to go over definitions again here. *Analytical* writing describes and reports, and it's what they did for homework. Writing *inspired* by art can be more free-form and creative.) We do this by reading an example of a poem that was written about a painting. (We use a poem called "Girl Powdering Her Neck" by Cathy Song and show a reproduction of the painting). Then we ask the students to spend ten minutes writing something inspired by the piece of art they wrote about analytically for their homework assignment. This means not concentrating on color, shape, etc. but maybe telling a story, or writing a poem. We share this writing.

The rest of the final session is spent making copies of the students' art writing and compiling it into books. We distribute copies, decorate our front and back covers, take Polaroids and write bios for the "authors page."

At the end, everyone picks their favorite piece of writing to read aloud one more time and we eat cupcakes (the most artful snack).

Student Work

ON "MIRROR" BY ROY LICHTENSTEIN

"This sculpture is very unique. It is called "Mirror." The sculpture is by Roy Lichtenstein. Since you can't see the color in my sketch, I'll tell you what colors are in this fabulous mirror. The color on the little stick thingys is black. The color on the line on the edge is yellow. The first wavy line is blue, and on it is another wavy thing that is white. The little squiggly line attached to the second sticky line is also white. Before I read the title, I didn't know it was a mirror. I thought it might be just a circle with shapes. This sculpture makes me feel wiggly and shaky. I like this sculpture a lot."

POEM INSPIRED BY "MIRROR":

It swivels and curves
As if the turns
Are the face moving
About the mirror
When the face is
Gone the swivels
Are too
The curves and
The turns
Are the face
Lurking around
And I will
Tell you all now
That there is no face ...
At all

For the face
Moving around is
Only a shadow
Moving this way
And that to
Create the curves
On the mirror.

—*Sabina Young, 10*

HOW TO WRITE A COMIC

by TODD POUND & JENNY TRAIG

4 hours

Materials: Costume supplies (optional)

This class is great for students who think they don't like to write, because it lets them tell stories through pictures. It's a grand tradition. Visual storytelling has been around forever—just take a gander at some hieroglyphics or cave paintings. Before you know it, a few words creep in, and boom, you're telling a story using both text and pictures, like a true *artiste*. Of course, text and pictures need to co-exist peacefully on the page. This class shows students how those elements can work together to produce great stories.

We'll be honest: the part of this class everyone likes best is the drawing. It helps if you have a real live artist (amateur or pro) to illustrate points on the board. The plot diagram comes alive when it's being sketched out right before your eyes using atomic alligators and nuclear fish. Character development becomes very engrossing when you have an artist right there, sketching out exactly what the class dictates: "A miniature giraffe! With a mohawk! And hoop earrings! Wearing a tutu, on roller skates, with flames shooting out of its nose!" If no artist is available, take a deep breath and do it yourself. We bet you're a better artist than you think.

Session One: Character

We start by asking for a volunteer. This hapless student is then outfitted with a couple accessories—maybe just a hat and glasses, or maybe a wig and feather boa. We ask the class to describe the character they see before them. "Librarian!" They shout. "Movie star!" "Crazy lady!" We ask why. "Because she is wearing glasses, so she must be smart." "She's dressed like a celebrity." "Normal people wouldn't wear that."

We use this to illustrate a point: they were able to get all this information from just two little accessories. In comics, you have to keep the text brief, so you need to communicate things like character using a visual shorthand. How they look, how they talk, their name—all these things will let us know who they are. The Character Design handout (page 23) goes over this in detail, so we distribute that and go over it with the class. As for drawing characters, we remind them

that simplest is generally best. They're going to have to draw this character over and over, and penciling in a hundred legs or a thousand freckles gets tiresome. The most famous characters are generally pretty basic. We start to sketch a few characters on the board and ask the class the shout out the answer when the recognize them: Batman, Mickey Mouse, Bart Simpson. Usually, they can guess from just one or two strokes, from the hairline or the ears alone, which is why these are such great characters.

 SUPERTEACHER BONUS ACTIVITY: *Have the whole class design a character together. It can be anything: a rhino with a mohawk and tutu, a lion-gator hybrid with braces and rollerskates, a talking banana. To keep things fair, you may want to have the students write character features (like "braces," "sunglasses," "braids," "funky boots," etc.) on scraps of paper, then place them in a bowl. Sketch the character on the board, adding features you've drawn from the bowl. As you're drawing, invite the class to come up with the character's backstory. How did this crazy creature come to be? What are its likes and dislikes? Fears and loves? What's its name? What does it do for fun?*

After forty minutes of discussion the students are usually pretty eager to get to work, so we turn them loose to create their own characters. First, they draw them using the model sheet (page 24). This is what the pros use, to make sure the character stays consistent from frame to frame. Students are instructed to draw their character from a few different angles, e.g., from the front, side, and back. The notched lines will help you make sure the character stays the same height, with the same length arms. We talk about the concept of "heads high," basing your character's height on the measurement of his or her head. Superheroes are generally about eight heads high; normal people are about five; Calvin of *Calvin and Hobbes* is about two. If they finish early, they can practice drawing their character in different moods: happy, angry, excited, scared.

Next we distribute the Written Model Sheet (page 25). Here, the students list all their character's qualities. It helps them flesh out the character's personality and keep track of things, so if on page one we learn that he's allergic to chocolate, we don't see him eating a candy bar with impunity on page six.

Session Two: Story

In the next class we discuss story. We go over the plot chart handout (page 27). We talk about the concept of "backstory" —how did your character get to be the way s/he is? We discuss the backstory of Superman, Batman, and Spider-Man as examples. We limit the lecture to thirty minutes, because the students are eager to work. We hand out some blank panels (page 28) and they spend the next hour working on a first draft.

Session Three: Composition

In the final class we discuss composition, in both senses of the word—composing objects in a frame, and composing words on a page. We go through comic books to see how other artists compose. Is the POV (point of view) looking down, like a bird in the sky? Looking up, like a worm? What's big? What's small? What's in shadow? What's barely sketched out, and what's really detailed?

Then we teach them the cardinal rule of writing for comics: *keep it brief*. The reader gets bored if there's a big chunk of text, so you have to be concise and find other ways of telling the story—through art and dialogue, for instance. We talk about using satisfying words instead of wishy-washy ones. Brainstorm a few good ones and write them on the board. And we define the most important comic writing technique, onomatopoeia. We practice: What is the sound of a skateboarder crashing into metal trash cans? Of slipping on a banana? Of a mirror breaking?

Finally, we distribute more blank panels, and the students show us everything they've learned. We are always blown away. When they've finished and time permits, we photocopy everyone's work and bind it into a class comic book with a blank cover the students can decorate themselves. It's usually so good we could charge money for it.

CHARACTER DESIGN!

Creating characters is the most important part of writing a comic book. It's also the most fun! Here's how to do it in four easy steps:

1. Decide what your character will be: a man, a woman, a child, an adult, an animal, an alien, an ice cream scooper ... anything at all. You can base your character on a friend, a family member, a pet, a famous athlete, or even a fictional character from a story you like. Once you've got your hero, you'll also want some supporting characters like sidekicks and mortal enemies. Look around you to find examples of characters you might want in your story. Remember, your characters will drive the plot, so it's important you really understand what makes them tick.

2. Think about your character's backstory. If she's a cranky field mouse, figure out why she's in such a bad mood. Is it because she hates the country and longs to live in the glamorous, glittering big city? If your character's a mutant, figure out what caused the mutation. Was it a nuclear accident? A food allergy? Think about all your character's likes and dislikes, strengths and weaknesses. Is he super-strong but afraid of bunnies? Is he addicted to sardines? These little details will make the character feel rounded and real. Broad, one-dimensional characters are fine in some comics, but it can be interesting to have more complicated characters too. Give your character some personality traits we might not expect. Maybe your superhero's hobby is pottery. Maybe your arch villain wears frilly ankle socks under his combat boots. Surprises are good.

3. Give your character a really cool name. Pick a superhero name like Surpasso or a normal name like Al. You could let us know that your hero is a good guy by naming him Valiant P. Whitehat, or you could play off our expectations by, say, making Angelica Goodchild an evil brat.

4. Sketch your brand new characters. The way the characters look will tell us a lot about who they are, so put some thought into their features, their figures, their clothes, even their haircuts. That doesn't mean you have to dress a nerdy character in plaid highwaters and goggles, but you can. You can also play against our expectations by making the seven-foot square-jawed giant a fraidycat. Use your characters to define the "tone" or "mood" of your story. Is it dark and scary or light and funny? The tone is created not merely by what your characters say and do, but also what they look like.

Here are some things to remember:

- We have to care about the characters, but we don't have to like them. We can love to hate them, too.

- You have to feel comfortable drawing your characters. Select a drawing style you feel confident about. Remember your characters are all just collections of geometric shapes.

- Draw them from every angle. Create a model sheet for reference. What does your character look like from the front? From the side? Draw them over and over.

- Study other characters. What makes Snoopy so cool? Wolverine? The Powerpuff Girls? What characters do you like? Why?

MODEL SHEET

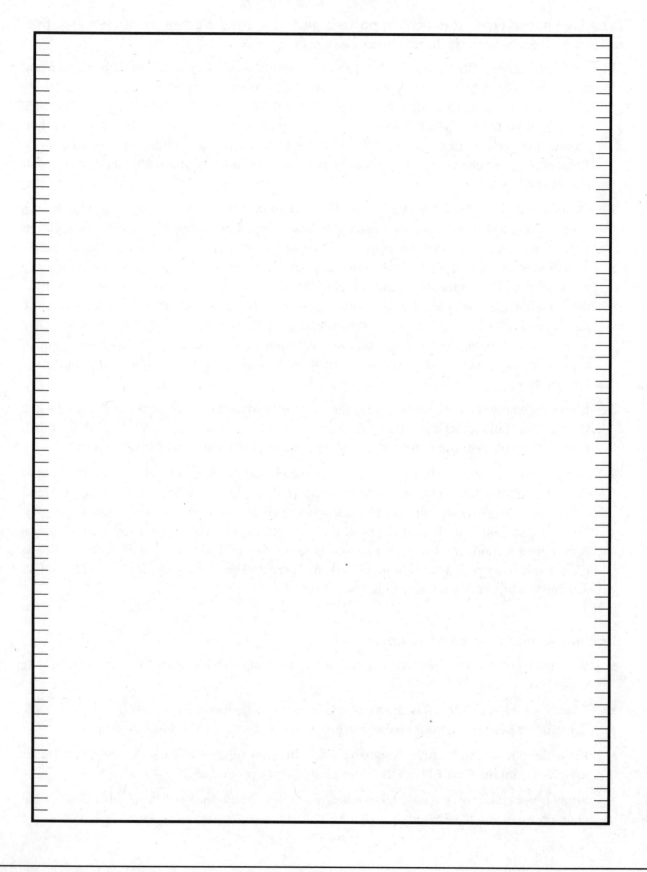

WRITTEN MODEL SHEET

Character's name:

Home:

Personality traits:

Greatest strength:

Greatest weakness:

Sidekick:

Other pals:

Arch enemy:

Love interest:

Backstory—how did he or she become who he or she is?:

Mission in life:

When he or she gets angry, he or she...

When s/he's happy, he or she...

What's in his or her refrigerator?

If he or she went to a karaoke club, what song would s/he perform?

HERE ARE SOME IDEAS TO GET YOU STARTED

You could base your comic book on a fairy tale and tweak it to make it your own. Turn Goldilocks into a foul-mouthed hillbilly and the three bears into super-intelligent, genetically altered animals who teach at the local junior college. Juuuust right.

Ghosts. Ghosts are great because they are ooky, kooky, spooky and easy to draw. Your comic book could be very serious and suspenseful (what does the phantom spector want?) or goofy. Maybe your ghosts are simply spiteful, doing no actual harm but annoying the living by replacing the shampoo with Miracle Whip.

Talking animals. Talking super-intelligent genetically altered animals!

Talking food. Here's a great idea: the secret life of groceries. Do a comic book about what happens in your refrigerator when the door is closed. Do the carrots and celery duel? Is the head cheese bossy? Does the salad dressing try to start a war?

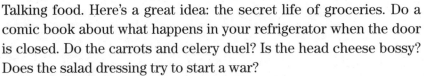

You could go the super-realistic route and do a story about an everyday event, like cleaning the bathroom. All kinds of magical, exciting things can occur while cleaning a bathroom.

Superheroes! Is anything better? They have powers! And such fashion sense! They're classic! You could play with the usual format by making your superhero very stupid, lazy, or cowardly. Here are some superhero rules to follow or break: 1. They must wear tights (boots are good, too). 2. They must have cheekbones. Prominent ones. 3. They are haunted by dark secrets. 4. They make witty puns while chasing after pesky villains.

(Sshhh! Alter ego.)

STRUCTURING THE STORY
A HANDY-DANDY CHART!

3. Climax

Archenemies battle! The clock is ticking—can the hero save the day before it's too late? We're on the edge of our seats!

Tidy Wave has Litter Bug where he wants him... but can he bear to touch the filthy fiend?

2. The plot thickens

The villain enters. Something fishy is going on here...

Who is turning Sparkle City into his own personal dumpster? Could it be that vile varlet, Litter Bug? And why does Tidy keep washing his hands?

1. Introduction

We meet the characters and explore the setting. On the surface, everything looks perfect... but is it?

Tidy Wave and his sidekick Squeaky Clean keep the streets of Sparkle City safe and spotless.

4. Denouement

The action wraps up. Things begin to fall into place. Loose ends are tied into neat little bows.

Tidy & Squeaky mop up.

5. Conclusion

The bad guys are caught and the heroes celebrate. Show's over! Now get your coats and go home!

Tidy slips on some fresh gloves and slaps Squeaky Clean a well-earned high-five.

HEY! You don't have to tell the story in order. You could tell it backwards. You could start at the climax. Or you could chop it all up. Artsy-fartsy!

Student Work

[*Some students prefer the challenge of telling a story in a single panel. We liked this one.*]

Total Chaos

—*Ethan Hall, 11*

MAKE-BELIEVE SCIENCE

by Amie Nenniger

1 hour

Materials: Candy corn (or substitute), dish of water, items to test for floatability (toys, paper clips, etc.), chocolate kisses, one copy of the handout packet (pages 32–35) for each student

Did you know that salt water and salt combine to form cotton candy? Or that kittens, if fed the proper diet, can fly? Well, it's not true, but who cares? It's interesting! At 826 Valencia, we believe the study of science shouldn't be bound by facts, formulas, and the laws of physics. If you agree, you'll love this lesson plan. First we learn some completely fictitious, but totally enthralling, scientific findings. Then we use our newfound knowledge to write some science stories, which we compile into a pseudoscientific journal. Students leave with their own science journals, a head full of untruths, and, we hope, a new enthusiasm for creative play.

This is a great lesson plan for kids who think they don't like to write. Our version is designed for younger children, with lots of drawing and simple writing tasks, but it could easily be modified for an older crowd by asking for longer paragraphs and fewer pictures.

We start class by distributing the handout packets and telling the students they'll need to take a new name. Adding the suffix *–enschpreckenschpiel* to your existing last name is a good step towards scientific acclaim. The students write their new nom de science on the cover of their scientific journal (page 31).

Then we roll up our sleeves and start experimenting. Following the prompts in the handout packets, we learn some made-up chemistry, astronomy, physics, and anatomy and biology. We spend about twenty minutes on each subject.

Chemistry: The students learn that chemists are in charge of equations, a fancy word that explains how everything in the world adds up. They volunteer equations they know (inevitably math, i.e. 2 + 3 = 5). We discuss how equations can also use words, like red + yellow = orange. We can also use our words to describe other combinations, some of which are quite silly (a hummingbird + a book = reading really fast). Then we break to fill in the Chemistry page in our handbook (page 30).

Astronomy: Sure, scientists use microscopes, and telescopes, but there is an even easier way to catch a glimpse of the galaxies. Studies have shown that nibbling on candy corn makes it possible to view life on other planets. Everyone enjoys a piece of candy and squints at light fixtures until the inner workings of Jupiter are revealed. Then we turn to the Astronomy page of our handbook (page 33), where students are asked to describe the setting and its inhabitants with words and pictures.

Physics: Kids take a variety of objects (coins, toy cars, pompoms, corks, and erasers are great test samples) and record what happens when the object is tossed in a bucket of water. Then we turn to the Physics page of our handbook (page 34), where the junior scientist must record an observation and explain why this occurred. Why did the object splash? Was it afraid of water? Boats float, so the rule of rhyme explains that goats, coats, quarter notes, and sore throats will float too!

Anatomy and Biology: The human body is a mystifying organism that allows us to stand still with a running nose. No one really knows how digestion works, but here is our best guess: When you eat food, you chew it up and then it swings on a trapeze and splashes into a basin behind your lungs, where it is washed clean of any impurities like germs or lint. Then, tiny hairdryers blow it off. Once it's dry, the food falls down a flight of stairs (which makes that rumbling noise). Once food is in the stomach, it is carried off by a well-trained pack of miniature squirrels that deliver nutrients to your cells. If kids don't believe this tour of the digestive system, they are encouraged to eat a chocolate kiss, then turn to the Anatomy and Biology page of the handbook (page 35) and carefully record the morsel's path through the body.

For some extra science flavor, you can list and define some very scientific words for the students to include in their reports, like *ergo* or *quod erat demonstrandum.*

And that's it! At the end of class, we teach the students the secret scientist handshake (waggling fingers) and congratulate them on all their important work.

THE JOURNAL OF PARAFICTITIOUS SCIENTIFIC INQUIRY

WITH CONTRIBUTIONS BY

PROF. _____ENSCHPRECKENSCHPIEL, PHD.

CHEMISTRY

Chemists are in charge of EQUATIONS. Equations explain how everything in the world adds up. For example: yellow + blue = green; rain + mud = worms.

_____ + _____ = _____

_____ + _____ = _____

_____ + _____ = _____

_____ + _____ = _____

_____ + _____ = _____

_____ + _____ = _____

_____ + _____ = _____

_____ + _____ = _____

_____ + _____ = _____

ASTRONOMY

Everybody knows that carrots are good for your eyes. But candy corn is even better. This one time, after we ate a whole bag, we could see Mars! We discovered Mars is made of butterscotch pudding and ruled by kittens. Eat a piece of candy and then tell us what you see on Jupiter.

Describe Jupiter: _____

_____

_____

_____

_____

_____

This is how it looks:

The creatures that live on it are… _____

_____

_____

_____

_____

_____

And this is how they look:

PHYSICS

Recent research in our laboratory bathtub leads us to believe that some things, like marshmallows, cheese, and dump trucks, float because they are afraid of water. We've also discovered that all green things sink, because green things are lazy. Try placing a few items in water. Record whether they sink or float, and why.

Item #1: _____

SINK or FLOAT? _____

Why? _____

_____

_____

Item #2: _____

SINK or FLOAT? _____

Why? _____

_____

_____

Item #3: _____

SINK or FLOAT? _____

Why? _____

_____

_____

Item #4: _____

SINK or FLOAT? _____

Why? _____

_____

_____

ANATOMY & BIOLOGY

Did you know these anatomy fun facts?

• The knee bone is actually connected to the cha cha cha bone!

• Adult humans have 253 teeth!

• There's more hair in your nose than on your whole head!

What happens to the food you eat? We're not sure, but we think it's carried off by tiny squirrels who live inside your belly. What do you think?
Eat a chocolate kiss and describe what happens.

First, the chocolate kiss goes to the _____ ,

where it _____ .

Then, it goes to the _____ ,

where it _____ .

Finally, it goes to the _____ ,

where it _____ .

Here's a picture of what happens:

Student Work

Chemistry

Chicken + potato = a potato with wings and a beak.

—Colette Aro, 8

Cat + dog = bite.

—Anthony Cabral, 5

Astronomy

Jupiter is ...

"Lots of cats. It's just like [Earth], but everyone is a cat, including George Washington."

—Laine Aro, 6

"It has little pieces of sand and when you step on them, they make sparks. [Jupiter's creatures] look a little different than all the creatures on this earth. They have big ears, bigger than hippo or elephant ears."

—Anthony

"It looks like a chandelier with light bulbs."

—Colette

Physics

Objects that sink or float in water, and why:

"Cork. Floated. It's very heavy, and heavy things float."

—Anthony

"Toy zebra. Sank and floated. It can swim, but when it doesn't swim it sinks."

—Colette

Anatomy

The digestive path of a piece of chocolate:

"First, it goes to a shark. Then, it goes to the ocean, where I eat the shark. Finally, I hit the shark on the head, and he gives the chocolate back to me."

—Anthony

EVERYONE'S A COMEDIAN:
WRITE YOUR OWN JOKES AND RIDDLES

by MARCY ZIPKE

2 hours

As you've probably noticed, elementary students are stand-up comedians in the making. Their inventory of jokes (such as riddles or knock-knock jokes) is impressive. In this lesson, we put these comedic skills to work, aiding the development of metalinguistic awareness (a working understanding of the constraints posed by our language). Puzzling over—and writing your own—riddles is a fun way to learn about language as well as an important step in achieving fluent writing and reading comprehension. All we need to have handy for this lesson are a few joke books and a children's dictionary and/or thesaurus.

Start by telling a few jokes in which the humor depends on language manipulation. The riddles can turn on a word with more than one meaning:

What kind of bed never sleeps?
A river bed.

How do you stop a skunk from smelling?
You hold his nose.

Or the riddles can depend on the way you arrange the words in a sentence:

What did the boy say when he was told that
his dog had been chasing a man on a bicycle?
Don't be silly! My dog can't ride a bicycle.

Ask if any of the kids have riddles to share. When everyone is sufficiently hooked, explain that it is easy to write your own riddles, all they have to know are some words that go with a favorite sport or activity.

As an example, have the kids chose an activity to write riddles about (baseball works really well). Brainstorm a list of words associated with the activity.

Example: Baseball

Bat	*Umpire*	*Catcher*
Ball	*Player*	*Coach*
Bases	*Outfielder*	*Diamond*
Plate	*Shortstop*	*Uniform*

Now explain to the kids that a homonym is a word with more than one meaning. Homonyms make the best riddles because you can ask a question that seems to be about one thing but really turns out to be about another. Have the kids find and explain the homonyms in your list.

Example: Baseball Homonyms

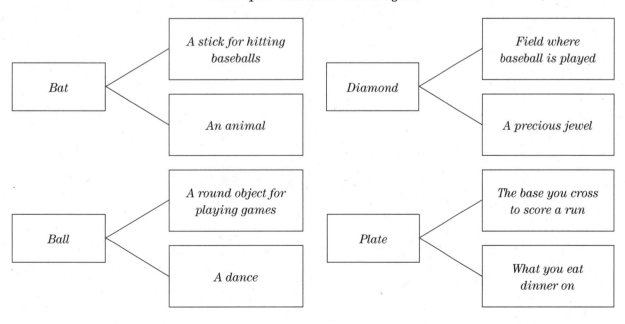

37

Now it's time to make up the riddles! Remember that only the question or the answer will really be about baseball. Here are some real third-graders' baseball riddles:

Why was Cinderella the worst player on the Yankees?
Because she couldn't go to the ball.

Why is a catcher such a good dinner guest?
Because he is always cleaning the plate.

Why are the Red Sox the coolest people on a hot summer day?
Because they have lots of fans.

Why does it take longer to run from second base to third base than from first base to second base?
Because there's a shortstop in the middle.

Why do frogs make the best outfielders?
Because they are good at catching flies.

Where is the biggest diamond in Chicago?
Wrigley Field!

Why did the policeman run out onto the baseball field?
Someone was stealing second.

Homophones (words that sound alike but are spelled differently and mean different things) work really well for writing riddles too. Start by brainstorming some pairs:

Hare/Hair
Bare/Bear
Dear/Deer
Meet/Meat

From here, the kids can write riddle questions that resolve both of the definitions:

What do you call rabbit fur?
Hare hair.

Older kids can make up riddles from expressions or idioms:

What did the calculator say to the student?
You can count on me!

When the kids have written riddles they like, encourage them to record the riddles in a small notebook or on folded pieces of paper, with the riddle on one side of the page and the answer on the other. Illustrating the answers with a funny drawing is always fun too. The kids will each leave with their very own personalized riddle book!

Want more? The following two books are excellent for aspiring comic writers: *Fiddle with a Riddle* by Joanne E. Bernstein; *Funny Side Up!* by Mike Thaler

IF I WERE A KING OR QUEEN: CREATING YOUR OWN COUNTRY

by J. Ryan Stradal & Bob Jury

5 hours

All children live in their own world—albeit one restrained by the mores and demands of unfair, illogical adults—and the rules, wishes, and parameters of this world are often only expressed piecemeal, as in a desire to stay up until midnight or a secret wish for a horse in the garage. This exercise lets students transcend all that.

When we explain to the students that they'll be creating their own country from scratch, many start working before we're even done explaining the guidelines. Fortunately, the setup is short and simple: we go over the aspects of what makes a country, we spend a few hours creating our ideal nations, and then we share them, United Nations–style, with our fellow world leaders.

We've found that the students need little guidance beyond the introduction, although they do request an audience for their cartographical innovations (more on this shortly).

The first things we explain are a country's components, which the students then invent for themselves in whichever order they choose. They are:

Name of Country: The naming of one's country, though difficult, should be tackled first because it suggests boundaries that make the infinite scope of nation-building seem less daunting. We've found that the students opt for simple, declarative names that suggest a theme (e.g. Jungle World, Red and Blue Land) or hybrids with actual places (e.g. Boston, D.C., or Kittyville, California).

Who's in Charge? Now's a good time to engage your class in a brief lesson about different kinds of government: monarchies, dictatorships, democracies, republics, empires, parliaments, etc. What kind of government will they choose for their country? What will they call its leaders? Supreme Queen, Tribal Chief, King Awesome, Dude(tte) in Charge, Duchess, Prime Minister, and El Presidente are all great choices. No students have ever chosen someone other than themselves to head their fictional country. Real-life authority figures rarely figure at all in these worlds, and when they do, they're usu-

ally demoted to a menial position. Try not to let it get to you.

Map: After you've shown the students a quick example of a fictional map on a dry-erase or chalk board, this portion of the exercise will be tackled with alarming alacrity and resounding imagination. Certain patterns will emerge: public repositories of money (usually in the form of rivers or lakes), buildings constructed from highly perishable comestibles, and sprawling personal estates (one student's eight-bed, six-bath mansion ultimately proved to be on the modest side and needed to be revised).

We go over the fictional map and, naturally, we see many variations on its themes. We blend the political, the topographical, and the edible, disregarding scale, mold, and zoning ordinances. The students often explore beyond these suggestions, inventing spectacular landmarks (a Tree of Life losing a war of attrition with a tornado) and unique urban centers (many students create cities populated exclusively by some their favorite animals).

Flag: Many students immediately gravitate toward designing their flag, utilizing a palette that would cause accidents at the U.N.'s carport. We need few to no examples; the students often generate flags as if they were waiting their whole lives to do so.

Description: This is the World Almanac entry. What is the population? What languages are spoken? What do people wear? Who is the most popular writer or musician? We explain that this is where the students can express their tastes and make their country truly subscribe to their own desired logic. We do not consider any pet-to-human ratio too outlandish.

Decree of Absolute Laws: We tell the students that for once, they can make all the rules, and for many, this is at least as fun as drawing the map. Harsh tax codes are not unheard of, and parents, teachers, and siblings often experience a severe curtailment of civil liberties. However, many students also eliminate the insulting practice of charging money for food, so life for adults in these countries isn't a complete downer.

What's Next: Once we've guided the class through an explanation of each component, with examples, the next few hours are primarily composed of one-on-one consultation with students who are either stuck on a detail or have an exciting innovation to share.

In a project like this with few parameters, it can sometimes take the students a while to adjust to the idea that the aspects of this fictional country can be as far-flung as they wish them to be. We answer many questions pertaining to logic and boundary, such as: Can one trillion people fit on an island shaped like a teddy bear? (Of course!) If Matthew's map has a black hole, can Emily's have a white hole? (Why not?)

At the end of class, we ask the students who are so inclined to do a short presentation on their country for the edification of the other heads of state. This often emboldens some of the kings, queens, princesses, and lords who were initially hesitant to do so. Then we place the completed work in a royal binder for safekeeping and easy transport. They are now ready to make their new country a part of the world.

FIVE SUGGESTIONS
FOR COUNTRY-BUILDERS

1. If you're having trouble with your map, ask yourself: What is your favorite food or beverage? Name anything you would like to have in close proximity or in great quantities, like a root beer lake, or an ice cream iceberg.

2. Are there any laws you currently consider to be unfair? Now is your chance to set the world straight. You can also decide how many school days you have a year, what is taught in school, and, naturally, if there even is school.

3. Consider dividing your country into different states or territories if you can't fit everything into just one nation. You can also banish or assign certain things to islands, like vegetables, snow, homework, pizza, or chores.

4. Take a look at the student sitting next to you. Does your country have relations with theirs? Are they peaceful or problematic? Will Puppy Town and the Snowcone Island renew their peace talks this year? At last, it's your call.

5. Design a coat of arms, logo, or symbol to put on your flag. Consider a representation of your favorite animal or pet. Nothing gets the point across at a border crossing better than a giant hamster.

WORD PORTRAITURE

by JENNY TRAIG

1 hour

Materials: One live model, preferably in a funny outfit

This is one of my very favorite lessons because it involves a live model and costumes, which automatically makes it unbelievably fun.

We start class by giving a brief history of portraiture (see below). We keep it heavy on the show and light on the tell, using art books. We show several different kinds of painted portraits, from the *Mona Lisa* to *Madame X*, noting things like background and symbolic accessories. Sometimes we read a few of Gertrude Stein's word portraits. Then we turn the students loose to create their own.

The model (usually in an interesting get-up) sits at the front of the class doing whatever she chooses. Some knit; some read; some just sit there. For the next twenty minutes, the students sketch her, using words instead of paint.

We encourage them to use as much detail as possible. "What, exactly, is the color of her hair? Is it yellow-orange like nectarines, or as gray as pencil lead?" We invite the students to draw conclusions from the evidence in front of them, embroidering as much as they like. "What are her hobbies? If she doesn't wear a watch, what can we infer from that? What do well-worn shoes say? What does she do for a living? Is she a spy or a librarian?"

Sometimes students want to share their observations with the class. We stopped encouraging this after one student shared, "He's old, he's bald, and he has a big butt." But when things go well, it's just lively. "She wants to look old-fashioned," the students observed, in one recent class. "She looks crazy!"

This particular model sported a lovely burgundy velvet dress, tasteful heels, and a Dali-esque handlebar moustache. There was much discussion of the authenticity of the facial hair, and much debating on both sides. Was it fake or was it real? The debate was settled at the end of the class when the instructor found the moustache stuck to her shoe. Fake.

The second part of the exercise is to distribute the handout (page 43–44) and have students write portraits about people they know or famous figures. We encourage them to experiment with different forms or invent their own (they seem especially fond of the acrostic poem, the start of each line spelling out their subject's name). When we have time, we like to frame the finished product. It makes a lovely gift.

A BRIEF HISTORY OF PORTRAITURE:

It's hard to say exactly when the portrait was invented. Painting dates back to cave times, but they mostly depicted things like hunts, which, since they didn't have cable, was about as exciting as life got. Later, we start to see people depicted, but usually they're idols or royal representations, not individuals. In the Middle Ages we see lots of painted people, but they're almost always religious figures. Why? Only the Church could afford to commission art. (Portraiture may be the most commercial art form, because it's normally paid for by its subject. This is not necessarily a bad thing. Consider charging your subjects for their word portraits.)

Then came the Renaissance. Now it was the aristocracy who had the money. This was the birth of portraiture as we know it. The rich threw down their cash, and, months or years later, went home with lovely framed representations of themselves. The idea has remained the same ever since. The form changes—demand for portraits by poorer folks led to silhouettes and miniatures; the invention of photography made portraiture accessible to just about everyone; and modern art abstracted and refracted the whole thing. But the general principle hasn't changed since the Renaissance. In the early part of the twentieth century Gertrude Stein invented the word portrait, which puts this principle into words instead of paint. It's very interesting, and it's what we're going to do today.

WRITE YOUR OWN. EXPERIMENT WITH STYLES.

Portraits can be painted in all different styles: abstract, pop, pointillist, etc. They can be written in different styles, too. Here's a list of six good ones. Pick your favorite one, think of a subject (your dog, Dad, best friend, whoever) and write it up. A long paragraph should do it, but if you're inspired you can write more. If you're really inspired, try several different styles.

1. Hagiography

Hagiography is a very fancy word that means "biography of a saint" and it's a fun format for a word portrait. Write about your subject as though s/he were a saint. Use surreal, mystical imagery. Here's a sample: "St. Britney first heard the calling when she was nine years old. 'Disney,' the angels whispered, so the family packed up the Dodge and drove to Orlando."

2. Advertisement

Write your portrait as an ad. Remember, you're selling something here, so you want to be over-the-top and cheesy as all get-out. It should read like commercial copywriting, energetic and clichéd: "Looking for a fun person to eat lunch with? Look no further. Alice Mackenzie is all that and more. She chews with her mouth shut and shares her potato chips. She can shoot milk out her nose, and her funny stories are sure to make you do the same. Alice Mackenzie—America's Favorite Condiment!"

3. Newspaper Article

This is a good format because being in the newspaper is so exciting. You could do your portrait as a celebrity profile or as straight news ("Local Boy Declared Wrestling's Biggest Fan"). The obituary is a convenient format but your subject might not take you wanting them dead very well so we think it's best avoided.

4. Negative Relief

You could write a portrait like a negative of a photo, describing the subject by writing only about what s/he is not: "Ellen is not a tall woman. She is not blond and she has never had a tan. When she buys a chocolate bar she doesn't eat it all at once. She has never skied, but if she did, she would prefer cross-country to downhill."

5. Abstract

Picasso's abstract portraits are all nose. You could do the same thing in written form by emphasizing one feature above all others, writing just about your subject's forehead or feet. Or you could be like Gertrude Stein and list a series of unconnected things you associate with the subject, giving the reader an overall sense of what s/he's about: "Pearl buttons. Buttered toast. Crumpled napkins and house dust. Thank-you notes. Ginger ale without ice. On rainy days, the door swells."

6. Caricature

Caricatures are the most fun to write but also the trickiest. Pick your subject's most important one or two characteristics and exaggerate them absurdly. (Award yourself ten bonus points if you know this technique is called "hyperbole.") If you're writing about someone you know, it's probably best to exaggerate their good characteristics rather than their bad ones. No one wants to read that they have the largest nostril flare-span in North America. But they would love to know they have the bounciest, best-behaving hair since hair was invented.

Student Work

Klara

Klara is not tall. She overslept this morning. She was late for school and late for breakfast, but she's never late for dinner. Klara always wears glasses. She never sees right. She always wears a white dress. She tries to act old-fashioned. When she's angry, she always gives a loud scream, but when she screams, her beard falls off.

—Kira Saks, 8

A Terrifying, Boneless Rock

Boneless, gray, hard, heavy, rough, moldy. It's not grass. It is not anything but a weird, cold, big, stinky, book-reading, writing, million year–old rock that is terrifying and also hurt.

—Radford Leung, 9

OH, YOU SHOULDN'T HAVE, REALLY...
OR, HOW TO WRITE A JON SCIESZKA PICTURE BOOK

by JON SCIESZKA

1 hour
Materials: One Jon Scieszka book
(The local library should have several.)

Imitation is said to be the most sincere form of flattery. It's also a great way to start writing.

When I was a kid, I discovered Jack London's stories. All of my stories from that year featured brave dogs "bounding" through hazards of every sort. The "bounding" seemed vital. Later stories from my Edgar Allen Poe Phase were sure to include at least one misshapen dwarf, a surprise ending, and the word "dreary." My Kafka Period and my *Mad* magazine Days seem to have collided and fused to form my current style.

So the basic idea of the class is to show one of five Jon Scieszka picture books (listed below), read it, and then use it as a model for kids to imitate. It's a near-foolproof plan because (1) it's nothing more than an organized version of what kids naturally do on their own and (2) the writing challenge is easily adapted to fit the ability of each individual student. The concrete and literal writers can copy the story directly. The more sophisticated writers can write their own variations.

I would imagine starting the class by showing a Jon Scieszka picture book and announcing, "We have finally discovered how Jon Scieszka writes his books. Special agents learned that Mr. Scieszka is a sucker for flattery. He loves it when kids imitate his writing. So when the agents promised that kids would imitate his writing if he told them how he wrote his books ... he spilled his guts. If you promise to imitate him, we can reveal his secrets."

This is a perfect time to bring up the aphorism, "Imitation is the most sincere form of flattery." Discuss.

Read the selected book. Choose from:
The True Story of the 3 Little Pigs!
Baloney, Henry P.
Math Curse
Squids Will Be Squids
*The Stinky Cheese Man and Other Fairly
    Stupid Tales*

Then distribute the corresponding handout, which explains how I wrote it (pages 47–49). Remind the writers of their promise to flatter me with imitation, and brainstorm how they might write their own stories using the story that was just read as the model.

If you want to really keep imitating the Jon Scieszka writing model, explain to the students that I never draw the illustrations for my stories. I write them, then hand them off to someone else for the illustrations. I would be doubly flattered if they did the same and drew some new pictures for the stories they read.

THE TRUE STORY BEHIND
THE TRUE STORY OF THE 3 LITTLE PIGS!
HOW TO WRITE A FAIRY TALE FROM A NEW POINT OF VIEW

"**I**t wasn't my fault."

That's what I was thinking the wolf would say if he got to tell his side of the Three Little Pigs story. I thought about how the wolf would explain knocking down those pigs' houses, then let him explain.

What would different characters in other fairy tales say if they got a chance to tell their own version of their story? Here are some thoughts to get you started:

I'll bet the witch had a perfectly good reason for fattening up Hansel and Gretel.

I wonder what the stepmom thought about goody-goody Cinderella?

The three bears must have some interesting opinions about Goldilocks that didn't make it into the official version.

What did the seven dwarves really think about Snow White?

THE TRUE STORY BEHIND *BALONEY, HENRY P.*
HOW TO WRITE AN INTERGALACTIC TALL TALE

Tall tales are stories of wild exaggeration. The stories about Paul Bunyan, John Henry, and Pecos Bill are tall tales.

Anybody can write a tall tale. It's a lot like making up a really outrageous bunch of lies. Say you are late for school one day and your teacher asks you why. You could say, "I was attacked by a gang of hungry sea lions." That would be an interesting beginning to a tall tale. But if would be an even more interesting tall tale if you pretended you were from outer space and translated the words "sea lions" into another language. Then your tall tale would start, "I was attacked by a gang of hungry *seelowen*." (That's German for *sea lion*.) Which is exactly what I did to write *Baloney, Henry P.*

So make up your wildest and craziest excuse why you were late for school.

Translate some of the key words into other languages.

Presto—you have an Intergalactic Tall Tale.

Internet translating dictionaries are great places to find your Intergalactic words. Dictionaries and those funny little pocket travel books are good Intergalactic word tools too. And for some reason, the most Intergalactic-looking words seem to be Finnish or Dutch.

THE TRUE STORY BEHIND *MATH CURSE*
HOW TO WRITE A FUNNY MATH STORY

Anybody who has ever had to answer those math word problems can tell you where I got the idea to write *Math Curse*. I just wondered what would happen if one day everything turned into a math problem.

Use whatever math you are studying, and make up problems and answers about your life. Use addition, subtraction, multiplication, division, fractions. Don't forget true/false questions, multiple choice, and greater-than and less-than.

For extra credit, imagine and write what might happen if everything in your life turned into a science experiment, an art assignment, or a history quiz.

THE TRUE STORY BEHIND *SQUIDS WILL BE SQUIDS*
HOW TO WRITE A MODERN FABLE

Okay, I admit it. I took stories my daughter and son told me and turned them into fables. Is that so wrong? This guy named Aesop did it hundreds of years ago. So I thought I should too.

Fables are stories about people and the weird, annoying, funny things they do. But in fables the people are changed to animals, and there is usually a moral at the end. That way you can write about your friend Jessica who annoys you by always chewing your pencils, and not insult her because your fable is about a beaver.

Think of something annoying or funny or strange that a friend does.

Change their character into an animal, or a breakfast cereal, or a Madagascar hissing cockroach, or whatever you think is most like them.

Add the moral you would want that friend to learn from your fable. For instance: chew a pencil, lose a friend.

THE TRUE STORY BEHIND *STINKY CHEESE MAN*
HOW TO WRITE YOUR OWN FAIRLY STUPID TALE

I already admitted how I thought it was fun to goof around with one fairy tale and turn it into *The True Story of the 3 Little Pigs!* So after I did that, it got me thinking—wouldn't it be even more fun to mess up a whole bunch of fairy tales?

And that's what I did.

Fairy tales usually have pretty obvious characters, plots, and action. You've got your princesses, your princes, kings, queens, witches, trolls, giants, dragons, stepmothers, and magical animals. You've got your magic spells. You know how most of the stories go.

So why not try to mess up the stories in as many ways as possible? Change one character. Reverse the plot. Twist the magic spell.

I started with thinking what would happen if the little old lady ran out of gingerbread and made the little man out of something else?

What if Rapunzel decided to do something different with her hair?

What if a not-very-smart giant told his tale?

What if Sleeping Beauty woke up early? You would have your own Fairly Stupid Tale.

BODY LANGUAGE: KINETIC WRITING

by ANGELA HERNANDEZ

1 hour
Materials: Island props
(Optional, but a coconut, seashells, beachwear,
sunglasses, and sunscreen are recommended.)

This lesson gets everyone up and moving, so it's great for students who have trouble staying in their seats. It's a good way to explore different forms of storytelling, and it can be adapted for other subjects as well. I've also used it in my U.S. History class to review material. Letting the students get out of their seats and act out the lesson really helps them connect.

This class might also work well for the second language learner. For many second language learners, gesturing often helps facilitate the communication process and boosts confidence when speaking their non-native language.

Here's how it works:

Pass out the handout (page 51). The prompt invites students to create a desert island story. Give the students ten minutes or so to write. Because this is such a physical lesson, it's great to bring in physical props to inspire creativity. Let the students touch a hairy coconut, smell sunscreen, or listen to a shell. Sunglasses or a beach hat might help get them into character, and the props can lead to some inventive improv.

Next, have the students come to the front of the class one at a time, and act out their story, using only movement, facial expressions, and the island props—no words. (You could also have students trade papers, if they're squeamish about acting out their own story.) Then have the class guess what the story was about. Let's see, there was armpit scratching, funny faces, and running in circles.... Was it about a monkey dance troupe? An allergic reaction? Hyperactive toddlers?

Finally, have the student read the story out loud so the class can see if they guessed correctly. Ah, so it *was* about a monkey dance troupe after all! Fine work!

AN ISLAND ADVENTURE

Last week, I was out sailing, when all of a sudden there was a storm! My boat was shipwrecked on an island! I wandered around, and you wouldn't believe what I saw....

Tell us what you saw here. What did you smell, hear, feel? How did you react? Were you scared? Excited? What did you do? Then what happened?

_____

_____

_____

_____

_____

_____

_____

_____

_____

_____

_____

_____

_____

_____

_____

_____

_____

_____

_____

_____

_____

_____

KID CAFÉ: ZANY MENU WRITING

by BONNIE SCHIFF-GLENN & SOPHIE FELS

2 hours

Materials: One folder for each student

This yummy workshop has two parts. In session one, the participants create a zany restaurant through some spirited collaborative menu-writing. Session two allows the participants to independently decorate their new menu and describe daily specials in a blank insert. In our lessons, we do both parts on the same day, with volunteers printing the menus as we pause for a snack. The two parts could easily be done on consecutive days, however, to allow time for printing and preparing the menus and inserts.

Session One: The Restaurant

The students gather around us, and we explain that they've been assigned, as a team, the task of designing a new restaurant, complete with all of its signature dishes. The mysterious chef who's presented them with the task, we tell them, is somewhat unique: he is capable of making anything, real or imagined, from the most delicious to the most disgusting dishes. He's asked for a challenge, and they are the ones to provide it for him. What will they ask him to make?

We go through the menu-writing course by course, discussing new vocabulary as necessary ("beverages," "appetizers," "entrées," and so on). We remind the team that their concoctions need not be reasonable and may be the kind of thing that they'd find in a favorite science fiction story or cartoon rather than on their own dinner tables. Potions and curse-infused dishes are often favorites. Each student writes down a fabulous dish creation. The students then give their idea to our menu editor, who takes them home and types up a master menu with each student's dish listed. These will be distributed in the next class.

The students tend to want to come up with a name for their establishment first, but we've found that saving this task for the end is preferable: as they are created, the dishes themselves often begin to suggest a name.

Session Two: Today's Specials

Once the menus have been completed, edited, and printed, a copy is made for each child. To approximate the sturdy style of typical restaurant menus, we glue ours to colored two-pocket folders, with the pockets cut off beforehand. Colored oaktag, construction paper, or file folders would work just as well. We make sure, in our layout, to include room for decorations and illustrations of favorite dishes, which we have the students complete as we are helping them paste the menus onto the folders.

Each student receives an additional sheet entitled "Today's Specials" with headings for Appetizers, Entrées, and Desserts—but no dishes! This is an opportunity for students to add inspirations that may have come to them since the original writing or ideas that, for whatever reason, did not get into the menu.

That's it! Bon appétit!

SPY SCHOOL

by KATE PAVAO & JENNY TRAIG

1 hour

Materials: One copy of handout packet (pages 54–60) for each student, costumes, lemon juice, toothpicks, fruit

Most people have no idea how much writing spies actually do. Everyone thinks spying is all martinis and high-speed boat chases. The fact is, spies have to write all the time. There are cases to file, forms to fill out, memoirs to pen, and more paperwork than you can imagine. This class prepares students for future careers as highly literate covert operatives. It also gives them lots of practice observing and describing. And boy, do they have fun.

This lesson does require a fair amount of prep. You'll need to make a copy of the training manual (pages 54–60) for each student. You'll definitely need a whole bunch of fruit and some index cards. Yes, we said fruit. And if you happen to have some items for disguises to bring in—like hats, scarves, or sunglasses—that would be great. Bonus points for lemon juice and toothpicks (for invisible ink). And if you can find a volunteer to dress up strangely and pay your class a visit, you'll have a lesson your students will never forget.

Here's how class works: We distribute the handouts and welcome our recruits to Spy School. All students are encouraged to take an alias, so we spend a few minutes going around the room and asking everyone what their new code name is. Then we get down to work.

The first thing we learn about are the tools of the trade. We spend about ten minutes going over "The Spy's Toolbox" (page 55) in the handbook. This is a lot more interesting if there are actual items on hand for the students to check out, so we usually show things like funny hats and goofy glasses. We ask a few brave students to model them, showing how easy it is to completely transform your look with just a few small accessories.

Next we move onto cryptology. We turn to the "Codes" section of the handbook (page 56) and learn all the different codes: the Numbers Code, the Caesar Cipher, the Magic Five Code, and the Da Vinci Code. This takes ten minutes or so. When time permits we mix up a batch of lemon juice for invisible ink as well. Then we give the students an assignment. Using the prompt on page 57, they have ten minutes to write a coded message for our agent in Brazil. The students trade papers with their neighbors and try to crack each other's code.

Next we bring out the fruit. We turn to the "Gathering Intelligence" (page 58) section of the handbook and give each student a piece of fruit (usually an apple or an orange). Their assignment: for the next ten minutes they have to observe every little thing they can about their fruit, taking notes and making a sketch. What makes this apple different from all other apples? Is there a bruise? A black spot? A hole? Does it have a stem? A sticker? What's the color like? Is it uniform or mottled? When the ten minutes are up, the students all hand over their fruit and the teacher places each piece of fruit on a card with the student's name on the other side. Then, one by one, the students come up to see if they can pick out their piece of fruit.

Next, we eat the evidence.

Finally, it's time to put all our new spy skills to the test. We turn to the "Official Spy School Case File #1" (page 59) in the training manual. All of a sudden, a mysterious person (usually a cooperative colleague, friend, or parent) comes into class dressed strangely and behaving even more strangely. She may mutter or drop things. All of these things are clues. For the next fifteen minutes the students fill out Case File #1, observing as much as they can about this mysterious visitor. Who is this person? And what is she doing here? Is she a double agent? A fellow spy trying to send you a message? Or is she just plain crazy?

Spy School is almost done. Only one thing remains: the debriefing. We go around the room, asking the students to share their theories on the identity of the mysterious visitor. Then we turn to the "Debriefing" section in the training manual (page 60) and invite the students to make up a cover story. They certainly can't tell their parents they were spying all morning. They've been practicing their nonfiction writing; now they'll get a chance to practice writing fiction, making up a convincing tale about the nice, safe, non-spy-like things they did instead.

CLASSIFIED TRAINING MANUAL

THIS TOP-SECRET MANUAL
BELONGS TO _____

If that's not you, put the book down right now and back
away, or we will find you! You have been warned!

Why are you still reading this? Put it down!
And by all means, don't open it!

THE SPY'S TOOLBOX

Disguises

You definitely need a disguise. In general, it's better to blend in with an outfit that doesn't draw too much attention, but that's not much fun, so if your spy uniform involves a cowboy hat and a feather boa, that's just fine with us. Here are some basic incognito supplies that provide instant camouflage:

Glasses: The bigger and darker, the better.

Scarves: Provide instant coverage. Also, they prevent sunburns.

Hats: Easy and portable.

Wigs and false moustaches: Not very subtle, but fun.

Funny teeth: Change your whole look instantly! Buckteeth are especially good.

Hardware

Yes, yes, it would be wonderful to have a shoe phone and a lipstick camera, but the clever spy doesn't need to rely on high-tech gadgetry. That stuff is for amateurs! You can make your own spy supplies from stuff you already have at home. Here are some useful materials:

Scotch tape: Want to know if anyone has been snooping in your room? Place some Scotch tape on the door, high up or low down, where no one will notice. If it's torn when you get home, you'll know someone was snooping.

Dixie cups: The classic listening device. Place one against a door or wall and you can hear what's going on on the other side. If you have two cups and some string, you can make a low-tech spy phone to communicate with your fellow agents.

Hair: Drape a hair over your journal before you leave. If the hair has moved when you return, you'll know someone was peeking.

Milk cartons: Make your own periscope from an empty milk carton and a hand mirror. You can see what's going on around corners!

Resources and Further Reading

You might enjoy these books: *Harriet the Spy* by Louise Fitzhugh; *Stormbreaker* by Anthony Horowitz; *Encyclopedia Brown* by Donald J. Sobol; *From the Mixed-up Files of Mrs. Basil E. Frankweiler* by E. L. Konigsburg; *Spy Science: 40 Secret-Sleuthing, Code-Cracking, Spy-Catching Activities for Kids* by Jim Wiese and Ed Shems; *Crime Scene Investigations: Real-Life Science Activities for the Elementary Grades* by Pam Walker and Elaine Wood

CODES

Number Code

Assign every letter a number. You can use a simple formula, like A=1, B=2, or something more complicated, like A=1, B=4, C=9, D=16, etc. Then write your message in numbers instead of letters. What does this say? Hint: 20=T and 15=O.

20 15 1 19 20   9 19   20 1 19 20 25.

Caesar Cipher

This code was used by Julius Caesar. Simply substitute the letter three places down the alphabet for the letter you actually mean. So, A=D, B=E, C=F, and so on. What does this say?

EULWQHB VSHDUV

Magic Five

To decipher this code, circle every fifth letter and ignore the rest. What does this say?

STSRMHTGHYDRJUFIOKMEPUJHESDLKTDRPOSNJDRMKOBGELPVCLSRBVL

The Da Vinci Code

This code is simple: just write backwards. Write from right to left and flip all the letters. Use a mirror to read it. This is how Leonardo da Vinci wrote everything! What does this say?

Can you read this?

Invisible Ink

Write your message using a toothpick dipped in lemon juice. It will dry invisibly. To read it, have an adult help you iron the letter on a low setting (be careful not to singe the paper). The heat will make the letters appear.

SPY SCHOOL NEEDS YOU!

Spy School needs to get a very, very, very important message regarding our bubblegum supply to our agent in Brazil. However, if the message fell into the wrong hands, the results would be devastating! Catastrophic! An international bubblegum disaster! Imagine how messy that would be!

We need you to write the message in code. You can use one of our crackerjack cryptology methods or make up your own. Write your message here. When you're done, give it to a fellow agent and see if s/he can solve it.

_____

_____

_____

_____

_____

_____

_____

_____

_____

_____

_____

_____

_____

_____

_____

_____

_____

_____

_____

_____

GATHERING INTELLIGENCE

To be a good spy, you need to be a good observer. You need to be able to look at a suspicious person or a crime scene and quickly make a mental note of all the important details: Does he have freckles? Eyeglasses? Tattoos? A funny walk?

You need to be able to describe these valuable pieces of information accurately so that your bosses back at headquarters can read your report and understand exactly what you saw, what you heard, what you smelled, what you felt with your fingers—perhaps even what you tasted.

Prepare for an on-the-spot test! Pencils down! Spend some time really sniffing, measuring, comparing, inspecting, tapping, and staring at the object your instructor gives you before you begin writing and drawing.

After carefully observing my secret object, I would say it:

_____

_____

_____

_____

_____

_____

_____

It looks like (go ahead and draw a picture here):

OFFICIAL SPY SCHOOL CASE FILE #1

On _____ , 20__ , I, Agent _____ , was dispatched on a top-secret mission of the highest importance. It was something, all right. Here is what I observed:

The subject(s) looked like this:

_____

_____

_____

_____

Here's a picture:

Here's what the subject(s) did:

_____

_____

_____

Here's what I overheard the subject(s) say:

_____

_____

_____

Putting it all together, I draw the following conclusions about the identity and mission of the subject(s):

_____

_____

_____

DEBRIEFING

The final phase of any spy mission is the debriefing. This is where you lie about what you actually did. You can't tell your family you were chasing international double agents all day! They would go crazy! Instead, make up a nice boring story about spending your day organizing the sock drawer, or sweeping.

It was a beautiful day, perfect for calm tidy activities in which no one gets hurt, like…

_____

_____

_____

_____

So that's what we did, all day. Boring? No! Who could get bored spending the day in such a safe manner? Let me tell you a little more about this exciting activity!

_____

_____

_____

_____

Yes, it was very exciting indeed, and we worked up quite an appetite. We had a nice nutritious snack of milk and…

_____

_____

_____

_____

And then we took a nice quiet nap. It was all very nice and perfectly safe. And if you're wondering how I got that little hole in my shirt, it's quite simple. I…

_____

_____

_____

_____

MIDDLE SCHOOL
LESSON PLANS

WHINING EFFECTIVELY
OR, HOW TO PERSUADE YOUR PARENTS

by TAYLOR JACOBSON & ABIGAIL JACOBS

6 hours
Materials: Four adults for a last-session panel

This workshop teaches students to write proposals so convincing no parent can resist them. We have tested them on real parents, so we know. We've seen students exhibit ironclad persuasive reasoning as they've tried to change their bedtime, raise their allowance, or increase their candy quota. It's quite impressive.

Session One

We begin with a brainstorm on what we think *persuasive* means. This usually gets a lot of very interesting answers. We talk about what makes writing persuasive, why someone would want their writing to be persuasive, when and where persuasive writing is used, and what it means to persuade someone. The kids get pretty riled up when they start to understand they might really be able to talk their parents into *anything* if they craft the right argument.

We emphasize the difference between persuasive writing and opinion writing. This is sometimes hard for them to grasp but we try to work through it by defining emotion vs. reason. We give examples: "Raw eggs are disgusting" is an opinion. "Raw eggs are a proven health risk" is persuasive. "Fourteen-year-olds should be able to drive" is an opinion. "In many countries, fourteen-year-olds are safely permitted to drive" is persuasive. "The school day starts too early" is an opinion. "Studies have shown that teenagers' comprehension improves after 10 a.m." is persuasive. And so on.

We begin by going over the Five Commandments of Persuasive Writing. They are:

1. Know your audience

Are you trying to persuade your parents? Your teachers? Your friends? Society at large? Tailor your writing to your audience. Don't use slang with your teachers; don't use stiff, formal language with your friends.

2. Choose your position, and prepare for the opposition

State your opinion clearly. If you truly know your audience, you probably already know their opinion on your topic, and can counter it: "While some parents may think kids are likely to lose an iPod, research shows that's an extremely infrequent occurrence."

3. Back up the argument with research

We tend to get asked "Can we make the research up?" here, so a brief discussion of what research is may be necessary.

4. Don't state your opinion unless you can back it up with good arguments

We remind them: don't confuse facts with what you see as the truth.

5. Restate your point and summarize your supporting points

A little repetition helps drive your argument home.

Next, we read an example of good persuasive writing and an example of not-so-persuasive writing aloud (pages 65–66). We let the students tell us which one is good and which one is bad and why.

If time permits, we spend some time brainstorming topics and methods of research (statistics, interviews and quotes, examples). Topics usually involve persuading parents to buy something (GameBoy, cable TV, cell phone, puppy); or allow something (walk home from school alone, have a sleepover, forgo homework one day a week).

The assignment for the first class is to bring your topic, a brief definition of your audience including their opinion on the topic (if you already know), three strong points in your favor, and three possible counterarguments.

Session Two

In the second session we roll up our sleeves and work. We read what the students have written so far, then fix what needs fixing. If you have time to meet one-on-one with each student, great. If not, peer editing can be really helpful.

Usually, what the essays need at this point is more research to back their arguments. We look for answers on the Internet. We also look for some good experts for students to interview and help them draft questions. Their assignment is to have the essay finished for the last class.

Session Three

In the last session, we put our persuasive papers to the test. We bring in a panel of "parents and parentlike experts" to whom the students present their work. The panel for our last workshop included a teacher, a journalist, a writer, and a self-described parent-persuading expert.

Each student stands up and presents his or her persuasive paper. The panel then comments on the style, writing, delivery, and overall persuasiveness, keeping in mind the parts and steps of a persuasive essay that we have discussed throughout the workshop. Feedback usually sounds something like, "At first I thought, 'Is this kid crazy? There is no benefit to video game playing that could persuade his parents to buy him a Nintendo GameBoy.' But you completely persuaded me with your statistic that linked video game playing with higher standardized test scores. If I were your parents, I would buy you one today." Music to our ears. Success!

A NOT-SO-PERSUASIVE ESSAY

Dessert should always be served before any meats, fruits, and especially vegetables because dessert is definitely the best part of any meal. I mean, who can argue with the yumminess of cookies, cake, and ice cream as compared to spinach or meatloaf? I can't and I'm sure you can't either. Let me tell you why you think that dessert should always be served first at every meal and you will certainly have to agree with me when I'm done.

First of all, we have the issue of how delicious dessert really is. As far as I can tell, everyone feels this way, so I shouldn't even have to convince you. Anyone who likes vegetables better than dessert is nuts—and I don't mean the kind of nuts you'll find in some chocolate brownies. I have asked most of my friends and they agree with me on this point: dessert tastes better than any other part of a meal. So, why shouldn't we get to enjoy dessert first and the other stuff later? Well, we should, which is what I'm trying to tell you here.

Aside from how good dessert tastes, we need to talk about how bad other kinds of foods taste in comparison. Nutrition, schmootrition—spinach just plain doesn't taste good and everyone knows it. Besides, if I'm really supposed to eat something as unappetizing as spinach, shouldn't I be allowed to eat an appetizer of double fudge ice cream first? Every restaurant menu I've ever seen serves appetizers, so there's no reason we shouldn't do the same thing at home.

My last point is probably the most important one, so listen up. By putting dessert at the end of a meal, you risk running out of time before you have to go to bed. That's right: all that time you spend eating eggplant, asparagus and—if you're really unlucky—liver and onions, you could be eating dessert. But instead, due to the unreasonable rules placing dessert at the end of a meal, you sometimes have to wolf it down at an unreasonable pace due to time considerations. I don't know about you, but my bedtime is 9 p.m. *sharp*, so after spending an hour and a half pushing lima beans around my plate (that makes it look like you've eaten more than you have) I never have enough time to properly enjoy my dessert. That is not only unfair to me, but it also is kind of dumb.

In summary, dessert should be eaten first because of the following:

1) It's the best
2) Other food is very often the worst
3) It's the only way to enjoy dessert at the leisurely pace at which it should be enjoyed.

Thank you for your time and consideration. I expect our next meal together to reflect the changes I have outlined above.

A GOOD PERSUASIVE ESSAY

Children should be allowed to eat dessert before salad, main course, and vegetables at dinnertime because it improves their overall happiness, it assists in digestive functions, and it allows parents to spend less time washing dishes. Many parents think that healthy foods such as salad or vegetables are more important to a child's well-being, but recent studies have proven that consumption of dessert first is beneficial in more ways than one.

First, contradictory to the belief that a healthy balance of proteins and carbohydrates aids digestion, it is the sticky sugar found in most desserts that coats the belly and allows for improved absorption of nutrients. In his best-selling book, *Digestive Functions*, the well-known digestive scientist Dr. Stomach Acid says, "basically, the stomach is happy when it eats dessert and therefore, more able to digest other, less satisfying foods such as salad and vegetables." Dr. Acid strongly supports the primary position of dessert in the meal and suggests that brownies, ice cream, and cake are the most beneficial desserts to serve on a regular basis.

Furthermore, eating dessert first improves children's overall level of happiness, making them more pleasant to be around, nicer, and more responsive to their parents. Children who eat dessert first have been known to clean their rooms more often and assist their parents with household chores. Sally Smothers, a fourth-grade student at San Francisco Elementary School, notes, "If my parents served dessert first, I would be so excited that I would wash the dishes after every meal and help my brother with his homework. In fact, I might even volunteer to walk the dog and clean my room once a week."

Finally, when salad, main course, and vegetables are served before dessert they often leave a messy residue on the plate, forcing parents to use new, clean plates when they serve dessert and therefore increasing the number of plates they must wash. But when dessert is served as the first course of the meal, there is no residue left on plates because dessert is so delicious. Therefore, the plates can be reused immediately for the other courses of the meal. Only one plate used means fewer dishes to wash. A recent study conducted by the Institute for Parental Relaxation (IPR) found that nine out of ten parents prefer doing "almost anything else" to washing dishes. Further, in his essay, "Dessert is Tasty: Researching Dessert and Its Benefits for Parents," Dr. Green Beans agrees and says, "serving dessert first would result in reduction of plate usage by no less than 50 percent. This is a clear indicator that serving dessert at the beginning of the meal would benefit parents as much as it would please their children."

In conclusion, the benefits of serving dessert before the main course clearly outweigh the drawbacks. With this one small change to the order of food consumption, parents could help make their children happier and healthier, all the while improving their own lives.

EAT THIS ESSAY: FOOD WRITING

by Susie Kramer & Laura Scholes

4 hours
Materials: One bag of groceries,
small snacks (e.g. olives, peanut butter and jelly on crackers),
"magic writer's fuel" (popcorn and Raisinets, optional)

Any lesson that ends in a feast is automatically a winner. This one is also great because it makes students think about memory and imagination, and the connection between the two.

The idea behind this lesson is that memory is one of the best tools for writing, but it can also be elusive. Food has the unique ability to call up long-buried memories and emotions, so writing about your eating experiences, both delicious and disgusting, is a great way to exercise the memory muscles. Food writing also demands the use of precise sensory detail and strong active verbs.

Session One

We teach this session in a two-hour block, but if that doesn't suit your schedule you could easily break it into two one-hour sessions instead. The class begins with a bag of groceries. We pull various foods out of the bags—artichoke hearts, peanut butter, fruit cocktail, what-have-you—and the students give thumbs-up or thumbs-down for each item. Usually they want to defend or explain their reactions too. This is a fun way to generate some excitement, and it helps the students see what a personal matter food really is.

After that we get them talking a bit about why they like to eat. "Because it's fun" seems to be the most common answer, which is great, because that's part of the whole point of this workshop—to explore our social and emotional associations with food. We tell them there are three connections we will be exploring:

- Between yourself and the food you eat

- Between other people and the food they eat with you, prepare for you, etc.

- Between yourself and other people.

Using the tools of writing, we're going to see how all of these things fit together as a part of your personal identity.

At this point, with all the talk of food, the students are usually pretty hungry. Each student gets a little plate with two bites—peanut butter and jelly is a good bet, and then something like olives, which elicit a huge range of reactions. The students close their eyes and try each food, then free-write for two minutes on their experience of this food, both right now and in their memory. We encourage them to get as specific as possible: the feel of the sticky peanut butter on their teeth, the reason they first ate it, the most memorable time they ate it. Then a few students share their written responses out loud.

Next we see how other writers have tackled the subject. The poems "Good Hot Dogs" by Sandra Cisneros [1] and "This is Just to Say" by William Carlos Williams [2] are great examples. They're sort of like love letters (to hot dogs and plums, respectively), but they are also both about the relationship between two people. We read them aloud and ask: How does each poet feel about the food involved? How do they each feel about the other person mentioned in the poem?

Then we ask the students to make two lists: one of their favorite foods and one of their most hated. Next to each, they write a few adjectives or phrases that come to mind (sweet, bitter, slimy, greasy, seeds, juice, grandma, school, whatever), and the reasons they like or dislike each food. This gets their personal relationships with food down on paper in a bare-bones kind of way.

This segues nicely into another short reading, the essay "Mint Snowball" by Naomi Shihab Nye (page 69), which we read aloud. We ask the students: Which of the foods on your list is your mint snowball? Which do you associate most strongly with a person in your life?

We ask the students to look at their lists and choose the food that sparks the strongest reaction, the most vivid memories and associations. Once they've

---

1. In Cool Salsa: Bilingual Poems on Growing Up Hispanic in the United States *(Henry Holt, 1994)*

2. At http://www.americanpoems.com/poets/williams/1047

made their choice, they break out on their own to draft a rough version of a story associated with this food. We tell them to close their eyes and think back to the most memorable experience of eating the food, preferably when the relevant friend or relative was present (for the eating or the preparation). Tell the story of that moment or meal. Imagine where you were in detail when you ate that food, the taste of each morsel. Don't use just taste and smell—use all the five senses to describe the scene. Why was this particular experience so memorable?

This is a good time to encourage the students to be as descriptive as possible. Instead of "The mango was sweet," we want to read, "The mango was so sweet it almost made you wince. It was as orange as a sunset. The orange flesh stuck to my face and made me look like a clown. My mother laughed when she saw me."

It's amazing the variety of responses students give. One boy wrote about watching his grandmother make *pupusas*, waiting for the tortilla to puff up into a little dome. "When this taste ends, I'm in hell," he wrote. Another boy wanted to write not just about one food, but about the last time he would see his Cub Scout friends, when they decided to throw orange soda, Pepsi, whipped cream, chocolate sauce, three kinds of ice cream, and sprinkles in a glass and drink it down. It seemed like such a great idea, he said, but the drink was way too sweet, and the memory of that last moment with his friends is full of sadness and disappointment.

We send the students home with an assignment for the next session: they're to interview the important person associated with their chosen food and, if possible, take part in the preparation of that food. If the important person is unavailable for comment, it's okay to interview another friend or family member. We ask them each to bring in a recipe and a sample of the special food for our finale feast!

Session Two

The second session of the workshop is mostly used to revise the students' initial drafts, using the material they gathered during their interviews. We do it in two busy hours, but you could easily break it into several smaller sessions. The work is powered by an enormous bowl of "magic writers' fuel," which is a mixture of popcorn and Raisinets. This concoction boosts their creative juices, helping them come up with amazingly vivid and spectacular detail.

We like to use mini Post-It Notes as a revision tool. The students each get ten or fifteen Post-It Notes. Then, using the results of their interviews, they write a sentence on each of the Post-Its and decide where these can be inserted into the story. They can also use the Post-Its to add another layer of sensory detail. With every mention of the food in question, students can add another detail about what it's like to eat that food (like, "The strawberry seeds from Grandma's pie got stuck in my teeth and didn't come out for days"). Every time the important person in question appears, they can add another detail about what that person was like ("Grandma always said my name like it had five syllables. Her strawberry pie made me feel loved and comforted"). By the end of this, their pages are totally yellow with Post-Its, and they can type their revisions, incorporating the additions.

Now is a good time to talk with the kids about *structure*. We encourage them to think of their first draft as the middle of the food memoir, so what they need next is a *beginning* and an *end*. We talk about what the beginning should do and what the end should do, and we give them ten minutes to work on each one. They're usually able to come up with their own answers to what a beginning should do. *Introduce* your reader to the topic. *Hook* your reader in. It helps to look back at "Mint Snowball," at how Naomi Shihab Nye pulls the reader in with her astoundingly vivid description of eating the snowball itself.

What should the end of the food memoir do? It should *connect* everything together. It should offer some *new idea* that leaves the reader thinking. It should have *punch* (images or phrases that really knock the reader's socks off). At this point, the students can ask themselves: What does all of this mean to you? Why are these memories important to you—who you are and who you are becoming? That's what they need to express with their endings.

We spend the rest of the workshop putting all the parts together—the initial draft, the Post-It additions, the actual recipe, and the new beginning and end. When they're done, each student reads his or her finished memoir after serving the food that goes with it. This is a wonderful way to culminate the workshop, because the kids can enjoy their own eating experiences while listening to their classmates' words.

 SUPERTEACHER BONUS ACTIVITY: *Copy everyone's food essays and recipes and bind them all into a very literary class cookbook!*

MINT SNOWBALL

My great-grandfather on my mother's side ran a drugstore in a small town in central Illinois. He sold pills and rubbing alcohol from behind the big cash register and creamy ice cream from the soda fountain. My mother remembers the counter's long polished sweep, its shining face. She twirled on the stools. Dreamy fans. Wide summer afternoons. Clink of nickels in anybody's hand. He sold milkshakes, cherry Cokes, old-fashioned sandwiches. What did an old-fashioned sandwich look like? Silver spigots on chocolate dispensers.

My great-grandfather had one specialty: a Mint Snowball, which he invented. Some people drove all the way in from Decatur just to taste it. First he stirred fresh mint leaves with sugar and secret ingredients in a small pot on the stove for a very long time. He concocted a flamboyant elixir of mint. Its scent clung to his fingers even after he washed his hands. Then he shaved ice into tiny particles and served it mounded in a glass dish. Permeated with mint syrup. Scoops of rich vanilla ice cream to each side. My mother took a bite of minty ice and ice cream mixed together. The Mint Snowball tasted like winter. She closed her eyes to see the Swiss village my great-grandfather's parents came from. Snow frosting the roofs. Glistening, dangling spokes of ice.

Before my great-grandfather died, he sold the recipe for the mint syrup to someone in town for one hundred dollars. This hurt my grandfather's feelings. My grandfather thought he should have inherited it to carry on the tradition. As far as the family knew, the person who bought the recipe never used it. At least not in public. My mother had watched my great-grandfather make the syrup so many times she thought she could replicate it. But what did he have in those little unmarked bottles? She experimented. Once she came close. She wrote down what she did. Now she has lost the paper.

Perhaps the clue to my entire personality connects to the lost Mint Snowball. I have always felt out of step with my environment, disjointed in the modern world. The crisp flush of cities makes me weep. Strip malls, poodle grooming, and take-out Thai. I am angry over lost department stores, wistful for something I have never tasted or seen.

Although I know how to do everything one needs to know—change airplanes, find my exit of the interstate, charge gas, send a fax—there is something missing. Perhaps the stoop of my great-grandfather over the pan, the slow patient swish of his spoon. The spin of my mother on the high stool with her whole life in front of her, something fine and fragrant still to happen. When I breathe a handful of mint, even pathetic sprigs from my sunbaked Texas earth, I close my eyes. Little chips of ice on the tongue, their cool slide down. Can we follow the long river of the word refreshment back to its spring? Is there another land for me? Can I find any lasting solace in the color green?

—*from* Mint Snowball, *by Naomi Shihab Nye*

Pancakes for Lunch

It was a Sunday afternoon in the summer and my dad was cooking pancakes and bacon. We had just gotten back from my cousin's house, so we were starving. Everything was good until my dad left for work and my younger sister, who was seven years old (I was nine), started cooking on a chair. I could tell from other experiences that this was no different. She stirred the bacon and flipped the pancakes but she did it every ten minutes, so it was as black and blank as a computer screen. I heard my sister say, "Ryan, we've got a problem!" It smelled like a firework had been set off in the kitchen. The smoke was gray and silver like the grease in a car. And all the smoke alarms were going off. Ever since that day, she has never cooked pancakes and bacon again. But what will happen next Sunday, or the Sunday after that? I wonder how much longer the curse will last? Five years, ten years—for the rest of her life?

—Ryan Loughran, 12

MEET YOUR PROTAGONIST!

by RYAN HARTY

1 hour

Here's a lesson I like to use near the beginning of a course. Students like it, and it gets them thinking about sophisticated fictional elements like character and plot—often without even realizing it! Most of the time, it encourages them to write good, engaging stories in which important things happen.

I begin with the discussion of a good, engaging published story in which important things happen—maybe something the whole class has read. As we discuss, I raise the question, *What does the main character want?* (In almost all good stories, of course, the protagonist wants something.) Another question: *What is the main character afraid of?* (Again, this should be evident.) You can talk about whether the character gets what they want in the end; whether they avoid the thing they're afraid of; how students feel about the outcome. (If they like the story, they'll have plenty to say.) Then I ask, *Why might desires and fears be important to consider when writing a story?* Invariably they know: it makes the story exciting, it gets us involved, it makes us want to know what will happen, etc. They're thinking about conflict, narrative drive, plot, etc. (And in fact with older students, upper-level high-schoolers, say, it can be an opportunity to introduce this kind of vocabulary.)

Now we discuss the main character in further detail. *How does the writer let us know who she is?* With descriptions, they say, with dialogue, with the character's thoughts and actions. (They are becoming experts on characterization.) *What are the most important things we know about the character?* They shout them out: her parents just got divorced; she has a pet Chihuahua; she's afraid of Amanda Petruzzi, the class meanie; she loves the color purple.

Now it's time to create our own character. We do this first as a group. Here's the template:

> Two desires
> Two fears
> One secret
> Eight very important things

I start with the basics. *How old is the character? Boy or girl?* (You might want to do a boy and a girl, so all students can identify.) *What's his/her name? Where*

does he/she live? These are not your eight very important details, just basic facts.

Now have students to come up with desires and fears, encouraging them to be as specific as possible. For example, it might be interesting to know that the character has a crush on a boy at school, but if we know that she's in love with Rodney Rapunzi, a quiet boy who knows all the answers in math class, we know a good deal more about her (and we have a better idea of what her story will be like). Likewise, whereas most boys worry about being humiliated in class, if our guy is worried about his new corrective eyeglasses, or his embarrassing cousin Dmitri from Lithuania, we get a better sense of what his world is all about.

Fill in the important details. Ask students about the character's family, friends, teachers, school, etc. Write down what they shout out, again encouraging them to be specific (and asking clarifying questions, if necessary). Write down more than a dozen details, then have students pick the eight most important ones.

Secrets are essential. They create a sense of intimacy between character and reader, and they often point to the heart of a story. *What do we know about this character that no one else (or almost no one else) knows?*

So now you have a character. Here's an example, this one based on an upper-level high school class (middle-schoolers will have much sillier characters, which is great):

> *Matilda Gleeson is thirteen years old and lives in Redwood City, CA.*
>
> *She wants a new Guess watch to replace the one she recently lost .*
>
> *She wants to see her father more often than she does (which is almost never).*
>
> *She's afraid she might be losing touch with her best friend Amanda.*
>
> *She's afraid she's going to have her mother's (large) nose.*

Her secret is that she sometimes goes to the neighborhood where her father lives with his new wife and her kids.

She is smart, but she doesn't try hard in school (she's afraid her friends will think she's a loser).

Her favorite teacher, Miss Alvarez, once read one of Matilda's short stories aloud in her English class.

She loves her little brother, Matthew, but is sometimes mean to him when her friends are around.

She has a pet cockatiel named Charlie.

She likes to stay up late at night reading the Narnia books (though she thinks she's too old for them).

A few times, since the divorce, she has heard her mother crying in bed.

Her grandmother lives two blocks away; Matilda likes to visit, because Grandma is fun and never pries.

She dreams about moving to France and becoming a photographer.

Ask students what kind of story they'd like to read about this person. See how sharp their instincts are. In most cases they'll know right where the heart of the story lies. They might want to see the girl spying on her father's family, for example. They might want something to happen with the brother, or with the best friend, or with the mother. *Where should the story begin?* They'll have lots of ideas. Depending on how old they are, you might take a few minutes to discuss writing scenes vs. summary, showing vs. telling. Or you may just want them to write. You can have everyone write about the character you've created, or they can create characters of their own, using the template (this is what I usually have them do). If they create their own characters, you can have two or three of them read theirs aloud, if there's time.

GET YOUR HAIKU ON
by Daphne Gottlieb

1 hour (or more)

Sometimes it's hard to love poetry. Some of it is really stuffy, some of it is really abstract and hard to follow, and some of it is so quaint it's cringeworthy. But there's one form that never lets us down—it's precise, it's snappy, and sounds as contemporary as anything even though it's a traditional form thousands of years old.

That's right, we're talking about haiku. Haiku, with its traditional Japanese form: the first line has five syllables, the second has seven, and the third has five, for a total of seventeen syllables. Before you know it, you're done with one and on to the next.

You're also probably already a poet and aren't aware of it. There are haiku all around you. It's in the music you listen to:

Don't push me cause I'm
close to the edge. I'm tryin'
not to lose my head.
> *—from "The Message"*
> *by Melle Mel*

or how about

Tried to cool her down
to take another round—now
I'm back in the ring.
> *—from "You Shook Me All Night Long"*
> *by AC/DC*

or

Oops! I did it a-
gain. I played with your heart—got
lost in the game, ooh.
> *—from "Oops! ... I Did it Again"*
> *by Britney Spears*

Musical tastes aside, this is the kind of poetry we can get behind—poetry that speaks to our daily experience. You can drop all sorts of language from the world around you into haiku's form, from the instructions on microwavable food to classified ads from the newspaper to the most important: our own lives. Students are often somewhat daunted to write poetry because it's effeminate or stodgy or snooty. But by bringing in everything from song lyrics to shampoo instructions *(lather, rinse, repeat / lather, rinse, repeat, lather / rinse, repeat, lather)*, the mundane takes on the qualities of the sublime. And can be ridiculously funny. We have been surprised time and again teaching workshops—by high school weightlifters writing about pushing it to the point of failure in the gym; by after-school cooks giving us recipes on how to make the whole world better; by all the writers telling us about what's outside the window, in their day. That's the point of poetry at its best. That's why we love it.

Ready to get your haiku on in your own classroom? The handout on page 74 has four haiku variations for your students to try: group haiku, speed haiku, an unhaiku haiku, and a haiku battle. Enjoy.

THINGS TO DO WITH HAIKU

Given the short form of haiku, it's possible to take ten to fifteen minutes and have a bounty of poems result. The key to writing, sometimes, is finding permission to speak—song lyrics and shampoo bottles sort of grant that these haiku are everywhere, and hey! Anything anyone writes will be better than those! What do you see every day that people need to know about?

1. **The Tanka**
   Honoring the old tradition of tanka (see A Brief History of Haiku, below), each student writes a haiku (5-7-5) and passes it to another for the tanka (7-7) addition. You could stop here or keep going, and pass it to yet another student for the 5-7-5 hokku, then to another for the tanka, and so on. This is a traditional renga, in which one completes another's work.

2. **The 3-Minute Topical Haiku**
   Begin the day with haiku. Write a topic on the board (like "lunch menus" or "P.E." or a current event). Everyone writes a haiku on the topic. These can be posted in a blog, in a chapbook, in whatever collected form is interesting.

3. **Write a Haiku from ...**
   Advertising. From a cereal box. From something in the newspaper want ads. From your iPod. From your math book. From a love note. From your wildest dreams. Once you know how to find poetry, it's always there.

4. **The Haiku Battle**
   Three flags. Two haiku. Two students come up and do an MC-style haiku battle. After hearing both, the flags vote. Whoever gets the most flags wins. The haiku battlers are replaced with two more students, and the flags are passed to other students.

A BRIEF HISTORY OF HAIKU:

In addition to being a formal form of poetry, haiku also depicts a certain moment—that of a world in transition. Originally about the observation of nature in flux (as in the case of great masters Basho, Buson and Issa, in Japan's Ido period of 1600-1868), haiku originally derived from the form of *tanka*, which had a structure of 5-7-5-7-7. Between the 9th and 12th centuries, one person frequently would write the first three lines, then pass the poem on to another writer for completion. The first part was called *hokku*, or "starting verse" and became what we know as haiku. Americans, as we are wont to do, co-opted it and changed it. When the Beat Poets found haiku, they threw the 5-7-5 out the window when they needed to, as well as the examination of the natural world, and focused in on what they saw. When they wanted to make the syllables work out, they'd add an "er" or an "um". This is not only legal but applauded. Make up the rules. What changed you today? What's important to say? You've got 17 syllables. Go.

TINY TALES

by JENNY TRAIG

1 hour
Materials: Tiny items to eat and show (optional)

This class is a celebration of tiny things. For an hour or so, we eat tiny cakes, drink tea from tiny cups, and write tiny stories that consist of just a few paragraphs. It's a great way to teach students the basics of story-writing, because everything is on such a small and manageable scale.

I begin class by telling the Parable of the Candy Bar. When I was about six my mother instituted a fabulous weekly ritual. Every Friday, I was granted the candy bar of my choice. The first few weeks I went for the Charleston Chew. It was the biggest. But it was not the best. All that stale strawberry nougat—it took hours to eat, but it felt like years. It was awful. After a few weeks I got wise and started choosing smaller treats. Best of all were the fancy, tiny chocolates: walnut-sized truffles, flinty toffee fingers, fat pecan turtles, sugary cubes of fudge. This is the parable of the candy bar, and this is the lesson: small is good.

Oh, sure, there are some tiny things that aren't so great—bugs, mold spores, pimples, mini-quizzes—all of these things are very bad. But most tiny things are very, very good, and tiny tales are very good indeed. Tiny tales are like the little chocolates. They are dense and compact and rich. They can be savored or gobbled up quickly. A tiny tale isn't a synopsis. Tiny tales are like elves: all the fingers and toes of a large person are there, only smaller. They are enchanted and magical.

Tiny tales just as colorful and evocative as a longer story. They are like jewels, faceted and sparkly. They are convenient and portable and fast.

I tell the class chocolates are my favorite tiny thing, and ask the class to share theirs. Ladybugs? MP3 players? Jelly beans? All great.

Once we are primed to appreciate tiny things, we get down to work writing our tiny tales. We begin by going over the handouts together. First, we learn what elements every story needs (page 76-77). It's got to have a plot, a setting, and characters. We take turns reading the handout aloud, and I ask the students to give me good examples. I want to know: Who's your favorite character? What book has the best setting? The most interesting plot?

Then we go over the next handout (page 78) together and learn how to shrink a story down. This is where we practice editing. With younger students, you might want to skip this step. For older students, it's a great introduction to revising.

Finally, story ideas in hand (page 79), I turn them loose. They write for ten to twenty minutes. Some students will want to write more than one tiny tale, and that's just great.

If time permits, and you have some bookmaking skills, you can help the students turn their tiny tales into tiny books. They make good gifts.

WHAT EVERY TALE (EVEN A TINY ONE) NEEDS

1. A Plot

You should probably have a plot. The plot is the point of the whole story, the main thing that happens. So, for instance, in *Cinderella*, the plot is Cinderella's attempts to go to the ball and meet her prince. Here's how to build a plot yourself:

A. Start with the **introduction**. Introduce the characters and the setting.

B. Next, the **plot thickens**. Show us that things aren't as simple as they seem. Maybe one of the characters has a secret, or maybe someone new and mysterious comes to town. Maybe people start fighting, or maybe they start to fall in love.

C. Now for the most exciting part: the **climax**! Here is where all your really interesting stuff happens. The clock is ticking ... will the hero reach the baby crawling toward the cliff before it's too late? We're on the edge of our seats!

D. ... and then, start to **wrap things up**. (This is also known by a fancy French name: *denouement*. Let's all say it together: *day-new-MONT*.) The action winds down. The fighting couple makes up. The mystery is solved.

E. Finally, write your **conclusion**. The bad guys are caught, the good guys congratulate each other, and everyone makes up. The end.

This is the basic plot structure. Once you know how to do it, you can break the rules. You can tell your story backwards or out of order. You can tell a story that's all introduction, all climax, or all conclusion. You could tell your story as a list or a recipe or a book report or a how-to. Knock yourself out.

2. A Setting

Your story has to take place somewhere. That said, you don't have to write a whole lot about it. But if you like settings, by all means, go nuts. Bring on the misty meadows, the creaky mansion, the dark and stormy night. If you're *really* into scenery, your tiny tale could be *all* setting. No characters, no plot, just setting. If you do this kind of miniature right, the setting *becomes* the plot and the characters. Ooky, kooky, spooky.

3. Some Characters

In a tiny tale, you don't have much time for character development. You have to convey the essence of the personality in just a few sentences. Here are a few tips:

Give your characters great, expressive names. Here are some good ones: Duane Spiffy, Violet Lasagne, Bucky Dent, Bianca Suede. You can let us know the main character is brave and true by naming him Gallant Goodguy. Or you can surprise us by, say, making Sweetie Pie Goldenchilde a mean old crone.

If you want a mysterious tone, you can skip names altogether, like this:

"She'd never seen this doctor before, she was sure. But that pale skin, that glittering overbite ... it was all familiar, familiar as baby food, old as a fossil, like a memory she could no longer recall.

He rolled up her sleeve and swabbed her arm with iodine. 'What good veins you have,' he observed. 'You'll make an excellent patient.'"

You have to describe your characters quickly, but you don't have to be flat and predictable. They can be complicated and surprising. One way to round them out is to give them some unexpected, contradictory personality traits. "Duane was a bad dude" is not nearly as interesting as "Duane had two hobbies: petty vandalism and crochet."

The way your characters talk also tells us a lot about them. Who might say these lines?

"I'm your worst wilderness nightmare, little camper!"

"Darling, that dress makes you look three feet wide."

"I ain't never flown a rocket ship, but how hard can it be?"

HOW TO SHRINK A STORY

The first step is to get your story down on paper, however it wants to come out. Hopefully it contains everything we just learned about: plot, setting, characters, etc. Once you've got something to work with, go back and edit it down. Editing is like washing in hot water: it cleans up the story and shrinks it down.

When you're editing, remember the first law of tiny tales: Every word has a job to do.

Think of it this way: you've got three dollars. Each word is a penny you want to spend wisely. Here's a guide to getting your money's worth.

1. Get rid of all the wishy-washy words. These guys are the first to go:

> *seems to*
> *kind of*
> *about to*
> *started to, began to*
> *almost*

2. Use single words instead of longer phrases when possible: "much" instead of "a lot of," "rarely" instead of "not very often," etc.

3. Go on repetition patrol. The first draft is usually full of repetition. Cut stuff like this:

> *The aerobics instructor was plump* ~~*and chubby*~~.
> *The podiatrist was sleepy* ~~*and exhausted*~~.
> *They were confused.* ~~*They didn't know what to do.*~~

4. Use strong, satisfying words. Here are some good ones. I like them because they do the work of several words:

> *dank* (makes me think of *dark* + *stank* + *rank*)
> *fetid* (makes me think of *stinky feet* + *putrid*)
> *florid* (makes me think of *flowery* + *ruddy*)

5. Every event, every detail, every character should be there for a good reason. If it doesn't advance the plot, or make the story funnier or moodier or more mysterious, then cut it. Bye bye, water balloons that don't explode! See you later, boring guy with no good lines! Hasta mañana, pointless aside about bananas!

6. Remember: What's missing can be just as important as what's there. The pauses between sentences, the details left out, the mysteries unexplained—all these can be useful tools.

HERE ARE SOME IDEAS TO GET YOU STARTED

1. Mysteries

Mysteries make great tiny tales. You present the mystery, sort through the clues and consider the possibilities, choose an outcome, and that's it. Small mysteries make the best tiny tales. Leave the international spy stories to James Bond and instead track down the missing hairbrush or the substitute teacher's secret identity.

2. Short Histories

Write a short, informative history of anything you want. It doesn't have to be true. In fact, it probably shouldn't be. A short history of freeze tag, of bubble gum, of bobby pins or cat litter—all these would make great miniatures.

3. How-Tos

Write a tiny tale with a weird format: the text on a bottle of conditioner, the assembly instructions for a toy or game, rules, or a recipe.

4. Case Files

Medical case files, dental case files, police case files, veterinarian case files—all these make fine tiny tales. Here's a great idea: *hairdresser case files!*

5. Letters

The letter format is great for tiny tales. Your correspondents can be international penpals trying to track down a missing jewel.

6. Moody Blues

These don't necessarily tell as story so much as describe a mood. Write a moody little piece about a haunted lake or an airless summer day.

7. Big Moments

Big moments make great little stories. Think of an interesting character and then think what the biggest moment in her life was: the eighth grade spelling bee, an unusual trip to the flea market, a single perfect meal. It can be happy or sad, wistful or ecstatic.

8. Serials

The best. The best! Serials are like a rope of pearls. One tiny tale leads to the next. Here's a great setting for a serial: summer camp. There's a hundred stories right there.

HOW TO TURN LIES INTO LITERATURE

by EMILY KATZ

2 hours

We can all tell lies. But telling a good lie requires thought and creativity. It requires the people involved to have personalities, dialogue, and character traits. It requires movement, setting, and plot development—which makes it a lot like good writing. In this class we learn to turn lies into literature.

It helps to begin lying right from the start. As I arrive, I heave down my belongings and greet students with, "You wouldn't *believe* the mess I just went through," or "Guess who I just ran into?" These are both, of course, lies—the trip that regularly brings me to the classroom is perfectly ordinary, and nowhere near as interesting as the story I'll tell them now.

Next, it's the students' turn to fib. For the duration of the lesson I give students the option of going by a different name and creating an alternate identity for themselves. We go around the room and everyone says a few sentences about who they "are." This can include likes/dislikes, what they did right before class, their favorite band, etc. Then we jump into writing exercises. Spend ten minutes on this first prompt: *make a list of things that are true*.

When that's done, if you like, you can spend a little while having the students read aloud from their lists. Then, have them spend ten minutes writing on the next prompt: Make a list of things that are lies.

These will probably be a little more fun to share. The lies they create can be outrageous or simple. A few of the best ones I've heard come out of this exercise are: "I am the walrus," "When my older brother eats, he gurgles," and the cryptic "Enough is enough." (This one provoked a lot of *oohs* and *hmms*).

Finally, we move onto our last prompt: *make a list of truths* and *lies*.

They do not need to designate which is which, and in this exercise students begin to recognize how the two can run together to make great stories. Lies very often begin with a grain of truth, and even after they turn into great big whoppers, you can usually spot a little truth in there. We talk about how the fluidity between truth and lies can make us better writers. I remind the students that they don't have to be intimidated by the prospect of inventing characters and plotlines, because they can begin simply with what they know and can then move in any direction they like.

This is a good point to sit together and read some examples of authors who use lies quite successfully. I like to read a passage from the novella "Honda" in the book *Not a Chance* by Jessica Treat, in which the main character, a compulsive liar, gets caught up in her own thoughts, which are a web of humongous lies. She creates a really detailed, intricate story that is very far from reality, but ends up seeming kind of real because of the great lengths she goes to make everything work out right. I ask the class if they think this story begin with a lie, and what the lie might have been.

Next we break up and work independently. The students pick an item from their lengthy collection of lists and build a story. Some students opt to begin their thinking with a "spider map," putting their own lie right in the center and brainstorming parts of the story visually. I remind them that the goal is to make the stories complete, outrageous, and as detailed as possible. They can include dialogue, characters, distinct personality traits, and of course, a setting and movement. I emphasize the importance of plot and remind them that they can just make one up, and they can make the ending up too. It doesn't matter if the end results are long or short, as long as they are imaginative and baldfaced.

HOW TO FINE-TUNE YOUR FALSEHOOD

1. **Borrow details from people you see**

   You can base a character on someone you saw one time on the bus, or someone that you can't imagine living his or her own life. A lot of students say they can't imagine their teachers doing anything but standing in the classroom. (What, they have homes?!) What does that girl with pink hair you see walking down 23rd Street eat for dinner? Who does your teacher tell about her day when she gets home from school?

2. **The setting you choose can be comfortable to you without being dull.**

   It is always nice to use a story setting that you know personally because it helps you to add rich detail, and might make the reader trust you more. If you don't want to set your fabricated story in outer space, that's okay. If you want to set it in the same city that you live in now, sure, go ahead. But perhaps instead of the plot unfolding on 24th Street, where you've lived your whole life, it can take place in another neighborhood, across the city, that you've driven through but haven't gotten to know that well.

3. **Use an outrageous piece of dialogue.**

   Your character is allowed to say things you would *never* say. Something outlandish. But fairly clean, please.

4. **Take a real-life situation and imagine how it came to be.**

   Or take a real-life situation and imagine where it could go. Fantasizing about the past or the future is a great way to get writing. In fact, that's much of what creative writing is based on: using a situation we've come to know, or a person we just can't understand, and figuring out why through creative thought. It is important not to let your conclusions rest—push them further, open more doors. Challenge your thinking, and imagine what might happen if things unfolded in a completely different way.

Student Work

Invisible Ted

There are really two people in this room. One of them is my friend Invisible Ted. Ted was born in London, England. He hates coffee and loves tea. I met him while I was at the wax museum. He was standing by the wax figure of Robin Williams. I went over to him and said, "Hey Ted."

"How can you see me?" he said.

"Duh. You're bright pink!" I said.

"What?!" he screamed in his odd British manner. "How can you? I'm invisible!"

"No, you're pink," I said. "Now you'll have to be called Pinky. How about a cup of tea, on me?"

"Sure," said Ted. "Say, what color am I now?" he asked.

"Pink," I said. "Still pink."

"Oh," he said. "I was hoping I could be blue."

"Yeah," I said. "Blue's cool."

We had a nice cup of tea. Then he asked me if he could come back to California with me.

"Sure," I said. "But people might laugh at you because you're pink."

"Don't worry," said Ted. "I am only pink to you."

"Okay," I said. So now he is here in this room. And he is laughing at all of the people who like coffee.

—Annie Paulukonis, 12

STORIES FROM THE YEAR 3005: SCIENCE FICTION

by ERIN JOURDAN

3 hours

We're not sure what lurks in the farthest reaches of outer space—marauding warlords, futuristic cities, mutant lizards—but we're pretty certain there are some good stories. In a world without gravity and oxygen, just about anything can happen. Purple skies? Root beer lakes? Why not? This class encourages students to let their imaginations run wild and describe what might be out there.

Session One

We start by encouraging the students to think about every detail of their made-up world. What do the inhabitants eat? Wear? What's the weather like? The topography? And who lives there? The handout on page 84 will help them flesh things out. Students in one recent class introduced us to worlds like Pizzatopolis, Metamorpho, Albinoland, Double Water World, and Mattressville. We were impressed.

Next, we move on to characterization. We're going to be writing a story later, so we need more than moons and rocks. We need protagonists and villains. First we discuss characterization. We talk about giving characters complex traits, talents, flaws, and interests to make them feel rounded and real. Next we do the exercise on page 85, which helps students create a dossier of information about their main character with details to make him or her fully rounded.

Once that's done I like to go around the room and have the students share. This is great stuff and it deserves an audience.

Session Two

In our next class, we move on to the real writing work. I give the students prompts, and then have them write for five minutes or so on each. Believe it or not, they usually want to write more! Having a prompt really helps—it gets some words on those blank pages so that they can blast off!

First they write a little bit about the world they made up in the last class using these prompts:

When I look at my planet I see ...
What I know about my planet is ...
When visiting this planet, don't forget to ...

Then we write about the character they created in the last class using these prompts:

_____ woke up and knew something was wrong ...
_____ was having a great day ...
_____'s biggest problem was ...

I love having students read in class, but if they are too sheepish, I read their stories anonymously myself.

The class can end here. Or, if your students are super-ambitious, you could have them write a short science fiction story about the world they've created. They should have lots of material!

INTERGALACTIC INTELLIGENCE DOSSIER

Our records indicate you have been gathering intelligence on a distant universe. Please describe this world.

Name of planet:

Describe the terrain:

Any geographical formations of note?

Describe the weather:

Describe the atmosphere, e.g. neighboring planets, moons and suns, etc.:

What is the best thing about this planet?

What is the worst thing?

What is the weirdest thing?

Any other important things we need to know about this planet? E.g., is it made of frosting? Is it an upside-down backwards world?

Describe its inhabitants:

Describe the laws of its society:

Do they know about earthlings, and if so, what do they think of us?

If you were going there, what would you need to pack?

INTERGALACTIC INTELLIGENCE DOSSIER

The University of Space Studies has learned you've been gathering intelligence on a particular intergalactic life form. We would like to know more. Please describe this individual.

Life form's name:

Species:

Appearance:

Age (in human years):

Any super powers?

Does it have a secret identity?

Does it have any pets?

What is in its pockets right now?

What are its fears and phobias?

Does it have a sidekick? Who?

Does it have an enemy? Who?

What does it dream of?

What are its personality quirks? Physical quirks?

What is the scariest thing that has ever happened to it?

Does it hate anyone? Why?

Does it love anyone? Why?

If you gave it a billion earth dollars, what would it buy?

Student Work

An Excerpt from "Sacrifice"

"Larry!" yelled a woman's voice, "come down to eat."

Suddenly some sort of black thing appeared at the top of the stairs. It resembled a stick figure, with a huge head and buglike eyes. He bounded down the steps two at a time, and once he reached the floor, proceeded to moonwalk to the kitchen.

"When will you grow up, Larry? The military needs men, not boys," his mother demanded.

"Yeah, yeah," Larry said absentmindedly.

As they began eating, a round, black blur came shooting down the stairs and crashed into the kitchen table.

"Harry, Garry, stop fighting. It disturbs us all," said Larry calmly as he pulled apart two beings similar to himself in looks. He looked at the broken table and the mess that his two siblings had created. He held out his hand over the mess and it instantly cleaned up.

As he finished eating he said, "All right guys, I have to go to school now."

"Bye!" they yelled in unison.

Larry stepped out of his house and into the desert. It was a moment he never liked experiencing, leaving the cool controlled climate of the indoors and stepping into the cruel unforgiving heat of the desert. On the way to school he passed dwellings similar to his, white circular domes rising up out of the ground. Today was a particularly scorching day; Larry did not even feel like moonwalking as was his custom. He just plodded along.

As Larry entered school a voice sneered at him, "Look, it's Larry the loser."

"Eat some Splurg and choke, Barry," Larry shot back as he entered the school.

From ground level, the school looked like a regular white dome. However, to accommodate all of its students it was buried deep underground.

As Larry walked into his class he was again reminded of the dreadful draft.

"Students, you all know of the upcoming military service," said Larry's teacher, Karry. "You all must serve, no excuses. If you try to escape the draft you will be imprisoned for life."

"Argh," Larry thought to himself indignantly. "I don't want to fight in the military. All I want to do is dance. I wish our Desert People and the Water People would stop fighting. Their constant fighting has made it so that I can't dance in peace. Now they want to make me fight. I am not a soldier, I am a performer."

All through the school day, Larry tried to formulate the best plan to use in order to escape the draft. Just as the school day was about to end, he saw the answer. Prince Jerry. He was the son of the king of the Desert People and could talk his parents into doing anything.

To be continued....

—*Ishaan Sengupta, 14*

RECESS FOR YOUR BRAIN

by CHRISTINA AMINI

1 hour
Materials: Magazines to cut up,
scissors, glue, construction paper

Writer's block? This lesson takes the pressure off and encourages wild storytelling, using magazine collages to inspire the narrative. It helps students make inventive connections and releases creative energy. One part visual, one part kinesthetic, and three parts imagination, it's fun for writers and non-writers alike. Just let the pictures be your muse.

We start by distributing the handout (page 88), which will guide us through the process of finding pictures and turning them into stories. Then we turn the students loose on our old magazines, with instructions to cut out four pictures of anything they want.

They can use the suggestions on the handout if they want a theme to guide their choices. Maybe they choose pictures of favorite objects. Perhaps they choose four orange images. Or maybe they close their eyes and choose at random. (We've found constraints are helpful for indecisive students.) The choosing part of the lesson could go on forever, so be sure to set a time limit. Five minutes should be long enough to make the search a little frantic and fun.

Let the students know *any* picture will work, so there isn't any pressure to choose (and fight over) the "best" images. They will be able to create a story out of anything they find. One of my students chose a picture of a butterfly and another of a computer and imagined that the butterfly was a secret agent with its own laptop. So there you go.

Once everyone has their images, the next step is to ask the students to arrange them into a loose story. Help them start thinking about how to connect images by choosing two pictures at random and asking them to dream up a possible story for them. "What could connect a shoelace and an allergy medication ad? Maybe a bad hike in the springtime and someone who can't stop sneezing?" Another example: "What could connect an image of a baby chick and a basketball?" Perhaps some kids play basketball, the ball goes into the bushes, and they find a baby chick? "Where might the story lead from there?"

Next, each student cuts and pastes the images onto construction paper. The images can overlap, they can be torn haphazardly—no rules here. Allow another ten minutes or so for gluing, and then present the next stage: writing!

Have your students spend at least fifteen minutes writing the story based on the pictures they chose. Usually, I ask that the students to write at least one paragraph, but often their imagination takes over and they write more. If I notice that someone is stuck, I ask them questions about the pictures and give them permission to make outlandish jumps in logic.

We close by asking volunteers to show their collages and read their stories. By now, hopefully, everyone is excited and inspired, and if they want to write more—we bet they will—we go over the "More Rules, More Stories" section of the handout and keep on creating.

FATE IS YOUR CO-AUTHOR!

Gather

Choose *one* of the following methods to gather your pictures:

- Choose four pictures you like.

- Choose four pictures you dislike.

- Choose a main character (a baby, a cuddly dog, an eraser, anything), and then choose other pictures that you think your character might like or dislike.

- Choose pictures based on color. Maybe you want to choose all red things: red roses, red shoes, the Golden Gate Bridge.

- Close your eyes and pick your images at random.

- Scavenger hunt: Find one person, one animal, one household item, one unusual thing.

Glue

Paste your images onto the construction paper in any order you like!

Go

Start writing about your pictures by combining them into one story. Crazy plots are encouraged!

More Rules, More Stories

A French group called the *Oulipo* (**Ou**vroir de **li**ttérature **po**tentielle, or "workshop of potential literature") uses constraints for all of its writing. Founded in 1960 in Paris, this group believes that formal constraints make for artistic liberation. Its members include Raymond Queneau, Georges Perec, and Italo Calvino.

Try one of the Oulipo's writing techniques:

- **The S + 7 Method.** With this method, you take a paragraph from a book or a piece of your own writing, and then circle every noun in it. Find a dictionary, look up each noun, and replace it with the seventh noun following it. Your new story will sound like the original, but will have an entirely new meaning! (Also good practice for identifying nouns and using the dictionary.)

- **False Translation.** Take a poem in a foreign language that you don't know and use the sound of the words and the way they look to "translate" it.

- **Lipogram.** A lipogram is a piece of writing that purposefully excludes one letter of the alphabet. One of the most famous lipograms is George Perec's *La Disparition*, a novel without the letter e.

Or invent your own!

I WROTE A GUIDEBOOK AND ALL I GOT WAS THIS LOUSY T-SHIRT: TRAVEL WRITING

by Susie Kramer & Laurie Scholes

6 hours
Materials: Tourist costume (optional),
travel guidebooks

Session One

For this workshop we swallow our pride from the get-go, because we show up to the first session in costume. A tourist costume, to be specific—Bermuda shorts, Hawaiian shirt, dorky hat, fanny pack, and so on. In this case, the fanny pack is stuffed to bursting with travel guidebooks. We get them from the library, since we need enough for the students to share in pairs or small groups.

To begin, we dump the guidebooks clumsily onto the desk at the front of the room and say, "We're planning a visit to [your town here], but these guidebooks are so dense and boring that every time we open them we instantly fall asleep. Since you kids live here, and you seem so kind and knowledgeable, do you think you can help us out?"

Then the students band together in pairs or groups of four. As a group, they prepare a written itinerary for us. We want to know: where should we go? How do we get there? What will we find? We ask them to be as specific and detailed as possible, and to choose the most interesting destinations.

The results of their trip-planning exercise can be used to compile a list of necessary elements for the guidebook. Eventually this list becomes a kind of table of contents for the finished product. We ask them questions about the purpose of a guidebook, since purpose is so important in this kind of informative writing. What do you think people look for in a guidebook? Why do people use them? A little group brainstorming leads to a list of the things readers want from a guidebook: information about restaurants, museums, landmarks, and so on.

Instead of lecturing about guidebook style, we ask them to read bits from the books they used in the exercise. Do we want our guidebook to be funny and irreverent? Chatty? Serious and comprehensive? It's fun to treat this as a kind of editorial board, and let all the kids weigh in. Usually they think the published guidebooks are dry as dust, so they're eager to figure out how to make theirs better. Define the different possibilities for style, then take a vote. Get specific: should

the guidebook be written in first or third person? Who is our audience? This is especially important; we encourage them to consider designing the book for kids their age, since they have an insider's perspective on what kids like to do.

Then we start talking about technique. How do these guidebooks make you want to go to the places they review? A member of each group reads the passage they chose out loud, and we ask them what makes the writing interesting and persuasive. Specific detail, sensory impressions, and authoritative language are three of the things we like to focus on. We remind them that as the writer, you're kind of like the tour guide waving that ridiculous red flag to make sure everyone on the tour follows you through Chinatown. But in this case, the red flag is your writing, and if somebody loses sight of the flag or gets tired of following it, you're in trouble. The reader has to trust you.

The handout (page 91) helps to wrangle all these ideas together and review them.

To wrap up, the students are instructed to think of their favorite place in town, the one place where they *must* drag all unsuspecting out-of-town relatives. They close their eyes, and we lead them through a sensory experience of this place. What do they see? Hear? Smell? Taste? Feel? This is just a list-making exercise; they will use all of these details for a full-fledged description later on.

For homework, we let the students loose on our city, instructing them to go visit the same places they just visited in their minds. They are to take notes on their travels, including of course the essential facts of transportation, admission fees, hours of operation, and the like.

Session Two

To warm up, the students write an imaginary guidebook entry about a made-up place. They can make it up themselves or choose an existing fictional place, like Oz or Middle Earth or Fraggle Rock or Candyland. We remind them about the stylistic choices we made last time, and also about the important elements of guidebook writing. Students can read these out loud, for practice listening to and recognizing the writing style the class has chosen.

Now we ask the students to take out the notes from their travels. Another meeting of the editorial board provides a chance to divide their chosen locations into the existing table of contents from the last session. The students can see the book beginning to take shape as each of their locations is filed under a chapter on the board. Some choices defy categorization—that pet cemetery, for example, was one of the toughies—but a "Miscellaneous Fun and Learning" chapter should suffice.

The rest of this session is all about the writing. Students compile their list-making work from the first session with the notes from their homework travels. It might help to review the handout on guidebook writing, and to conference with the students individually as they work. The Internet is a great tool here, as we like to encourage the students to fact-check their information. (A phonebook will work just as well.) Students who finish early become the art department; they start working on illustrations, printing photographs, and developing sidebar material. (Our favorite sidebar from a recent class: "How to Survive in San Francisco on Burritos Alone.")

If there's time and ambition, we like to assign the students to visit a place where they've never been but always wanted to go, and this is the subject of their second contribution to the guidebook. The assignment is the same as before: go to this second place and take good notes.

Session Three

The structure of the third session pretty much follows the structure of the second. We like to pass out a handout with examples from each of the previous week's entries; we use these to show what makes guidebook writing great. Most of the quotes we choose contain persuasive detail, the kind of thing you wouldn't know unless you'd actually visited the place in question. One student's french fries were pilfered by a renegade seagull at the zoo; his warning served as both a funny aside and a helpful detail. We also like to emphasize the wit and approachability of their natural written voices.

At this point we call another meeting of the editorial board to organize their new entries into existing chapters. We assign the necessary production duties (copying, collating, etc.). Some ideas for fun "extras" the students can contribute: a page of author information (compiled through interviews with classmates); "top ten" sidebars; a cover page; a table of contents. Once the students have finished writing and revising their second entries, they can get started on these extra elements. When everyone has finished a polished draft, we copy them all and bind them into real guidebooks.

The best thing about this workshop is that everyone takes home a fun and practical book. Their family and friends can use it, and every time it comes off the shelf, they'll feel proud.

BE A TOURIST IN YOUR OWN TOWN
HOW TO IMPART YOUR LOCAL WISDOM
ON CLUELESS OUT-OF-TOWNERS

Bon voyage! By the end of this class, we'll have produced together a fabulously fun and informative book for you to share with visitors to our great city. Here are some tips to help you along the way:

Goals of Guidebook Writing

1. **To inform** your readers about the place they intend to visit.

2. **To excite** your readers about the place they intend to visit.

3. **To assist** your readers in planning their travels, and in feeling comfortable once they arrive.

Essentials of Guidebook Writing

1. **Get your facts straight.** You don't want your readers to end up at Alcatraz when they're trying to get the zoo. Check and double-check names, addresses, phone numbers, and hours of operation. Also, give your readers helpful hints about the weather and other unexpected variables (it's cold in that thar zoo!).

2. Facts, shmacts! Facts are great, but your entries should also **make your readers want to have the experience**. Make them feel like they must eat an amazing local burrito *now*. Describe the creaminess of the guacamole, the sharpness of the salsa, the messy carne asada juices that run down your chin. This is what makes guidebook writing fun. Focus on the unique experience of being in your town—the sounds, smells, textures, and sights.

3. Speaking of sounds, smells, and textures, don't forget to **use incredible detail**. Be specific about the experience of your locale. Avoid vague adjectives like "super" and "cool" and "supercool."

4. **Remember your audience.** You should assume your readers have never set foot in your town, and maybe they never will. Make the experience lively, even for those who will never have it.

5. Be a good reporter. When you're out on the town visiting your hot spots, take lots of notes. **Don't just write down the nuts-and-bolts facts—also note your impressions and feelings.** (Not to beat a dead horse, but how 'bout those sounds and smells?) If you just hate taking notes, bring a recorder, and record your thoughts on tape.

6. **Know your stuff and be confident.** It's very important that your writing have *authority*—in other words, your writing should be confident and approachable. Your readers need to trust you if they're going to follow you all over a strange city.

7. A guidebook is more than just words. **Photos and drawings** can also help you tell your story. If you have a camera, great—take it with you. Otherwise, put your skills as an *artiste* to work.

Student Work

Around San Francisco

Exploratorium: "I advise you to bring extra money for the Tactile Dome, a mazelike structure where you must go through obstacles. The catch? You must go through while it is completely dark, seeing with only your hands."

—*Eric Chuanroong, 12*

Presidio Pet Cemetery: "While walking down the somewhat disorganized rows of homemade graves, you may visit Toka, or Kuro, King or Raspberry—even Bilbo Baggins, a white mouse."

—*Branduin Stroud, 13*

Embarcadero Center: "You sit outside on the tables and eat your food and enjoy the view of the Ferry Building. Watch out for your food—the pigeons like eating your crumbs!"

—*Dexter Tinmahan, 14*

Pearls International Beverages: "There are tapioca drinks from China that come in flavors like Green Apple, Strawberry, and Watermelon. There are also seasonal drinks like egg nog for the holidays."

—*Radford Leung, 14*

GRAMMARAMA: HOMONYM STAND-OFF

by MARGARET MASON

3 hours

Materials: Overhead projector and transparencies of handouts (optional, but helpful), timer, candy prizes

The word "grammar" may never inspire your kids to pull out noisemakers and party hats, but grammar doesn't have to be boring. This lesson turns grammar into an extreme sport. It's the Homonym Stand-Off!

Homonyms are the curse of professional writers and editors. They confound even intelligent, well-educated adults. They won't confound your students, however—your students are about to become homonym fiends.

These words will pop up again and again throughout students' lives, but it can be difficult to remember the discrepancies. The student handout that comes with this lesson provides mnemonic devices for each word set, introducing students to the idea of using mnemonic devices for any memorization exercise.

This is a very flexible lesson plan that spans about three class periods. It includes one day of in-class instruction, a quiz day, and a game day. You can leave a few days of study time between each lesson. Each activity involves the included homonym word list.

Session One: Instruction

You'll need:

- An overhead projector and transparencies of the student handout, *or* ...

- A blackboard where you can write words out as you discuss them

- Handouts for students to study at home, or you can have them take notes

Start by explaining what a homonym is and why it's important to learn the distinctions between words that sound alike but have different meanings. Tell the class that they'll be learning the differences and will be quizzed in preparation for the Homonym Stand-Off. Briefly explain what mnemonic devices are and how they can help students remember things more easily.

Review each set of words from the word list of your choice and go over any questions kids may have about the definitions and memory hints. Set a date for the quiz and distribute the handouts if you've decided to use them.

Session Two: Quiz

Be sure to grade and return the quiz before the Homonym Stand-Off so students know what they've missed.

Session Three: Homonym Stand-Off

This is where things get fun. The Homonym Stand-Off is a cross between charades, Pictionary, and a spelling bee. One student pulls a homonym clue out of a bag, and attempts to act it out or draw it on the board. His or her teammates must guess the word, and then you choose a team member to spell the word.

Of course, to win, everyone involved must know what the words mean and how to spell them correctly.

You'll need:

- A one-minute timer or clock with a second hand

- A chalkboard or whiteboard

- A bag of Hershey's Kisses or hard candy.

- A bag of individual clues you've written out in advance. Not all the words will work for this game, so just write out these:
  adaptor
  capital
  capitol
  compliment
  Earth
  earth
  hippie
  hippy
  loathe

naval
navel
pail
pour
poor
stationery
stationary
wrapped

How to Play:

- **Make teams**. Divide the students into two teams and let them choose their team names. Write each team name on the board.

- **Establish incentive**. Tell the teams that the winning team gets to choose whether to make the other team perform "I'm a Little Teapot," complete with actions, or get one Hershey's Kiss each for themselves.

- **Explain the rules**. You choose a student from the first team to select a clue. He or she has

one minute to act out the clue or draw it on the board while teammates guess. Once someone has guessed the word, choose another student from the same team to spell it.

Each team has the potential to earn three points per turn. They get one point each for:

- Guessing the word.

- Acting out the right word.

- Spelling the word correctly.

(Note: Before you ask a student to spell, let the team know whether their actor was acting out the correct version of the word by giving or withholding the point.)

- **Let the game begin**. Teams take turns guessing and spelling words until you run out of time. Winner takes all!

HOMONYM STAND-OFF STUDY SHEET

accept — to receive willingly, to approve, to endure. "I accept your conditions."

except — with the exception of. "I'll go any day except Sunday."

Memory hint: Except crosses out what you don't want. Accept means you'll take two.

adapter — a person who adapts things, books into screenplays, etc.

adaptor — a device that makes incompatible parts compatible. "That plug won't fit in the outlet, you need an adaptor."

Memory hint: The O in adaptor stands for outlet. Adapter ends in -er because most words for people who do things end the same way: baker, skater, butcher, player.

capital — a town or city that is the official seat of government; material wealth; an upper-case letter.

capitol — a building in which a state legislature meets.

Memory hint: A capitol is the kind of fancy building that makes you say, "Oh!"

complement — to make whole, to go well with something. "That painting complements your couch."

compliment — when someone says something nice, offers praise.

Memory hint: Compliments make people say, "I am the best."

Earth — the planet on which we live.

earth — dirt

Memory hint: The planet Earth is much bigger than a handful of earth, so the first letter is bigger too.

ensure — to make certain. "She ensured his safety."

insure — to make certain. "She insured his safety." But also: to provide insurance for. "She insured the house."

Memory hint: If you use insure, you'll always be right. "I am always right."

hippie — a liberal nonconformist.

hippy — having ample hips.

Memory hint: A hippy person's hips and legs make the shape of a Y. Stereotypical hippies are slim, like the letter I.

It's — the short way of saying "it is."

Its — the possessive form of "it."

Memory hint: "Its" is so possessive of the letter S that it won't even let a little apostrophe sneak in between. "It's" used to be two words, so the apostrophe butting in isn't such a big deal.

loath — reluctant, "He was loath to pass up the cake."

loathe — to despise, "She loathed her enemy."

Memory hint: The e on the end of loathe is for evil, which most of us dislike.

naval — having to do with a navy.

navel — having to do with belly buttons.

Memory hint: Al is in the navy; his uniform is naval.

pail — a bucket.

pale — light in color.

Memory hint: A guy who wears his swimsuit for the first time that summer is a pale male.

pore — to study carefully. "She pored over her books."

pour — to make liquid flow from a container.

poor — lacking money.

Memory hint: The U in pour is shaped like a bucket that collects liquid. Poor has two O's like little holes in your pockets. To pore over your books is a bore.

rapt — engrossed, absorbed.

wrapped — enveloped or covered.

Memory hint: Rapt is a short word, because the person who coined it had a short attention span. Wrapped has more letters because it has to cover something up.

stationery — office supplies, specifically writing paper.

stationary — to remain in a fixed position.

Memory hint: In stationery, the e is for envelope. Stationary is for everything else.

your — the possessive form of the word you. "Your bag, your clock."

you're — the short way to write "you are."

Memory hint: The apostrophe in "you're" is just saving a seat for the missing A from "you are." (He'll be back any minute.) "Your" is for everything else.

HOMONYM QUIZ

Word List

accept

except

adapter

adaptor

capital

capitol

complement

compliment

Earth

earth

ensure

insure

hippie

hippy

it's

its

loath

loathe

naval

navel

pail

pale

pore

pour

poor

rapt

wrapped

stationery

stationary

your

you're

Definitions

1. _____ Reluctant.

2. _____ The planet on which we live.

3. _____ A person who adapts things.

4. _____ A person with ample hips.

5. _____ Lacking money.

6. _____ Having to do with a navy.

7. _____ Office supplies, specifically writing paper.

8. _____ To make whole, to go well with something.

9. _____ To receive willingly, to approve, to endure.

10. _____ Dirt.

11. _____ Light in color.

12. _____ A building in which a state legislature meets.

13. _____ Makes incompatible parts compatible.

14. _____ To make liquid flow from a container.

15. _____ When someone offers praise.

16. _____ The possessive form of it.

17. _____ With the exception of.

18. _____ Engrossed, absorbed.

19. _____ To despise.

20. _____ A bucket.

21. _____ To make certain, and to provide insurance for.

22. _____ Enveloped or covered.

23. _____ An upper-case letter.

24. _____ To remain in a fixed position.

25. _____ Having to do with belly buttons.

26. _____ To make certain.

27. _____ The possessive form of the word you.

28. _____ An extremely liberal nonconformist.

29. _____ The short way of saying "it is."

30. _____ To study carefully.

31. _____ The short way to write "you are."

HOMONYM QUIZ ANSWER KEY

1. loath
2. Earth
3. adapter
4. hippy
5. poor
6. naval
7. stationery
8. complement
9. accept
10. earth
11. pale
12. capitol
13. adaptor
14. pour
15. compliment
16. its

17. except
18. rapt
19. loathe
20. pail
21. insure
22. wrapped
23. capital
24. stationary
25. navel
26. ensure
27. your
28. hippie
29. it's
30. pore
31. you're

FOUND POETRY

by HILARY LIFTIN

2 hours

We've found that poetry is a great way to teach kids to find humor, beauty, and meaning in the seemingly mundane. This lesson shows students that poetry can come from odd, unexpected places if you open your eyes.

Session One

We start class by playing a game based on "Exquisite Corpse," an old parlor game that the Surrealists used to create art in the beginning of the twentieth century. The class sits in a circle.

1. Student write their name on the back of a piece of paper, then turn it over and write a sentence. The sentence shouldn't be short or dull ("I am bored"). It should be long and interesting ("The night was dark and stormy, but Elinor thought she could get home by midnight").

2. Once students have written their sentences, they pass their pieces of paper to the left. The next person looks at the sentence his neighbor has written and, on the line below it, writes the opposite. So a student receiving: "The night was wet and dark, but Elinor thought she could get home by midnight" might write, "The day was dry and bright, but Ronile didn't think he could get home by noon." The second person folds down the top of the paper so the first sentence can't be seen.

3. The pieces of paper are passed again, and the third person writes a sentence that she thinks is the opposite of the second sentence, then folds the paper again so only her sentence is visible.

4. Pass the pieces of paper around the whole room (you can split class in two if it's too big), writing opposite sentences and folding the paper down once each time, until each student has written the last line to the poem he/she began.

When everyone's got their own paper back, students read their favorites aloud and talk about how their poems evolved. Why didn't the sentences alternate perfectly? Did anyone take "poetic license" (deviating from the form to achieve a desired effect)? Was it easier to figure out what to write on the page when someone else had already gotten you started? Do any of the poems seem to have a beginning, middle, and end? Does a meaning start to emerge?

Session Two

We hand out the poem "One Train May Hide Another" by Kenneth Koch (pages 100–101). Koch wrote this poem after seeing a sign near a railroad track saying "Caution! One Train May Hide Another."

We spend some time talking about how Koch found inspiration in the world around him. What is the original intention of the sign? Did Koch find extra meaning in it? What did it mean to him?

There are poems all around. When I was a camp counselor there was a day when the whole camp seemed to be descending into chaos. Kids were breaking their arms. People were playing pranks. It rained for a week straight and all the tents were leaking. I walked into the crowded, wet office looking for a pad of paper. I found one with a sheet that said at the top, "Will Somebody" To me this was a poem that perfectly captured the desperation of that day. Ask the class: what might a stranger coming into the camp and finding that piece of paper think was going on? Is it the beginning of a desperate plea? What happened to the person to distract him or her from continuing to write? Or is "Will" a person whose last name he or she couldn't remember?

Next we talk about where the students might find poems in their own lives: On bulletin boards? In notes home to parents? Does anyone have a found poem with them now?

Class ends with an assignment: Students are asked to find a poem-inspiring phrase in their own lives. It can be a sign, a random scrap of paper, or a tidbit of overheard conversation, about which they feel great poems could be written. In a follow-up class, students can put all their found poem ideas into a hat, and pull out a random bit of inspiration to write a poem in class with.

ONE TRAIN MAY HIDE ANOTHER

[*Sign at a railroad crossing in Kenya*]

In a poem, one line may hide another line,

As at a crossing, one train may hide another train.

That is, if you are waiting to cross

The tracks, wait to do it for one moment at

Least after the first train is gone. And so when you read

Wait until you have read the next line—

Then it is safe to go on reading.

In a family one sister may conceal another,

So, when you are courting, it's best to have them all in view

Otherwise in coming to find one you may love another.

One father or one brother may hide the man,

If you are a woman, whom you have been waiting to love.

So always standing in front of something the other

As words stand in front of objects, feelings, and ideas.

One wish may hide another. And one person's reputation may hide

The reputation of another. One dog may conceal another

On a lawn, so if you escape the first one you're not necessarily safe;

One lilac may hide another and then a lot of lilacs

    and on the Appia Antica one tomb

May hide a number of other tombs. In love, one reproach may hide another,

One small complaint may hide a great one.

One injustice may hide another—one colonial may hide another,

One blaring red uniform another, and another, a whole column.

    One bath may hide another bath

As when, after bathing, one walks out into the rain.

One idea may hide another: Life is simple

Hide Life is incredibly complex, as in the prose of Gertrude Stein

One sentence hides another and is another as well. And in the laboratory

One invention may hide another invention,

One evening may hide another, one shadow, a nest of shadows.

One dark red, or one blue, or one purple—this is a painting

By someone after Matisse. One waits at the tracks until they pass,

These hidden doubles or, sometimes, likenesses. One identical twin

May hide the other. And there may be even more in there! The obstetrician

Gazes at the Valley of the Var. We used to live there, my wife and I, but

One life hid another life. And now she is gone and I am here.

A vivacious mother hides a gawky daughter. The daughter hides

Her own vivacious daughter in turn. They are in

A railway station and the daughter is holding a bag

Bigger than her mother's bag and successfully hides it.

In offering to pick up the daughter's bag one finds oneself confronted
    by the mother's

And has to carry that one, too. So one hitchhiker

May deliberately hide another and one cup of coffee

Another, too, until one is over-excited. One love may hide another love
    or the same love

As when "I love you" suddenly rings false and one discovers

The better love lingering behind, as when "I'm full of doubts"

Hides "I'm certain about something and it is that"

And one dream may hide another as is well known, always, too.
    In the Garden of Eden

Adam and Eve may hide the real Adam and Eve.

Jerusalem may hide another Jerusalem.

When you come to something, stop to let it pass

So you can see what else is there. At home, no matter where,

Internal tracks pose dangers, too: one memory

Certainly hides another, that being what memory is all about,

The eternal reverse succession of contemplated entities. Reading
    A Sentimental Journey look around

When you have finished, for Tristram Shandy, to see

If it is standing there, it should be, stronger

And more profound and theretofore hidden as Santa Maria Maggiore

May be hidden by similar churches inside Rome. One sidewalk

May hide another, as when you're asleep there, and

One song hide another song; a pounding upstairs

Hide the beating of drums. One friend may hide another, you sit
    at the foot of a tree

With one and when you get up to leave there is another

Whom you'd have preferred to talk to all along. One teacher,

One doctor, one ecstasy, one illness, one woman, one man

May hide another. Pause to let the first one pass.

You think, Now it is safe to cross and you are hit by the next one. It can be
    important

To have waited at least a moment to see what was already there.

                              —*Kenneth Koch*

LAUGH YOUR HEADLINE OFF: WRITING COMEDY NEWS

by MELISSA PRICE

3 hours
Materials: Taped clips of The Daily Show,
copies of interesting pictures from the newspaper

I wanted to teach this class because I was disappointed with the coverage by the major news organizations. So I turned to *The Daily Show* and *The Onion* for their funny and passionate send-ups of the news. In this class we learn to follow their lead.

Session One

Class begins with an announcement: feel free to laugh at me, but not with me. They don't laugh. I don't blame them. Moving right along, we watch fifteen minutes of clips from The Daily Show. No one laughs until midway through the fourth clip. (Later I learn that most of the students had never seen the show until that day, so maybe they weren't quite sure how to take it—or maybe not everyone thinks "The Daily Show" is as funny as I do.)

Next, I distribute packets containing the following handouts: Nanette Asimov's "Dirty Dozen Elements of a Standard News Story" [1]; the Society of Professional Journalists' Code of Ethics [2] ; copies of ten stories from *The Onion's Our Dumb Century* collection; and excerpts from several *Daily Show* scripts. We take a quick look at the handouts, and then I deliver a short spiel about so-called "straight news" reporting and writing methods, explaining that we'll get to the comedy writing part of class very soon.

First, we discuss what the goals of journalism are and what the goals of humor are. We discuss objectiv-

ity, relevance, authority, sensationalism, satire, parody—all that good stuff.

Then we get writing! For inspiration, I distribute photocopies of pictures from the newspaper. There are: a gang of kangaroos, a huge snow sculpture of Thomas the Train, a woman trying to catch a bunch of potatoes on a plate, a famous actor in a fabulous dance pose, and a very tan old woman bearing an "I Heart Cuba" tote bag and holding an unlit cigar in her mouth. The students are supposed to write silly headlines for them. They certainly do.

Session Two

In our next session, we write even longer pieces. I distribute a list of headlines from twelve actual news stories (see page 103). The students pick one and write an *Onion*—style parody. If they prefer, they can invent their own: "Sixth Grader's Attempt to Make Friends Call Him by Cool Nickname Fails"; "Opinion Piece: My Dad is More Embarrassing than Yours"; "Math Teacher Admits: 'Yeah, You Guys Will Never Really Need to Know this Stuff.'" The result will be many column inches of grade-A comedy material.

 SUPERTEACHER BONUS ACTIVITY: *Compile all the students' articles into a parody paper, authored by the whole class, and distribute it to the school at large.*

1. At *http://www.highschooljournalism.org/teachers/teachers.cfm?id=33&ttid=29*
2. At *http://www.spj.org/ethics_code.asp*

REAL HEADLINES!

Write a story from one of the following headlines:

IT CAN BE DONE: SCIENTISTS TEACH OLD DOGS NEW TRICKS

—New York Times

RURAL COUNTIES KEEP AFLOAT WITH TAPE AND BUBBLE GUM

—San Francisco Chronicle

YOUNG POP STARS IN LOVE

—Los Angeles Times

LET'S NOT BE BEASTLY TO DALEKS

—London Observer

LOVEBUG RUMORED TO BE PART OF UNIVERSITY OF FLORIDA EXPERIMENT

—Southwest Florida Herald Tribune

MORE WIVES BRINGING HOME THE BACON

—Chicago Sun-Times

TOMATO WARS

—St. Louis Post-Dispatch

HOME RUNS DOWN, BUT WHY?

—Oregonian

DISPOSABLE, DANGEROUS—AND DUMB

—Philadelphia Inquirer

PATRIOTS ARE FREE TO GO SHOPPING

—Boston Globe

CAMILLA THE DUCHESS FINDS HER MAN

—International Herald Tribune

...or invent your own!

MY BORING LIFE

by MICAH PILKINGTON

2 hours
Materials: Sock monkey (optional)

It's been our experience that all middle-schoolers think their life is too boring to write about, and they couldn't be more wrong. Whenever we give them a prompt, they come up with some amazing stuff. The students in this three-session class knocked our socks off. We're sure yours will too.

Session One

The workshop leader begins by telling a gripping true story. In one class, the instructor relayed a traumatic event from her past involving a show tune performed in sixth-grade choir. She told the story, sang the song, and demonstrated the absurd choreography. We're sure you have a great story of your own. We identify the main events in the story we heard, then ask for a show of hands: Who else has done something embarrassing in public? Did anyone have a hard time adjusting to middle school?

We retreat to a big dry-erase board and ask the class a more general question: What are some changes that can happen in a person's life?

After we fill the board with ideas, we ask the class to write down everything they remember about three specific times their lives changed. Before we ask for volunteers to share their work, we introduce the Story Monkey, a friendly creature with special powers. Whoever possesses the Story Monkey has the room's undivided attention. We've heard some great stories from the holders of the monkey, from a rumble with a petting-zoo goat to memories of a beloved babysitter who died of cancer. When everyone has had a turn, we add a second step to the exercise: write down some problems you've encountered as a result of changes in your life. We end by discussing how conflict is the center of every story.

Session Two

We start by writing a few sentences of the most boring story we can think of on the board, then ask the class to fix it. We discuss different ways to do this:

- Does the story improve if we add details?

- How about adding action?
- Maybe more descriptions of sights, sounds, and smells?
- What about dialogue?

Now what does the story look like?

Next, we return the work we did in the previous session. Everyone picks one of the events they wrote about and rewrites it using the techniques we practiced on the board.

We finish this session sharing our work using the Story Monkey, offering feedback when it seems appropriate. We send the students home with a little bit of homework: to give their pieces a final polish.

 SUPERTEACHER BONUS ACTIVITY: *Because these stories are so incredibly un-boring, we think they deserve an audience. Superteachers may want to organize an after-school reading and invite the students' friends and families to hear their wonderful work. Photocopy fancy invitations to send home with the students, and schedule a practice or two to make sure the kinks are worked out.*

Session Three

The last session is our reading. It can be in-class, or, even better, after school, before an audience of friends and family. Before we begin, we remind the students how important it is that no one have any fun. Readers should speak in a whispered monotone, preferably while staring at the ground. We also caution against laughter, and advise the reader to glare at the audience if he or she receives any. After a few minutes of this, we admit that having fun is actually pretty important, as is making sure the audience can hear you.

Before we begin, we ask if anyone has suggestions on how to shake off nerves. Yoga? We do some as a group. Jumping jacks? Sure! A spazzy dance with your eyes closed? Awesome. We're ready. The reading begins, everyone is blown away, and off the students go, to continue their non-boring lives.

COLONEL MUSTARD IN THE LIBRARY WITH A CANDLESTICK: HOW TO WRITE A MYSTERY

by JULIANNE BALMAIN

1 hour

Materials: Miscellaneous objects (keys, costume jewelry, cups, photos, etc.)

Mystery stories are fun to write because they have a well-defined beginning, middle, and end. This makes them especially satisfying to read. Finding the answer to a perplexing question feels good. Once you know who drank all the milk and why, you don't have to stay up all night wondering about it. The world is full of nagging questions that never get answered. In mysteries, we finally get to know the truth.

Most mysteries begin when the main character, often a grizzled detective but sometimes just a person who is excessively curious, discovers a question that urgently needs answering. This question is usually, "Who perpetrated this terrible crime?" It can also be, "What happened to this lost but very important object (such as a rich man's last will and testament) or person (such as the French Ambassador to Peru) or pet (such as the beloved parrot from the local café)?"

The middle is when the detective or curious person is on the trail, hunting for clues. Often one clue will lead to the next clue and so on until the mystery is solved. Very often, near the end, the detective runs out of clues and is temporarily stumped. This is a good time for the detective's sidekick or some other subordinate character to accidentally provide a hint. For example,

the curious person's mother could leave a note saying, "Jimmy stopped by to see you today." If we know it couldn't possibly have been Jimmy since Jimmy was with the main character the whole time, and therefore someone must have been pretending to be Jimmy, it's definitely a clue. What's more, whoever was impersonating Jimmy is a suspect.

Once the driving question of the mystery has been answered and all other "loose ends" tied up—a loose end is a minor mystery within the mystery—the story ends and everyone saunters off to have tea and biscuits, or whatever they like to have at the end of a good story.

Ready to give it a shot? To prepare, collect several objects and display them on a table at the front of the room. They can be ordinary objects, such as a key, a feather, or a coffee cup, or special items, such as a satin glove, a diamond brooch, an antique photograph, or a treasure map.

You may also want to assemble a cast of three to five suspects using photographs cut from newspapers and magazines. Alternatively, choose several volunteers and decide the basic attributes of their characters as a group. Then distribute the handout (page 106), let your students loose, and watch the mysteries unfold.

WRITE YOUR OWN!

Using the objects on the table as clues, write a mystery story with a beginning, middle, and end.

Step one: Where?

Imagine a setting. Where would you like your story to take place? An exotic locale such as Mexico or Paris can be intriguing, but your own neighborhood works too. Mysteries happen everywhere.

Step two: Who?

Who will investigate the mystery? Using a detective makes things particularly easy, since it's in their nature to go around asking questions.

To get the story started, write a sentence or two establishing who the main character is, where he or she is, and what he or she is doing. For example: *"Sabrina opened the window overlooking Puerto Vallarta. She was glad to be on vacation, far from her job as a detective."*

Step three: What happens?

Now you need is a crime. Think of ways to bring your detective in contact with the crime and the objects on the table. For example: *"Across the street, a man was stuffing an enormous bag overflowing with bills into the trunk of a tiny car. Sabrina had never seen so much money. Where could it have come from? As she watched, he jumped into the car and sped away. Another man ran up after him, cursing loudly."*

Step four: Clues and suspects

Look around for clues. Is there any evidence? Are there any witnesses? Who might have a reason to be involved in the crime? Have your detective question suspects and see what they say. Could they be lying? Does something they say lead to the next clue or suspect?

Step five: Resolution

The best part of any mystery story, and the hardest part to come up with, is the final insight that triggers the "ah-ha" moment, when the detective finally knows what happened. How does your main character discover the truth? You may want to finish by finding a way to prove your detective's guess is correct. Does the guilty party confess? Is she caught in the act of committing another crime? Does she make a mistake that reveals her guilt once and for all?

Alternate method: You could also try writing a story by going in reverse: starting with your resolution and working backwards.

Extra credit: Create a pseudonym. Like an alias, a pseudonym is a false name mystery writers sometimes use to make themselves seem more mysterious. Write a brief description of your pseudonymous persona, including where he or she lives, what qualifications he or she has for writing the story, and anything else noteworthy.

FIGHTIN' WORDS: DEBATE FOR BURGEONING MIDDLE-SCHOOL TYPES

by DOUG WILKINS

2 hours

Students naturally take to debate. They are at the perfect age for being contentious and holding opinions of some sort. The trick is to channel their inclination to engage in what a friend of mine once referred to as "Oh yeah?" debate, as in "Oh yeah? Well, well, um, yer a dope." Not the kind of thing that gets libraries built, if you know what I mean.

Session One

Every debate class should teach students that

1. A debate considers a general resolution. This is debate-speak for the issue being argued, and it is usually formulated like this: "Resolved, that preparing for war will guarantee the elimination of peace." Students do not get to choose the side they will uphold.

2. Interscholastic debate has two sides, Affirmative and Negative. Affirmative *must* uphold the resolution, while the Negative only needs to oppose the Affirmative (a subtle difference of responsibilities, but a good one to know).

3. At age something-teen, few students are credentialed experts in a given field, so *published* evidence comes in handy and should be used in the debate. Saying "I heard about it somewhere" is not an adequate method of argumentation.

4. Organizing one's arguments and keeping track of the opposition's arguments is crucial to victory, so flowsheeting, a form of debate note-taking, is a key skill to learn.

And that's probably enough to get things started. Next: flowsheeting!

Flowsheeting is one of those things that everyone should have been taught prior to age 15. That ain't the case, currently. Yet it's simple: A flowsheet is a paper database where columns contain speeches, and rows contain arguments. (This is a great point at which to use the expression "line of reasoning.") Some debaters use two colors of ink to keep track of the two sides of the debate, and most flowsheeters use arrows to connect the arguments as they flow across the paper (hence the name "flowsheet"). And, yes, if the debate is extensive, debaters use more than one sheet of paper.

A SAMPLE FLOWSHEET

Here is a sample of a flowsheet taken during a debate about serving junk food during ballet performances. Notice the separation of speeches into columns and of arguments into different rows. Notice also that the arguments "flow" from left to right.

Affirmative	Negative	Affirmative	Negative
1. Junk food improves the experience	No, it doesn't Smells bad Is messy	Does, too! Smells great! Disposable	No way! Rancid!! Disposable is bad
2. Better than the usual food they serve	Fat & ballet don't mix at all!!!	Cucumber sandwiches? Forget it!!!	What's the life expectancy of fast-food eaters?
3. Besides, dance is just plain silly; it's for weenies in tight outfits	Dance is difficult; requires stamina	Aw, it's just a bunch of hopping & stuff for losers	When was the last time Mr. Couch Spud here walked anywhere?

Session Two

Setting up a classroom debate is pretty simple. Write a well-considered resolution before class (*do not* let the students write one, unless you're willing to spend another hour of your life hearing a discussion of the harms of smoking cigarettes or some other threadbare issue), spend ten minutes or so teaching the basics of flowsheeting, split the class into Affirmative and Negative, with the two groups on opposite sides of the room, and then start the debate. Affirmative starts (kind of like white getting to go first in chess), and then the speeches alternate between Affirmative and Negative. The teacher should preside over the session and ensure that some modest attempt at Robert's Rules of Order prevails. If you're really brave, announce a winner of the debate with five minutes to go and explain your reason for selecting the winning side.

Of course, it's much more educationally valid to do this repeatedly, checking the strength of the evidence the students bring (make this homework—the Internet has made elementary research a breeze), inspecting the reasoning they employ, reviewing the students' flowsheeting, pumping up their delivery skills, and keeping things fresh by switching resolutions frequently.

Do this often enough and your country's political system just might improve. Now there's an intended outcome of which to be proud!

WRITING THROUGH THE SENSES

by VICTORIA Q. LEGG

1 hour

Materials: Sensory prompts (fabric, flowers, spices, etc.)

We like this lesson because it lets you write with your nose, ears, tongue, eyes and skin as much as your brain. Students leave with a poem to excite all the senses.

We start class by talking about what the senses are and the value of sensory detail. We distribute the "Using Your Senses" handout (page 110) and ask the students to share what they write.

Next we read a descriptive passage (page 110). We ask the students to close their eyes and visualize what we're reading to them. We allow the story to sink in, then read it again with all the descriptive detail removed. Then we ask the students to tell us what the difference was.

Next we practice using our senses. We bring in items to stimulate the senses: soft fabric to touch, tinkly bells to hear, spices to smell, bright flowers to look at, little candies to taste. We pass them around, asking the students to focus on what the materials feel, look, or sound like. We ask the students to share descriptions of the items and write them on the board. How would you describe the sound of the bell? The feel of the velvet? The smell of the cinnamon?

Next we turn the students loose to create some ideas of their own. We ask them to think about a vivid sensory memory they have and to write about it for five to ten minutes, being as descriptive as possible.

Once we're warmed up, we do some creative, sensory freewriting. For the next twenty minutes they write about whatever they want, as long as it starts with a sentence from the last exercise. Some might want to write about their family, and some will make up a sci-fi fantasy. It can be about anything at all. Since this is a creative exercise, we tell our students there are only two rules: the pen or pencil must be moving at all times, and they cannot erase or cross out lines. We encourage them to use as much detail as possible. Which blue, exactly? Bluejean blue or baby blue? Was the texture soft as velvet or rough like sandpaper? Was the sound a squeak, a crack, or a slam? Loud or soft?

The second part of the exercise is to have students reread what they wrote and circle those words and phrases they are most happy with. We set a short time limit, like five to ten minutes, so they don't spend too much time judging what's been written. We encourage them to trust their instincts. Have them recopy their circled words and phrases onto a new sheet of paper. Then they make a poem using the words they just copied. They can add connecting words but not new content words. They do not have to use all the words, and they can use them in any order they wish. We give the students about twenty minutes to complete their poems. When we have time, we have the students stand up and read their work.

USING YOUR SENSES

When we write using the language of the senses, we are describing the textures of life: what it feels like to be alive. The five senses are smell, sight, sound, taste, and touch.

1. Our world is sense and it fills us up. Think for a minute about what it feels like to have cool water running through your fingertips on a hot day or the smell of roasting chicken when you walk into the house hungry after school. Can you recall what soda bubble fizz feels like in your mouth?

2. We understand the world first through our senses. Remember how safe you felt when wrapped up in your mother's arms? We learn not to touch the hot stove because we know what the pain feels like when we touch something hot. Have you ever noticed how tense people are when a storm is brewing, the clouds getting dark and scurrying across the sky, and leaves swirling around on the sidewalk?

3. Sensory detail evokes emotional content and connects us to our past. Fill in the blanks:

   The touch of cool hands on your feverish forehead feels like _____.

   The smell of your very favorite food being prepared makes you feel _____.

SENSORY READING

With sensory detail:
When Julia woke it was already noon, and her bedroom was filled with warm yellow light, so heavy and thick it felt like an extra blanket. It was so cozy and appealing she thought nothing could make her get out of bed. Seconds later she realized she was wrong. That *smell* could make her get out of bed. What was it? The first thing she sniffed was a rich, dark blast of musk-strong coffee. Underneath that was a hint of sugary maple and the tang of batter: pancakes. She could hear something sizzling, too—what was it? Oh, there it was—the savory aroma of eggs frying in butter. Still groggy, she threw off the heavy covers and sleepwalked, zombielike, to the welcoming kitchen.

Omitting sensory detail:
When Julia woke it was noon, and her bedroom was bright. She thought nothing could make her get out of bed. Seconds later she realized she was wrong. She sniffed coffee. Underneath that was a hint of pancakes. She could hear something cooking, too—what was it? Oh, there it was—eggs. She threw off the covers and walked to the kitchen.

THE STORY OF ME: WRITING ABOUT YOUR LIFE AND YOUR FAMILY

by JASON ROBERTS

2 hours

Here's the theme of this workshop: *You don't have to wait until you're really old to write your life story!* You've already seen many surprising and memorable things, and a lot of people, events, and ideas have helped shape who you are (and who you're becoming). This workshop helps kids discover how fun it is to connect your experiences, your influences, and your family history, and see how it all adds up to the story of you.

We usually begin not with introductions but with a deliberately provocative exercise: the facilitator announces that he or she is the new alien overlord of Earth. Each participant is commanded, in turn, to explain why he or she should be allowed to stay on Earth to continue their life in progress, rather than be shipped off to the salt mines in the Glorgg Nebula. This exercise prompts them to start thinking immediately of themselves in terms of their qualities, actions, and affinities, rather than as a little bundle of biographical data. It starts them thinking about what they are, not who they are.

Next we ask a simple question: *What is your earliest memory?* This tends to bring forth some particularly vivid imagery—indeed, one's first memory is usually little more than a vivid image. We then proceed to place that imagery in an emotional context, asking for more details:

- What feelings come attached to that memory?

- Who's hovering outside of the scene? Where do you think your mom/dad/sister/brother were at that moment?

- Can you remember any vivid sensory images from this event—a smell, a taste, music, something you saw?

- Why do you think you remember *that particular moment*, and not something from the day before or the day after?

This last question typically sparks a lot of introspection—it's a new idea, the concept that there's a reason this specific memory has stuck in their head. Sometimes there's no clear reason; it's just a pretty image. But more often than not, the participants can be encouraged to see it in the light of their own emerging personality. A first memory about, say, coveting an older sister's toy might lead to a cascade of anecdotes about growing up in the shadow of a sibling.

By now it's time to start writing these memories down. To help their essays take shape, I encourage the participants to imagine their Story of Me as a sort of recipe: *these* people plus *these* events made it possible for me to be who I am and who I'm becoming.

Here are some other questions I regularly pose during the workshop to help the process along:

- Can you think of some decisions your parents and grandparents made, long before you were born, that helped shape who you are?

- If one or more of those decisions hadn't been made, what kind of person might you have been instead?

- Did luck and chance play a part in their stories? What accidents of fate put them on a path that resulted in you?

- What are your biggest interests now? Can you trace the birth of those interests?

- How are you different from your parents?

- How are you alike?

- How are you different from who you were five years ago?

- If the kid who was you five years ago showed up in your room for a day, what would you do with her/him?

- What would you tell her or him?

- What things did you believe when you were younger that you now know to be wrong?

- Where you ever unjustly accused of something you didn't do?

- Did you ever do something you shouldn't have done without getting caught?

- Did you ever unintentionally hurt someone else's feelings? When did you realize you had made a mistake?

- What's the most trivial thing that, for some reason, means a big deal to you?

- If you could relive a single day, which day would it be?

- If you could erase a single day, which day would *that* be?

Student Work

Let Them Feel the Music

This all begins before I was born. My parents, who lived in Japan back then, were both interested in music, and were in a band. One day my dad visited my mom at her house, but she turned him down by saying that she was busy. My dad sadly departed, leaving something for her in front of her door. After he had gone, my mother had looked outside and saw a lunch that was still warm; it was made by my father. My mom felt bad for turning him down and she tried to chase him, but he had already gone. My mother had been very impressed with my father. After that, they met at music-related parties and started dating each other.

Back then, it was the trend to go to either India or to America. Their band decided to go on a trip to America since they knew a friend there, unlike in India where they would be all alone. One by one, the band members went to America. My father caught up with my mother later, and they decided to make our home here.

I think that one of the things that was passed on to me was the love of music. You might think that teenagers only listen to pop music, but I like to listen to other music, too. I play the double-bass and the piano. I want to make up a song that might change someone in some way, and let them feel the music that I love.

—*Aiko Sakai, 13*

YAAAAAAAHHHHHHHH!!!!!!!

If I were to relive one day, it would be the day that I went to the Santa Cruz Beach Boardwalk with my friends Ryan Baba, Eric Yen, and Alexander Wong. We had a limited time of two and a half hours, so we tried to do as much as possible. First we went on the Typhoon. It's very cool, but a little scary. Alex and Eric didn't go on because they said they would get sick if they did. After a couple of other rides, and a swift breakfast, we decided to go on the main ride, the Giant Dipper. This is the main attraction, and there is always a huge line. We had to wait about fifteen minutes to go on one ride. I knew it was worthwhile.

We finally got on. As we buckled our seats, we locked ourselves securely. Then the cart went through a pitch-black tunnel as everyone screamed. Then we started to climb the long uphill. At the top, the people looked like pebbles. Before I could utter a sound, the cart jumped down.

"YAHHHHHHHHHHHHHHHHHHHHHHHHHHHHHHHHHHHHHHH!!!!!!!!!!"

Everyone yelled as we went down. My heart was jumping. I felt like there was no gravity for a second. I kind of flew in midair, and the only thing holding me was the buckle. Though it's a scary feeling, it gets you no matter how many times you get on. It was so fast, I only could see a blur of the rails. It was so cool, and I felt like it was the best moment of my life.

—*Yukhi Sakai, 11*

EVENTUALLY DIE "

READ OUT LOUD

AFTERWARDS, EVERYONE SHOULD WIPE THE SWEAT OFF EACHOTHERS' BROWS + WRITE AN INSPIRATIONAL QUOTE ABOUT **COURAGE** OR WHATEVER! IT'S GOOD TO BORROW OTHER PEOPLE'S QUOTES, UNLESS THEY'RE CONVICTED FELONS ON "60 MINUTES," BUT IT'S WAY MORE FUN TO MAKE UP YOUR OWN + GO AROUND QUOTING YOURSELF IN THE THIRD PERSON. I MADE UP "ALL WITNESSES EVENTUALLY DIE" TO KEEP MYSELF FROM WETTING MY PANTS OUT OF FEAR ALL THE TIME. GOOD LUCK!

--ERIKA "MAD DOG" LOPEZ

CUT THE TRUTH ALONG THESE LINES

R.I.P.

"THE GUY WHO SAW WHAT YOU DID LAST NIGHT"

IN THE PRESS ROOM: CELEBRITY IN YOUR CLASS

by ERIN NEELEY

2 hours
Materials: Faux celebrity

Teaching middle-school journalism can be a real treat. The students are engaged, and they're learning great stuff: how to craft a good lead, find a hook, and ask the Great Question. To engage them even more, we've developed this fun lesson plan for a live-action simulated press conference.

The first thing you'll need is a volunteer to play a faux celebrity. Maybe she'll pretend to be Venus Williams, discussing her recent Wimbledon performance, or maybe he'll pose as Nick Cannon, promoting his latest film. The volunteer should be someone the students don't know, or there will be too much temptation to giggle.

The volunteer should be prepared to answer the following questions:

- Where are "you," i.e., the faux celebrity character, from?

- What do your family and friends think about your transition to fame?

- How did you get that big break?

- How has your life changed?

- What was the first major thing that you purchased?

- What is an average day like for you?

- What is the occasion for this press conference? Did you just win a title or an award? Are you promoting something?

Costumes and background really help. Students love it when our faux famous baseball player has some real facts about the bat, or when our fake rock star can talk about the guitar. Students tend to egg this sort of thing on, and in a funny way, these little details will add to the "validity" of their reporting.

The next step is to help the students prepare. We spend some time discussing the fundamentals of good questioning. What makes a good question? What makes a bad one? We encourage them to formulate questions that don't have yes-or-no answers, that aren't too obvious, that might catch the celebrity off guard. We encourage digging a little, but remind them not to get too personal. A really juicy question that demands an answer with detail is ideal.

Research is important too, so we have the students do a little fact-gathering on the faux celebrity's background and field. For example, if the faux celebrity is a crocodile hunter, we have them research crocodile hunting on the Internet. If he's an Olympic gymnast, they read up on that.

Finally, it's time to have our press conference. The faux celebrity arrives and starts taking questions. Begin with a quick, fun introduction that gives a little bit of background, like mentioning that he's the leading hitter starting out the season or holds the record for most strikes in a single game.

Students ask questions by raising their hand, and every student must ask at least one. Remind them that each question must be original—no repeats. However, follow-up questions are encouraged. Students should be taking notes the whole time, because they'll be asked to write a story as soon as the press conference is over.

The Q&A session should last about twenty minutes. The faux celebrity concludes with an inside tip or some words of inspiration, and leaves to much applause.

Then it's time to write. Give the students twenty minutes to write a draft of a story using the information they gathered in the press conference. The handout on page 118 will help them structure it. Their story should include the five W's and an H (Who, What, Where, When, Why, and How) and have an inverted-pyramid structure and pull quotes, as described in the handout. Once they have drafted a full article, give them an extra ten minutes to write a strong lead (if they don't already have one), to choose a great pull quote, and to create a headline.

If you have time, you can have students break into small groups and read each other their stories. Have them discuss the strengths in each individual story and what could be added to make the story even stronger. All students should find one really standout feature in each article to share with the class.

To end class, bring the faux celebrity back in, and allow him/her to hear a standout feature from each student's article as we close our press conference down and the flashbulbs cool for the day.

 SUPERTEACHER BONUS ACTIVITY: *Publish the students' stories in a special-edition newspaper complete with pictures! Inviting students to illustrate or photograph the subject is a good way to draw in reluctant writers.*

READ ALL ABOUT IT!

A good news story answers the following questions:

Who is the story about? (Let's say it's about a tennis champ.)

What happened to them? (Maybe she just won the U.S. Open.)

Where did it happen? (In New York.)

When did it happen? (Last week.)

Why did this take place? (She won because she was the strongest player.)

How did it happen? (Describe the winning match.)

Your story structure should be in an inverted pyramid, like this:

**Give the most important information
in the first paragraph. It should
only be two or three
sentences
long.**

In the next few paragraphs, you'll go into more depth, and give more details. By the end of the story, you should have provided all the information the reader needs.

You'll want to pepper the story with pull quotes. These are the quotes from your interviewee that add flavor and convey important information or emotion. Here's a bad pull quote: "Gray's a nice color." Here's a good one: "I don't know what possessed me to spend $5,000 on a hunk of cheese, but when I caught a whiff of that Roquefort I just knew I had to have it, no matter the cost."

HIGH SCHOOL
LESSON PLANS

DETAILS (GOLDEN), CHARACTER (IMMORTAL) & SETTING (RURAL INDIA)

by DAVE EGGERS

6 hours

This is the lesson I usually give on the first meeting of my evening high school writing class. My classes are two hours long, and for this first session, I'm trying to do the following things:

- Get the students thinking about specificity in their writing

- Get them thinking about the value of personal observation

- Get them better acquainted with each other (in my class, the students are from all over the Bay Area, but this is just as useful in a setting where the students all think they know each other)

- Get them started on a short story that challenges them to solve fairly sophisticated problems of setting and motive

Note: Any portion of this two-hour plan could be used alone. Most steps could easily take up a 50-minute class period. The time guidelines are only included if you happen to have a two-hour, or two-class-period, block of time available.

Step One: The Power of Observation *(12 minutes)*

Start with the head of a stuffed crocodile. Or something like that. 826 Valencia is next to a store that sells taxidermied animals, so I usually go over and borrow one of their crocodile heads. Whatever you choose to use, this object should be something fairly unusual, but it should also be something that the students have seen before. Now—without showing the students the object—pass out blank pieces of paper, and ask the students to draw the object. For example, if I have the stuffed crocodile head hidden in my desk, I would tell the students, "You have five minutes to draw a perfectly accurate rendering of a Peruvian caiman (a type of small crocodile)." The students will laugh, but you will be serious. They have to get down to business, and draw that crocodile.

After five minutes, most students will have a pret-ty sorry-looking crocodile. They will have drawn the animal from memory, trying to recall if the crocodile's eyes are on the top of their head, or the side, and if the teeth are inside its mouth or protrude out the sides. Collect the drawings and show them to the class. Guffaws will follow.

Now take the actual crocodile head out, and place it somewhere where all the students can easily see it. Now ask them to draw the Peruvian caiman again, using the actual animal as a model. After five minutes, you'll see a tremendous difference. Where there was guessing and vagueness and error in the first drawings, there will be detail, specificity and accuracy, now that the students can refer to the genuine article. They'll see that the eyes are actually on top of its head. They'll see that the eyes are like a cat's — eerie and many-layered. They'll see that the snout is very long, very narrow, and very brittle-seeming.

Step Two: Apply the Lesson of the Peruvian Caiman to Any and All Writing *(5 minutes)*

The lesson is pretty clear: If you draw from life, from observation, your writing will be more convincing. It doesn't matter if you're writing science fiction, fantasy, or contemporary realism—whatever it is, it will benefit from real-life observation. Is there a street performer in the novel you're writing? Go watch one in action. Is there a short-hair terrier in the story you're writing? Go observe one. Is there a meat-eating venus flytrap plant in your poem? See how they really do it. Nothing can substitute for the level of specificity you get when you actually observe.

Step Three: Knowing the Difference in Details *(25 minutes)*

My students and I talk about the three types of details. With different classes, we've given these three types different names, but here we'll call them:

—*Golden*

—*Useful*

—Not-so-good

Now let's try to define them, in reverse order so we have some drama:

Not-so-good: This is a very nice way of referring to clichés or clunky descriptions or analogies. First, clichés: If there's one service we can give to these students, it's to wean them off the use of clichés. Clichés just destroy everything in their path, and they prevent the student's writing from being personal or original. He was as strong as an ox. She ate like a bird. His hands were clammy. She looked like she'd seen a ghost. There's just no point, really, in writing these words down. When students can tell a cliché when they see one, they become better critical thinkers, better readers, smarter people. When they learn to stay away from clichés in their own writing, they're on their way to becoming far stronger writers. The other type of not-so-good detail is the clunky one. His legs looked like square-cut carrots. Her dog was like a blancmange crossed with a high-plains cowboy. This is, in a way, preferable to a cliché, but it's so strange and hard to picture that it disrupts the flow of the story.

Useful: These are descriptions that are plain but needed. His hair was orange. Her face was long and oval. These pedestrian details are necessary, of course. Not every description can be golden. Speaking of which:

Golden: This is a detail/description/analogy that's singular, completely original, and makes one's subject unforgettable. She tapped her fingernail rhythmically on her large teeth as she watched her husband count the change in his man-purse. In one sentence, we've learned so much about these two people. He has a man-purse. He's fastidious. She's tired of him. She's exasperated by him. She has large teeth. Golden details can come about even while using plain words: Their young daughter's eyes were grey and cold, exhausted. Those words, individually bland, are very specific and unsettling when applied to a young girl. In one key sentence, a writer can nail down a character. This is a sample from one of my students, describing a man she saw in the park near 826 Valencia: He wore a beret, though he'd never been to Paris, and he walked like a dancer, as if hoping someone would notice that he walked like a dancer.

Working this out with the class: Getting the students understanding the differences between these three kinds of description is possible with an exercise that's always good fun. Create a chart, where you have three categories: Not-so-good; Useful; Golden. Now give them a challenge: come up with examples of each. Tell them that they need to conjure examples for, say:

The feeling of traveling at 100 miles per hour.

The students in one of my classes came up with these:

Not-so-good: *like flying; like being on a roller-coaster; so fast you want to puke; like being shot out of a cannon*

Useful: *terrifying; dizzying; nerve-racking; hurtling*

Golden: *like being dropped down a well; as the speed grew, I heard death's whisper grow louder and louder*

The exploration of these types of description can last a full class period, for sure. If you want to keep going, consider this one game I use sometimes. This takes the concept to a new level of fun.

Optional Game *(25 minutes)*

Take twenty-five sheets of blank paper, or one for every student in the class. At the top of each—leaving plenty of room below—write something that might need description: the smell of a grandparent; the sensation of a first kiss; the atmosphere of a funeral home; the taste of a perfect apple; the look on the eyes of someone who's just seen a car accident. Now, pass these out, one page per student. The task is to come up with the best (Golden) description or analogy for each prompt. It works like this: Student A might start with the "smell of a grandparent" sheet. Student A then spends a few minutes trying to come up with the best description he can think of. When Student A has written something down, he passes the paper onto Student B, and Student A receives another one that's been passed by Student C. The next paper Student A gets might be "the taste of a perfect apple." Student A then spends a few minutes on that one. If he comes up with something, then great.

If he doesn't, he can pass it on. Each student writes their own analogy below the rest of the descriptions. The final object is to come up with the best description for each prompt. I usually give the students 25 minutes, so those 25 minutes are pretty madcap, with the papers flying, the students searching for the prompts that inspire them. At the end of the 25 minutes, each prompt might have 10-15 descriptions written below it. The teacher then reads all the descriptions aloud, and the students vote on which one is best. Whichever student wins the most prompts is feted in some appropriate way.

Step Four: Interviewing Your Peers While Observing them Shrewdly *(15 minutes)*

Start by telling the students that they're going to interview each other for fifteen minutes. The students will be paired up—try to pair up students who don't usually talk to each other much—and they'll find a quiet place to talk. One will interview the other, and after seven and a half minutes, they'll switch. Before getting them started, talk about what sorts of details are useful in defining a character, making that character singular and intriguing. They'll be applying what they know from the caiman exercise, and also using good interviewing techniques, to immediately get beyond the "Where do you go to school" sorts of questions. By asking good questions and observing closely, the interviews should produce strong results very quickly, now that the students know that they're looking for golden details.

Step Five: Immortalizing Your Subject *(30 minutes)*

Once each student has notes about their assigned peer, you can do one of two things:

The Simple but Essential Character Sketch

You can ask them to simply write one-page character sketches of their peers, which should be compelling, true, well-observed, and (of course) beautifully written. This alone is a very worthwhile assignment. When these are read aloud, the interview subject benefits from what in most cases is the first time they've ever been thus defined. It's strange but true: it's pretty rare to have someone observe you closely, write about your gestures and freckles and manner of speech. In the process, the interviewer improves their pow-

ers of observation, while the interviewee blushes and can't get the words out of their brain. And these two students get to know each other far better than they would almost any other way. It's a good way to break through cliques, create new bonds of understanding.

Place Your Subject in Rural India (for example) The lesson works pretty well either way, but something extraordinary happens with this second part, the curveball part. At this stage, after the first 15 minutes, hand out pictures to the students. These pictures, one per student, should depict some unusual, strange, foreign, bizarre, or historical setting. Usually I make copies from old LIFE books about the various cultures of the world. Thus some student might end up with a picture of a Swedish farm, a royal Thai court, a Nairobi marketplace, or a scene from rural India. Then tell the class that they need to a) Use the details they've gathered about their classmate; and then b) Place that student in this foreign setting. The writers then need to concoct a reason that their character is in rural India, or in Barbados, or Grenada, or in the drawing room of a Scottish duke. This requires the writer to imagine this new/ strange world, and also solve the problem: What is their character doing there? Are they stuck, are they trying to leave? How would this student react to being lost in a marketplace in Nairobi? Who or what are they looking for?

If you have some time, or want to expand the exercise, have the students research their location a bit. Even by using the picture alone, they are using their observational powers, but with the added benefit of some book-oriented or internet research, they can conjure ever-more convicing settings.

I have to admit that I came up with this exercise on the fly. I had no idea that it would work, but it did the first time I did it, and it always works. Here's why:

- The process of interviewing one's classmates is always appealing to the students

- The close observation makes both students, interviewed and interviewee, feel valued and singular

- The curveball of putting this person in a foreign setting forces the student outside their own school/home/neighborhood, and requires the solving of a fairly sophisticated problem: Who is this person and why are they here? The drama and conflict are built into the setting, and get a short story off to a quick and intriguing start.

A stellar example of one such exercise is on the following page. In their interview, 17-year-old Sally Mao's subject told her about some nightmares he'd been having, and mentioned having recently been to the hospital to visit his mother. Then Sally was given a picture of Bombay, c. 1970. From this, Sally created this story in about 20 minutes.

Student Work

Dust-silk Pouch

Up ahead, the road widens to reveal a slipshod blockade of cars, carts, and cargo. A yellow-curry smoke stews the engine of Mr. Kendall's van as he bites at the tail of jagged traffic. James, neck pressed against the seat, awakens from a sweaty dream to the grind of sound.

He has just suffered the same nightmare again. It gallops with him wherever he goes. He sees its lean legs and mane, its relentless tawny hooves swerving outside car windows, airplane windows, bedroom doors, its acrid breath clogging his nostrils, a familiar stench. The ride up the mountain has rattled his dreamscape like some monstrous cataclysm, magnifying his terror. This time the rodents had done it. They were wearing green uniforms, the whole lot of them. They swarmed, they crawled, they carried nooses, planks, kerosene, and razor-tipped whips. They were out for blood.

James asks, "Dad, what's a Nazi?"

"Eh? Are we having this discussion again?"

"What's a Nazi, what's a Gestapo, what are they?"

"A Nazi is a kind of monster," Mr. Kendall declares. "The kind that enslaves people, that performs cruel experiments. A Gestapo is their secret police."

"What kind of monsters are they? Are they some kind of furry creature? Rodents, maybe?"

"I wouldn't say that. But Nazis are less prevalent than they used to be."

"I just had a dream. It was the chipmunks, it was the rodents who made up the Gestapo, they wanted blood, Dad, they wanted blood, and they're right here in India—I'm not sure where but I think they're further up ahead. I'm scared."

Mr. Kendall laughs. "Well, son, who could really blame the rodents? The very term 'guinea pig' implies some sort of cruel and unusual experimentation. Yes, if rodents took over the world, they'd be out for blood."

His father's hands sweat on the wheel. "This may take longer than expected," he says. "The hospital is beyond this village. If I get this right, it'd probably be within the next two towns. I hope that's the one she's staying in. Otherwise, we're out of luck."

What they are waiting for James doesn't grasp. He fidgets, chews on imaginary gum, plugs his ears. Before this trip, India was a haze of cast-bronze Hindu idols, boiled-blood sunrises, young girls in jeweled saris and deep crimson makeup, and all that kind of exotic drone that keeps a dish of samosas spicy. But like any vision, this one has been extinguished. India isn't carved out of ivory. India bakes and suffocates. India is dirty, damp, and cauldron-colored. India sticks to the inside of his skin.

—by Sally Mao, 17

WICKED STYLE AND HOW TO GET IT

by MICAH PILKINGTON

4 hours

Maybe you've noticed—teenagers agonize about style. The same anxiety that goes into finding the exact right pair of sneakers goes into their writing. In our workshops they often ask us: how do you find your own authentic voice? This class helps them do just that.

Session One

On day one, we warm up to the topic by examining a few different writing styles. We read passages from a diverse group of books, from slangy (*Catcher in the Rye* is a good one) to comic (maybe some David Sedaris) to more formal (Henry James). We ask: Which do you like? Which doesn't work for you? Which do you identify with? Which puts you off and why?

Next we read the "Stylish Writing" handout (page 127), featuring the first paragraph of Jonathan Lethem's novel *Motherless Brooklyn*. Then we read an article from *The Onion*. After the students read them, we discuss the ways the style and the content work together to make a great piece. Would *Motherless Brooklyn* be as effective if it didn't rely on stream-of-consciousness? Would the *Onion* piece be as funny if it weren't deadpan? Then we ask: How you can use style and content to make your own writing better? What kind of word choices can you make? How do you structure your sentences? What kind of imagery can you use? We take suggestions and write everything down on a dry-erase board.

Enough talk; it's time for a writing exercise. We ask everyone to choose a scenario and describe it using an "inappropriate" style. We use the example of narrating a three-alarm fire using a slow pace and flowery language: "It was Sunday afternoon in the firehouse. Time for my tea. I just love tea, don't you? It's so fragrant and rich—it makes one feel like the Emperor of China! As I was saying, I was just about to have a cup of tea, when the alarm went off. Three of them, in fact. But before we get to that, let's talk about this: Earl Grey. Earl Grey is my very favorite kind of tea. I like it because you can enjoy it with breakfast, lunch, dinner, or all on its own. It goes particularly well with cookies, especially the rich buttery ones favored by the Scottish."

Everyone is invited to share their work, and the results are often thoroughly enjoyable and surprising. We were once treated to a pencil-sharpening scene reminiscent of Greek tragedy.

We end the first session with an out-loud reading from Charles Dickens' *Oliver Twist*—the scene in which Oliver first meets the Artful Dodger. Noting the difference between the narrator's voice, Oliver's voice, and the Dodger's voice, we send the kids home with an assignment: combine two voices in one scene and bring it in next time.

Session Two

On day two, ask the students to read their homework piece aloud. In one class, we got to hear a lively conversation between a businessman and a large, angry puppet. Next, we hand out two important short stories: Ernest Hemingway's "A Clean, Well-Lighted Place" from *Winner Take Nothing* and a winning entry from the annual Imitation Hemingway contest called "The Pains of Rain." [1] We read the first paragraph of each and discuss the choices made by the faux Hemingway and how they differ from, say, someone imitating Virginia Woolf. Then we ask the kids to write a quick description of their own writing style, citing influences, techniques, and things they'd like to try in the future, e.g. "I'm a modern Jack Kerouac with touches of Joyce Carol Oates. I'm into stream-of-consciousness narration, and I'd like to try my hand at magic realism."

Our last exercise as a class is a really fun one. On three separate pieces of scrap paper, each student writes down a character, a setting, and a line of dialogue. We gather each category and mix it up, then pass them back out. Now we write a scene using all three elements in any way we choose. We read the results out loud and usually it's so much fun that we do the exercise all over again.

At the end of class, we make a list of recommended reading. At 826, everyone made great suggestions, including *Tender Is the Night*, *The House of Sand and Fog*, and *How the Garcia Girls Lost Their Accents*. Stylish!

---

1. At *http://www.hemispheresmagazine.com/fiction/2000/hemingway.htm*

SOME STYLISH WRITING

Say you're writing a novel about a detective who suffers from Tourette's Syndrome. How do you start the first page? The first sentence? You could state the facts: "My name is Lionel, and I have a neurological disorder that is characterized by recurrent involuntary tics involving body movements and vocalizations and often has one or more associated conditions, such as obsessive-compulsive disorder."

But Jonathan Lethem is smart, so he does this instead:

WALKS INTO

Context is everything. Dress me up and see. I'm a carnival barker, an auctioneer, a downtown performance artist, a speaker in tongues, a senator drunk on filibuster. I've got Tourette's. My mouth won't quit, though mostly I whisper or subvocalize like I'm reading aloud, my Adam's apple bobbing, jaw muscle beating like a miniature heart under my cheek, the noise suppressed, the words escaping silently, mere ghosts of themselves, husks empty of breath and tone. (If I were a Dick Tracy villain, I'd have to be Mumbles.) In this diminished form the words rush out of the cornucopia of my brain to course over the surface of the world, tickling reality like fingers on piano keys. Caressing, nudging. They're an invisible army on a peace-keeping mission, a peaceable horde. They mean no harm. They placate, interpret, massage. Everywhere they're smoothing down imperfections, putting hairs in place, putting ducks in a row, replacing divots. Counting and polishing the silver. Patting old ladies gently on the behind, eliciting a giggle. Only—here's the rub—when they find too much perfection, when the surface is already buffed smooth, the ducks already orderly, the old ladies complacent, then my little army rebels, breaks into the stores. Reality needs a prick here and there, the carpet needs a flaw. My words begin plucking at threads nervously, seeking purchase, a weak point, a vulnerable ear. That's when it comes, the urge to shout in the church, the nursery, the crowded movie house. It's an itch at first. Inconsequential. But that itch is my whole life. Here it comes now. Cover your ears. Build an ark.

"Eat me!" I scream.

—From Motherless Brooklyn *by Jonathan Lethem*

Instead of describing Lionel from a safe distance, we get a vivid first-person account of what it feels like inside his colorful, uncontrollable brain. His disorder is a character in the story. He describes where it comes from, what it does, what it wants, and what happens when it's upset.

Also, because Lionel is obsessive-compulsive, he is driven to describe things from all possible angles in order to understand them. He uses five different metaphors to describe how other people see him. When he's talking about Tourette's, he can't stop listing things it does.

Cool, right? Now you try.

THIS CLASS SUCKS

by KAZZ REGELMAN & ANDREW STRICKMAN

6 hours

Materials: Sea salt, kosher salt, and table salt,
reviews from newspapers and magazines, a music CD and its published review

This class does not, in fact, suck at all. It's one of our very favorite workshops here at 826 Valencia, and not just because it involves food. It introduces students to different forms of criticism, preparing them for a swag-filled life as a reviewer. Here are the activities we do in class, all designed to help students be better critics and critical writers.

1. The Good, the Bad, and the Ugly

This short activity is a helpful introduction to critical and descriptive writing. Most students at this point understand that adjectives are the building block of description. But not all adjectives are created equal. As a group, brainstorm about adjectives that are overused, underwhelming, and slangy: *good, bad, awesome, cool,* and *sucks,* for example. These are just a few of the many "four-letter" words of critical/descriptive writing. It shouldn't take more than five to ten minutes to come up with a list of words that should be banned from most critical/descriptive writing (except perhaps when used ironically, as in the title of this class). Ask your students, what does the word interesting really tell them? Or *different*? Different from what? *Unique*—unique how? *Nice, good*—could these words actually help a reader visualize the subject?

2. When Is Salt Not Salty?

This exercise can be used in any writing class to stimulate the use of descriptive language, but it evolved out of a session on food writing we did with our students. We created a multi-course tasting menu for the students that consisted exclusively of salt. We used three different types of salt: sea salt, kosher salt, and table salt.

Students sample each salt one by one, by placing a few granules on their tongues. Encourage them to play with the salt in their mouths, to appreciate fully the tastes and textures. Kids love to make funny faces during this exercise and moan and groan when the sharp tastes are revealed. Make sure you have some water to drink in between each tasting. Encourage them to use as many of their senses as possible. What does each one look like, feel like, even sound like, as well as taste like?

After each tasting, the kids spend five minutes writing about each salt. Encourage them to use similes, metaphors, and descriptive writing—the only rule is that they cannot say the salt tastes salty. After each salt has been tasted and described, one last writing exercise has the students compare and contrast the salts. As a salt "critic," which would they recommend and why?

3. A Four-Star Exercise

After the students have done some writing of their own, we like to bring everyone back together for a group activity. We gathered some professionally written reviews and made copies to hand out to the students. We keep a teacher's copy that's complete, but on the students' version, we've whited out the stars or letter grade or whatever rating system is used. We used movie reviews from *Entertainment Weekly*, since they are brief but just meaty enough. You could use reviews of restaurants, movies, CDs, books, art, performances of any kind, even consumer products like cars, food, or clothing. Present a mix of reviews—some that pan the subject, others that praise.

Let the students discuss what grade they think the reviewer gave. Did the reviewer think it was well made? How about the service? Was the product a good value for the money? What is the target audience that will like this product? The writing in a well written review should reflect the grade given (and vice versa), but this will not always be the case in the reviews you read. You'll be surprised at how students interpret the writing in the same review: Some will swear the reviewer loved the film and gave it an A, while others are sure it got a D. From your key, tell them how the reviewer really rated it.

It also can be very interesting to read two contrasting reviews from different sources about the same subject. Why did one reviewer love it while the other hated it? Who would you believe and why? Which writing was more convincing?

Choose reviews that are appropriate for the age of the students, of course, both in terms of content and difficulty. Some helpful sources to start with include national magazines like *People* or *Entertainment Weekly*, which have numerous graded reviews meant for popular consumption. Also, local papers (and their online publications) are fantastic sources of reviews of everything from restaurants to film, music, and performances. Don't feel limited to local papers, either: check out *The New York Times, The Boston Globe, The Chicago Tribune, The Los Angeles Times*, or any major city paper.

4. Moving Outside the Comfort Zone

One of the most challenging things about writing criticism for a newspaper or magazine is that you can't only write about things you like, or things you know about. This, of course, requires an open mind and, occasionally, some level of research to craft a strong piece. So we talk a little bit about the responsibilities of the critic, and the qualifications a critic should have. Do you have to be a dancer to review dance? Do you have to be a chef to review food, or do you just need taste buds?

The exercise begins with a discussion about the special challenges of writing both negative and positive reviews. The best criticism *explains* what is wrong, or

right, with a particular piece of art, which frequently comes from a basic understanding of the piece's intent. A critic must understand the intent and context of a piece to judge it effectively and honestly. A critic cannot condemn something just because it falls outside of his or her own personal taste, or because it seems cool to be cynical. Each subject must be judged on its own merit.

The exercise then moves into a bit of show and tell. A piece of music is played that most students would not like—perhaps opera or avant garde jazz. The students then talk about what they heard. Was there *any* part of it that they liked? Could that appreciation be used to build an effective piece of criticism? Whether or not they liked it, did they feel it was skillfully executed? The next step is to allow them to use the Web to research the style of music and the performer or composer.

After they've spent some time researching, they should write a two or three paragraph review of the piece. (Play it for them again now that they know more about the style of music.) Cue them to specific things to listen for or places where they might need help hearing the nuance of a certain instrument or voice.

The final step in this exercise is to then show them a review of the piece they heard. How did a professional writer interpret the music? Do they agree with the writer? Where do they disagree?

THE ESSAY
by MEGHAN DAUM

1 hour

Let's face it, *essay* isn't the most exciting word out there (okay, it's more exciting than *rhombus*, but not by much.) Still, I'm weird enough that I've gotten my thrills out of essays since I was in high school. Why? For one thing, I figured out in tenth grade that it was easier to insert "profound" rock and roll lyrics by the likes of Sting and Elvis Costello (yes, I'm that old) into essays than into short stories. For another, I discovered that if you can summon the courage to write honestly and frankly about what you're really thinking, people will read it and say "Yeah! I feel the same way. I just couldn't figure out how to express it."

As you may already know, the word *essay* literally means "to try." When you write an essay you're not so much stating indisputable facts but trying to make sense of the world around you. There are lots of ways to do this; you can write about something you've experienced personally; you can document a specific event, such as an election or a political dispute or even a sports game, and use the facts to arrive at a broader conclusion; you can write about another person (it can be anyone from your best friend to your favorite musician—you don't have to know them personally) and talk about why that person is important to you. You can write comedy. That's right: stand up comedians are essayists in their own right. Anyone who ever had an HBO comedy special knows a thing or two about the essay form, even if they don't use the word *essay*. We can learn a lot from comedians.

I once wrote an essay called "My Misspent Youth." In it I talked about how, when I was in my twenties and living in New York City, I managed to get into a lot of debt even though I had a pretty good income and never seemed to buy expensive things. On the surface, this essay was a chronicle of how I managed to accrue this debt—student loans, rent, too many dinners out with friends. But that's only part of the story. What I really set out to do was use my own life as a way of talking bigger ideas. Most of those ideas had to do with certain glamorous beliefs many people have about living in New York. After living there for several years I eventually noticed that the stereotypical "starving artist" life we read about in books and see in movies isn't quite possible anymore (unless you actually want to starve, and that's not what "starving artist" really means). Due to economic forces, cultural shifts, and plain old real estate prices, it had become almost impossible to live the life of a genuine bohemian or artist in New York City. So my essay, even though it told my personal story and included many small details about my own life, was really about a larger phenomenon that affects many people. Yes, it's about me, but it's even more about New York City and, by extension, people all over the world who dream about living there. "My Misspent Youth" is an example of a personal essay. Even though it uses the word *I* a lot, it's not a memoir. The following handout explains that in more detail.

ESSAY FORMS FOR YOU TO TRY

1. The Personal Essay

When you go into the bookstore, you usually don't have to take more than eight steps before you get to a book that looks a lot like it could be someone's diary. These are called memoirs, and it used to be that they were written by famous people or, at the very least, people who had been alive for a long time and had done strange or interesting things. In the last ten years or so, even people in their twenties have started publishing memoirs. Like all books, some of them are good and some of them aren't, but as an essayist, I'm always reminding people this:

A personal essay isn't a memoir!

A personal essay is bigger, more complex, often harder to write, and, in my opinion, a lot more fun than a memoir. The reason people sometimes confuse them is due partly to that pesky pronoun *I*. When you use *I*, it can seem like you're talking entirely about yourself, but the truth is that *I* is a useful tool for talking about other stuff. When you use your own experience as a starting point for talking about other things—politics, movies, sports, music, whatever—you're using your mind to engage with the outside world.

For example: say you go to mall to buy a pair of jeans and everything you see is just dumb looking, gross, overdesigned, tragically trendy, whatever. In an essay you can talk not only about the frustration of not being able to find jeans, but use the piece as an opportunity to think and write about why designers and marketers have to change their styles every ten seconds. You could write about what it's like to be a member of the jean-buying public and how people who design and market things to teenagers get it wrong (or maybe they get it right; you can talk about that, too). In other words, a personal essay takes a small moment in your own life and uses it as a springboard for a discussion about bigger things in life. A pair of jeans turns into thoughts about marketing. A breakup with a boyfriend or girlfriend turns into an exploration of the changing rules of romance in society, or the irrational nature of jealousy, or the problems of communication. With personal essays, you're using yourself, the *I*, as a vehicle for talking about something that lots of people can relate to.

2. The Reported Essay

You can also write an essay that involves going out and collecting information, doing interviews, researching historical events, and learning about new things. Then you can weave all that stuff into an essay in which you express your opinion, too. This can sometimes be a little tricky, but it can also be really satisfying when you're done. Why? Because after you write a reported essay, you realize that not only do you know lots of new facts, you also know what you think about them. A lot of writers say they write in order to know what they think about something. That may sound strange—after all, don't you have to know what you think before you start writing?—but it actually makes sense. Writing is sort of an extreme version of thinking. So say you wanted to think really hard about something in your school, like a class election or the cafeteria food or how certain cliques got to be the way they are. You could just write about it from your own perspective (that would be a personal essay) or you could do some reporting (find out where the word *clique* came from, identify the different cliques in your school, interview members of the different cliques) and then write about it in a way that conveyed the information while also incorporating your own opinion. You can use the *I* if you want, but you also don't have to. For instance, you can say, "I think it's sad that people feel compelled to organize their entire social lives around the types of music they listen to," or you can say, "It seems sad that people feel compelled to organize their entire social lives around the types of music they listen to." Pretty simple, huh?

3. The Humor Essay

Like I mentioned earlier, many stand-up comedians function as de facto essayists (*de facto* meaning they're creating essays without necessarily meaning to). But when you think of what it takes to stand in front of an audience and string together a series of thoughts that makes sense, as well as makes people laugh, you see that it's a lot like what an essayist does. Often, the hardest part about writing a humor essay is getting started; once you find your "comedic voice," you're rolling. So start with something that seems hilarious or absurd to you. Then don't be afraid to go a little crazy. Does the term "Pythagorean theorem" strike you as demonic? Then imagine it *was* a demon. What would it look like? What kind of mayhem would it inflict on the world? What kind of ritual would be necessary to purge it of its evil spirits? In a humor essay, you can be as off-the-wall as you want. You can speak from your own point of view or, as though writing fiction, take the perspective of the subject you're writing about. And one very important thing: when you're poking fun at things, it always works better when you poke fun at yourself even harder. So poke away!

SCREENWRITING

by NOAH HAWLEY

3 hours

Screenwriting is very different from every other form of writing, and not just because there's the possibility that a famous actor will say your words while viewers stuff their faces with popcorn. Screenwriting requires an economy of language. There's no time to linger—you have to keep it moving. In novels, the rule is "Show, don't tell." But in movies, that's *exactly* what you have to do. This class teaches you to do it well.

Screenplays can take a long time to write, so we do the fast version. The assignment has each student create a list of characters and a script outline, then pitch the movie to the class. Pitching is a really important skill: much of the movie business is about the pitch. It's rooted in the oral storytelling tradition, and it's a great way to practice storytelling skills. If you want the real Hollywood experience, let the class give feedback.

The handout on page 134–135 shows you how to put a pitch together in three easy steps.

SUPERTEACHER BONUS ACTIVITY:
Have the students write a script for a two-minute movie. They can collaborate it or write their own. Then film it!

HOW TO PITCH A MOVIE
IN THREE EASY STEPS

Step One: Characters

The first thing you need to figure out is who you want your movie to be about. A bank robber? A spy? A cheerleader with a secret?

You also need supporting characters: friends, an antagonist, and maybe a love interest. Create a list of all the characters, with a brief description of each.

For your main characters, you want to figure out who they are, why they do the things they do, and why we're dropping into their lives at this particular moment. Why now? The more a character seems to be in crisis, the more vital the movie becomes. A movie about a bank robber on the day he has to get a bunion removed probably wouldn't be very interesting, but on the day he risks everything for a heist, you're pretty much guaranteed some excitement.

A final note: Never name a character Jack. There are way too many Jacks in the movies already. Bob, Bill, Randy, fine—but no more Jacks.

Step Two: Outline

Once you've figured out who your characters are, figure out their story. This means making an outline. In novels, you can sometimes skip this step, but screenplays really have to be outlined first. Outlining helps you see how each scene moves the plot forward. Unlike fiction, every scene in a movie has to be there for a reason.

The basic screenplay structure is three acts. In Act I, you introduce all your main characters and make us care about them. Introduce the problem and end the act on a high point, with things going either really well or really badly. As the movie proceeds, it's like bringing water to a boil. The energy and stakes have to go up. You're always dealing with setbacks. So in Act II, the tension builds. There are more and more problems. The end of Act II is the biggest setback of all, the crisis. Act III brings the story to a resolution.

Each act breaks down into many scenes. So your outline will be approximately 6-10 pages long and look like this:

ACT I

SCENE 1: Joe, a down-on-his-luck bank robber trying to go straight, is finishing up a hard day at work as a school janitor. On the way to the parking lot he says hi to a student in worn-out clothes—they seem to be friendly—and gives him a couple bucks.

SCENE 2: Joe tries to start his car, an old beater, but it's dead.

SCENE 3: Joe tries to take the bus, but realizes he's out of cash—he gave his last dollar to the kid.

SCENE 4: We see Joe finally arriving at his run-down apartment, obviously exhausted from a long walk home. On the door is a notice for eviction of nonpayment of rent. Joe looks like he can't take one more thing.

... and so on. You'll probably need around sixty scenes, depending on length.

Each scene breaks down into "beats." Beats are the moments, the actions in the movie: this happens, and then this happens, and then this happens. Those are your beats. So in our bank robber movie, he has a hard day at work (*beat*). He picks up after some rude students and mutters to himself, "I used to make $10,000 for an hour's work" (*beat*). We see his prison tattoo (*beat*). We see him be nice to a kid (*beat*). Each beat establishes something.

As you create scenes, it's important to think about why your characters do what they do, or their actions will ring false. What's the backstory on these characters? What's their motivation? If your main character is going to rob a bank, we need to know why. What does he need the money for? Is he just in it for the thrill? What's worth such a big risk?

The other important thing to remember is that you have to keep things moving. In each scene, you want to drop in as late as you can and get out fast. You don't need to show your protagonist driving to the bank, looking for a parking spot, locking the car, etc. Just cut in at the latest possible moment. The viewer can fill in the rest. Less is more, especially when it comes to dialogue. Audiences get stuff really fast. Sometimes a glance can replace a whole speech. And you don't have to have a character explain that she's a scientist if you just show her working in a lab.

As you do your outline you'll figure out the overall arc of the story. You start off with characters who are trying to accomplish something, and you need to decide if they'll succeed—do they rob the bank and get away, or do they get caught. Endings are tough in any medium, but especially in movies. Your movie needs to resolve itself, but it doesn't have to end happily, and it doesn't have to end the way we expect. What you want is resolution for the character. So even if our bank robber doesn't get what he thought he wanted—he doesn't get the money—his internal crisis is resolved when he realizes that he'd take the girl over the money. It's sort of amazing what you can do when people care about your characters. You don't have to satisfy their wishes. He doesn't have to get rich if he's going to be happy.

Step Three: Pitch it!

Once you've got your characters and your outline, it's time to prepare your pitch. A good pitch will make others love this movie as much as you do.

Your pitch should be three to five minutes long and should start off with a bang. You need to hook the listeners in right away with a character we care about. Keep them interested with a mystery, a problem, an exciting possibility. Using your outline, give the movie's story, but in the most interesting way possible. You probably don't need to mention the scene where the bank robber sits in his car, casing the Savings & Loan. But the scene where everything goes wrong (the alarm is going off, the bank employees are not cooperating, and the thief is having an asthma attack) is definitely something you should mention.

Screenwriting is a very collaborative medium, and you generally get a lot of input on your work. Sometimes it's beneficial. Sometimes it's frustrating: "I love your bank robber movie. What if it wasn't about a bank robber?" People will rewrite your work, and your ego has to live in a different place, but sometimes the criticism is helpful. You have to be flexible. That doesn't mean you compromise on what makes the movie what it is, but sometimes criticism will lead you in an unexpected, better direction.

And if you end up with a pitch that the class loves, maybe you should think about turning it into an actual script. Good luck.

MAGIC REALISM
by AIMEE BENDER

2 hours

What's magic realism? It's writing about a world that's mostly realistic, with a few magical elements thrown in, and students love it. In this class, they learn to create magic realist writing of their own. Writing with magic is fun, amazingly fun, because you can explore the consequences of one small but significant shift in the universe.

Begin with a short story: "The Very Old Man with Enormous Wings" by Gabriel García Marquéz, or "Hirschel" by Judy Budnitz, or "Jon" by George Saunders (which is long).

Talk about what happens when this shift happens. When a man shows up with wings, or when a baker makes people, or when there's teen demographic camp.

Talk about the connection between the two words *magic* and *logic*, which happen to share three letters but usually aren't thought of together. But they're so related! Magic relies on logic; we need to feel like the world makes sense, even if it's a different world.

Most of the exercises I have around this subject are building from the ground up, meaning the students can dive into a wild topic, and see what happens. Sometimes this ends up as absolute realism, which is fine, too.

Exercise one: Telling a Legend. Pass around two index cards. On one, write an element of nature. Brainstorm some elements of nature: waterfalls, carbon, palm trees, frogs.

On the second index card, write a verb. Not a fancy verb, a fairly basic verb. Depending on the group, go over verbs for two seconds, too. Then, pass nature cards to the right, verbs to the left. Each student ends up with an element of nature and a verb from two different students.

(Aside: I'm big on these index card passings because they really pop us out of our own mindsets, which tend to get fixed. Getting "dirt" and "jump" suddenly forces the brain to rethink the rules.)

Once all the students have two cards, tell them about Rudyard Kipling and "Just So Stories"—how each chapter told a legend. "How the ___ Got Its ___." Here, they are writing a legend too: "How the Cloud Got Its Balance." Some of them won't make sense—"How Fire Got Its Giggle," but in a way, that can be even better. Go around the circle, hear everyone's title. Then, let them write it out, see what they discover. Share a few after about fifteen or twenty minutes of writing time, depending on the group and age.

Exercise two: Creating a World. This one is more calculated, more about creating a world of magical realism from scratch. It works well for more logically minded students, but can cramp the style of those who don't want to think things through much in advance. Still, worth a try.

Have the students write down five small changes in the physical world, such as "Clouds are made of metal!" or "People grow two heads!"

For older kids or adults, have them also write down five customs, altered slightly: "We shake hands when we are hungry," or, "When someone sneezes, you feel blessed."

Have all the students read one of their altered rules of the physical world and one custom. These are fun to hear, and they usually spark the imaginations of students who feel stuck.

Then: consequences. Back to magic and logic. Have them pick one to write about. The writers have a chance here to build their own new universe, one that exists with this one rule changed. What are the consequences—to people, to religion, to money, to Los Angeles, to roses, to love, to everything and anything they can think of? They can make a list here, or just start describing the world to see if a story begins to develop. Maybe they find a character who doesn't fit in this world, for whatever reason, and see what happens. This is another good point to refer to the stories at the beginning again, as a way to see how other authors have done this.

Write and share!

WRITING FROM EXPERIENCE

by Stephen Elliott

2 hours

In this class students learn to transform the events of their lives—painful, funny, enlightening, embarrassing—into compelling fiction. The best part is that they learn something about themselves in the process. Their life experiences and how they respond to them make up their unique literary code—the greatest thing a writer has to offer. This class helps them get it down on the page.

The first thing I do is spend some time convincing students that borrowing from real life is OK. Students often feel that this is cheating—that in fiction, you have to make everything up. So we spend some time talking about all the great books that are based on real experiences, like *On the Road* and *The Bell Jar*. I bring up Charles Bukowski, who wrote sixty books directly from his own life. Bukowski was acutely aware that the reader is not the writer's mother and has to be won over with a good storyline and compelling characters. He took real elements and transformed them, turning true events into great writing.

Which brings us to our next issue: Who cares? Who cares about your stories? Why is writing about your life important? My answer: because you learn so much about yourself just from doing it. That's a huge benefit, and it's much more valuable than being published.

Sometimes students are worried about writing from experience because they're afraid to offend people they know. I remind them that writing and publishing are not the same thing. The time to worry about other people's feelings is at the publishing stage. In the meantime, don't let it limit the story. Keeping that in mind really frees you up.

Once they're convinced, we roll up our sleeves and get to work. The assignment: write a fictional story based on an event from your life. The handout on page 138 will walk you through the process, from finding something to write about to getting it down, punching it up, and revising it.

HOW TO TURN YOUR LIFE INTO GREAT FICTION

Step One: Find Something to Write About

Lots of students claim nothing interesting has ever happened to them, but that's just not true. Make a list of everything that has happened in your life so far. Now read the list over. What event brings up the strongest reaction for you? That's the one you should write about. It's something you haven't quite resolved, and it will have a lot of energy and life on the page.

Step Two: Get it Down

Now that you have your topic, start writing about it. Get it all down on paper. Don't worry about whether it's good or not. Don't hold anything back. Just get it down. We'll go back and fix it later.

Step Three: Punch It Up

Here's where we transform the true event into a really compelling tale. This is writing, not reporting, so we can make things up. Don't let truth get in the way of a good story. Let go and start creating. Look for ways to make it more readable. Condense characters or create new ones. Change the order of events or even their outcome. Change the ending if you want. This is your opportunity to live out the fantasy, to let the story end the way you want it to. What do you want to have happen to these characters? What are you curious about? Writing is like looking in a crystal ball. This is your chance to envision the future. How would it be changed if you'd done things differently?

As you punch things up, your priority is to keep things interesting. That means you need to come up with ways to make your characters charismatic. An easy way to do it: make your main character intensely interested in something. When they care about something—a person, a pastime, whatever—the reader will care about them.

Step Four: Revise

In the rewrite you're exploring subtext. You're looking for themes, things you might not have put in there intentionally. Maybe your story about learning to ride your bike mentions your big brother a lot. Maybe the story is actually about how much you miss him now that he's moved away. In the revision, you want to turn up those moments. You're also looking for ways to punch up any conflicts. Ask yourself: Did I end this scene too soon? Should I keep these people in a room together longer? That can be a pressure cooker. People want to relieve the pressure, so they let one of the characters out of the room. Sometimes it's better to keep them there and let the conflict happen.

That's it. Turn it in and be proud of yourself.

826 UNPLUGGED: SONGWRITING

by CHRIS PERDUE

2 hours

Many of us remember how passionate we were about music in our teens. Everything is changing so fast, your parents have no idea, you're too shy to talk to that girl or guy, and you feel like you're the first person in the history of this wretched earth to feel so confused and misunderstood. That is, until a certain song or album or artist says it all for you. You and Morrissey are right ... *there*. Music can express in a way that's unparalleled in any other medium. But getting started writing songs can be hard on your own. Students usually have the opportunity to do a fair bit of creative writing in school, and there are music ensembles, but there aren't so many chances to take a shot at writing a song, and to get good feedback about your creation. To be sure, although the desire to learn is definitely there, it can be challenging to get students to open up and participate in a songwriting class. Sharing your writing can be a big step in itself, but the idea of *performing* a song in front of your peers can be pretty frightening.

This lesson is designed to help get over all of that. One of the most important things to learn with songwriting, as with a lot of stuff, is to not take it too seriously. As a group, we'll come up with lyrics and melodies together, so no one is in the hot seat for too long.

First, the lyrics. We'll use a writing exercise called "Exquisite Corpse" (see page 99 for another lesson plan that uses this method). On a blank sheet of paper, someone starts by writing a phrase at the top. The next person writes their phrase below it, but before it's passed, they fold the paper over so the next person sees only one line before. And so on, until everyone writes a line. The exercise gets its name from one of the early rounds, played word-by-word instead of line-by-line: "The exquisite corpse will drink the young wine." It

often makes things more interesting to write sentence fragments that the next person has to complete. Or devise a rhyme scheme: number the lines, and specify that every even-numbered line has to rhyme with the odd-numbered line before it. Obviously, the finished product will most likely be all over the place. That's okay: the point is to have a lot of imagery and lyrical ideas with which to work. Now the students split into groups. Three to five students per group will probably work best. Assign each group a key for their song, or let them decide themselves. This will depend on the level of musical experience of the groups; for students with little musical experience, just stick with C major.

Next, each group writes down everyone's phone number. They then translate these numbers into the musical notes of their scale. For example, if your group is in the key of C, 1=C, 2=D, 3=E, and so on. For zero, use the leading tone -- in this case it's B. 9 is an octave above 2. So, in C, the phone number 867-5309 would be C-A-B-G-E-B-D. The groups should play each melody to see which ones they like, and then they can start working on setting the lyrics from the exquisite corpse to these melodies. At this point, you can help each group build chord progressions for their song based on their chosen melodies and their experience level.

The students should be well on their way. This exercise should supply them with plenty of seeds for their song, and they can take it in any direction they like.

 SUPERTEACHER BONUS ACTIVITY:
Record the songs, and issue a class CD!

Student Work

Exquisite Corpses from 826's Songwriting Workshop

blood red tears fell from her eyes, as thousands of doves fell from the sky.

but then as the sky darkened, the doves fell, causing the streets to flood.
    with blood.

the waves crashed through the streets of the ghost city, drowning a thousand
    invisible souls.

the fear of the west,

the fear of the world. just deadly water

that goes in my nose and smells of mango, and

lime because i need that smell

give it to me or go to hell

said the exhausted donkey, "I'm going to pass out

if I don't get some food soon!"

Curious George is extremely hungry—help him!

He must catch the flying cheeseburger.

Or else the world will combust in a million-kajillion tiny pieces.

But I jumped into a electric blue sports car and lived to see the next day,
    on Mars of course.

Through this surreal world, on Mars, I've seen satellites, astronauts,
    and the stars.

But the most interesting thing I've chanced upon has to be the gray and purple
    bug-eyed tentacled freaky Glarbon from Planet Z05.

The spaceship landed not a week ago

and already the aliens have eaten all the fro-yo.

I will take the fro-yo for you and me

the fair maiden played the kazoo with magnificent skill.

but her sweet kazoo melodies brought sadness, fear, and death.

as i walk among this forest of confusion, i think of you, with your sweet,
    sweet melodies

you are too pure to exist in mere mortal flesh, existing as the rippling golden
    notes released from a grand piano by a master pianist.

the notes bounce on the strings as the keys sink in.

we're gonna play some chess and i'll let you win.

i want to win at chess my friend

i really need the rules to bend

otherwise, i'm looking at a pretty stiff sentence

not a pretty loose elephant

[Hear songs composed in 826 Valencia's songwriting workshop at:
http://www.poundwise.net/826/songwriting2004.htm.]

CREATING CHARACTERS

by JONATHAN AMES

3 hours

This class helps students create characters in their stories that are well rounded, compelling, and vivid.

There are four basic building blocks to creating characters. All of them are essential and should be used almost as a checklist when reading over one's story:

1. The first thing you need to do is describe the character physically. As soon as they appear on the page, quickly let us know what they look like, how old they are, etc. Look at your favorite books and see how the writer gives a quick thumbnail description: "Amy entered the room. She was short with brown hair, and she'd just turned 17." Mention an odd characteristic, like a crooked tooth. Graham Greene would do this, and would return again and again to that detail. You can spin a whole character out of one little thing. That one detail will bring to mind the entirety of the character in the reader's mind. It's like being able to clone someone from a strand of hair.

2. Consider they way they speak. Make your characters' dialogue distinctive. Do they use slang? Are they rude? Vulgar? Are they taciturn or garrulous?

3. Next, enter their mind. Are they secretly nervous, although they act bold? Are they angry or timid? Show their thoughts, their secret ways of looking at the world.

4. Finally, have them take action. Do they run from trouble or lash out? Do they cry, steal, help others? The actions they take will reflect the kind of people they are.

Then we practice.

Exercise One: Creating a Toolbox

Give the students five minutes to write down the first and last names of every person they have ever known. It should be in paragraph form, with name separated by commas, not a linear list.

When they're done, ask them what the experience was like. Most people say they started with friends or family, and then this led to other groups of people, which in turn led to other groupings. That's exactly the point. I tell them that's half the reason we did this—it mimics the act of writing itself. We begin with an idea and then something else occurs to us. We start off describing a tree and then we end up talking about the bird nest in its branches. Writing is an association game.

The other reason we do this is that it provides everything you need to write stories and create characters. Here's your toolbox. The people you listed have all these different aspects, all these individual traits—red hair, missing teeth, shyness, big feet, bad breath. Like Dr. Frankenstein, you can draw from the different people in your life to build a new character. These people all have incredible stories, about luck and problems and divorce and death, and you can take bits and pieces of their stories and make your own stories out of them. Hemingway said, "Write what you know." And what we usually know in life are people. So in this list are the people you know and you can learn from them. They have all the ingredients one needs for stories: courage, heartbreak, loss, love, humor.

Exercise Two: The Elevator

Ask your students to pretend they're alone in an elevator. One other person comes in—someone completely different from them. Give them five minutes to describe this person in as much detail as possible. Then after that, have them skip two lines and do it again, this time switching places—pretending they're the other person, describing *them*. The first part is a great way to practice describing other people physically. The second part helps you learn how to get in another character's mind.

Exercise Three: Profiling

Have your students write an honest description of someone in their life. It can be a friend or a parent. Parents are usually very strong characters in our lives and that translates to the page and can make for a powerful piece of writing.

SPORTSWRITING—THE LIFE

by SAM SILVERSTEIN & JASON TURBOW

6 hours

The careers of professional athletes are measured in years, perhaps decades. Sportswriting, however, is a life. This workshop is meant to open students' eyes to the world of professional opportunities surrounding the games they watch.

Access to ballplayers is the hook. For our workshop the students are granted media credentials and conduct interviews in a Major League clubhouse, just like the pros. But the workshop is not all fun and games. In session one, we sort through possible angles and prepare for our interviews. Session two takes place at the ballpark and consists of collecting interviews and organizing notebooks. In session three, we read and react, as a group, to feature articles generated by the students in the interim. Professionalism is paramount and deadlines are enforced—just like in real life.

We've hung the class on access to the San Francisco Giants, but theoretically any sport/franchise will do the trick. It doesn't have to be a professional team; even Little League or the school badminton team can offer great stories. The key is a working relationship with the media-relations manager, whose job boils down to protecting his or her athletes from distractions. You will need to earn that person's trust to have any chance of prying a credential or three from his or her grasp.

You may also need to recruit some extra chaperones for session two. It minimizes strays at the ballpark and keeps the students in line. The potential for disaster in a Major League clubhouse should be minimized. And the entire point is for the students to have a good first impression of the profession. They can learn the sparky parts later.

Session One

In our first session we describe our jobs and tell the students what a sportswriter's life is really like. Yes, there are a lot of sports—but there's also a lot of writing. We discuss the sports beat vs. features and columns, big markets vs. small, high-school sports vs. major leagues, and how to break into the business. It might be worth making a call to your local newspaper to see if a sportswriter can come tell the class a bit about the job.

Next we talk "chops." We discuss what makes a good piece. How do you know a good story when you

see one? How do you find an angle? How do you balance entertainment against substance? We look through the sports section for good examples. We ask what grabs their interest and why. Then we touch on the basics of solid sportswriting, e.g., how to structure a story and write a good lead. For more tips, www.highschooljournalism.org is a great resource.

Then we get the students ready to start writing. We give them an assignment: prepare to interview a sports figure. If you have access to a local team, the students can pick a local player. If not, they'll have the fun of conducting an imaginary interview, so the sky's the limit—they can interview Ted Williams or Babe Ruth or anyone they like.

Before we turn them loose we go over interview basics. We tell them how to land an interview and how to act once you do. The first step is research. You need to find out as much as you can about your subject. Good places to start looking are on the Internet and in newspaper archives. Then we talk about writing good questions. Questions with yes-or-no anwers are out, as are really obvious ones. You want to ask the relevant question that no one else has thought of. You also want to ask questions that lead to other questions. It's important to keep the conversation going. Maintain good eye contact. Really *listen* for the story. Maybe you go in thinking you're interviewing a player about his batting average and the discussion veers off toward injuries. Maybe he has a past you didn't know about. Maybe *that's* your story instead. We also discuss taking notes vs. taping (both have their conveniences and hassles). Finally, we spend a little time on etiquette and dress. We know Oscar Madison was a sportswriter, but you probably don't want to show up to your interview dressed like him.

Their homework for tonight: research an interview subject and write up interview questions.

Session Two

For our second class we bring the students into the press box at the Giants game. Yep, this is pretty much the best class ever. But even if you don't have an in with a major league team, you can still have a sportswriting experience. Have the class convene at a school game or local sports event. Remind them that they're sportswriters for the night, so they need to dress and act the part. They're there to get a story. They can either report on the game or interview a local player (and use the questions they prepared in the previous assignment). They should be taking notes and thinking of good angles.

Their homework: write the story. It should be 800 to 1,200 words (just like a newspaper feature). They submit via e-mail against a real deadline.

Session Three

In the last session they get to experience the editing process just like a real sportswriter. This is definitely not as much fun as hanging out with ballplayers and eating nachos, but it's good for students to know that even the pros go through this process. Editors are like coaches for your writing, and they want you to win.

In our class we use peer feedback. Each student reads another student's work out loud, then we discuss it as a group. Was the angle successful? Were there good quotes and supporting details? Was the story well constructed, and did it hold the reader's attention? Then the teacher weighs in. If peer feedback sounds like a recipe for disaster with your students, you can just meet with them one-on-one.

Then they revise just like real writers do. Once they've got a polished piece, it's time to think about publication. We discuss outlets for their work: the school paper, the local paper, other publications. We show them an example of a pitch letter, and then we turn them loose, on their way to sportswriting stardom—or, at the very least, their first byline.

Grab Some Pine, Meat!

When Mike Krukow retired as a member of the Giants in 1990, he didn't exactly have his mind set on going upstairs to the broadcast booth and sitting behind a microphone. Instead, he transitioned from tossing shutouts to tossing salads.

He wasn't exactly a chef, but his job managing a restaurant kept him working long and arduous hours, without offering the direction he felt he needed in his life. Luckily for him, he wasn't the only one looking out for his future. Out of the blue, a phone call—which would kick off his broadcasting career—came from San Francisco.

It was the Giants, asking Krukow to fill in for then-Giants color analyst Joe Morgan. It started as a fifteen-game deal, but soon grew into sixty, and before he knew it, Krukow took a full-time seat in the broadcast booth. He has been the distinguished analyst of the Giants ever since.

Even though he was a pitcher during his playing days, Krukow's knowledge of baseball expands beyond the rubber. Not only can he break down the movement in Jason Schmidt's cutting fastball, he can also decipher the hole in his swing.

Initially drafted as a catcher, Krukow's experience with the offensive side of the game enables him to round out his broadcasts with a depth of baseball knowledge. He's also not afraid to call a game as he sees it, even if he risks offending some of his audience.

This summer at Pacific Bell Park, for example, a foul ball tailed down the right field line toward the stands. Giants right fielder Jose Cruz Jr. appeared to have a bead on it, but suddenly a fan stuck out his glove and snatched the ball away. Interfering with a ball in fair territory could have affected the outcome of the game, but the batter was ruled out due to fan interference.

"I was either going to call [the fan] a clown or an ass, and I opted for clown," said Krukow.

"Nothing's like playing," he said, "but broadcasting is the second-best job there is."

In a fourteen-year playing career, Krukow accumulated 124 wins with the Cubs, Phillies, and Giants. He made the All-Star game in 1986, when he posted a 20-9 record, including ten complete games and two shutouts. He spent the days he wasn't pitching studying big-league baseball, talking with teammates and coaches on the bench, and attending pre-game meetings.

"When I sat in the dugout, I wouldn't talk to pitchers," he said. "I would talk to hitters."

These days, should analyzing a hitter prove too much even for Krukow's experience, he only has to turn to his broadcast partner, longtime teammate and friend Duane Kuiper. Kuiper was a Major League second baseman for twelve seasons, three of which were spent with the Giants with Krukow. Between them, the pair has more than twenty-four years of big-league experience.

"If there is something I know that he'd be able to explain better than me, then I'll throw it to him," said Krukow. "Plus it sounds more conversational."

Known as Kruk and Kuip, the two have seen their popularity soar to the point that they even have their own dual-noggin bobblehead, released by the Giants last year.

"That's the secret of our relationship," said Krukow. "Kuip was one of my closest friends as a player. Now imagine being able to go to work with your best friend day after day. We're coming into your living room and there are two extended chairs there, and we're just talking baseball."

Despite years of success in the booth, a big-league coaching job still holds appeal for the ex-pitcher—just not enough to get Krukow to put on the uniform once again and have a seat on the bench. After he retired in 1989, then–Giants manager Roger Craig offered to make him the team's pitching coach. Krukow, however, is content where he is.

"I'd love to be a coach—I think any player would like it," he said. "I think I have things that I can tell and teach, but I basically get to do that every night on TV. So to me, being a broadcaster is as rewarding because of the way I'm received in the Bay Area. So, in a way, I am the coach."

It may seem that Krukow's lone desire in life is baseball, but he puts his family before his career. Like Giants broadcast partner Jon Miller, who has become the signature voice of ESPN's Sunday Night Baseball, Krukow has received offers to work for national media outlets, but he's too ensconced in the Bay Area to take on a bigger audience.

"Everyone would be flattered to be a national broadcaster, but I'm watching Jon do thirty transcontinental flights a year—it's a rough deal," said Krukow. "To me, I prefer to be known as the Giants guy and have extra time for my family and five kids. It couldn't conflict with what I do here. If it did, I really don't want to do it."

As a broadcaster, Krukow continuously strives to get better, even during his off days, and continues to improve his skills by listening to baseball commentators around the league. His favorite analysts include Morgan, Rick Sutcliffe, Mark Grant, Jeff Torborg, and Tim McCarver.

"They see the game differently and bring different things to the table. When I watch a ballgame, I look to get better," Krukow said.

One has to wonder if, after any of Krukow's 1,478 career strikeouts, he yelled one of his current catchphrases to his victim, now spoken to those who have been relegated to the bench after a tough at-bat: "Grab some pine, Meat!"

—Brian Cheung, 18

HUMOR WRITING: AN EXERCISE IN ALCHEMY
(FOR GRADES NINE THROUGH TWELVE, AND ESPECIALLY BRIGHT OR TROUBLED EIGHTH-GRADERS AS WELL. ALSO FOR SEVENTH-GRADE SAVANTS.)

by DAN KENNEDY

2 hours

There are a handful of misconceptions about humor writing; the first is that it must involve waiting around for a funny idea. The fact is, if one waits for a funny idea to come, one will most likely never get around to writing something funny. So picture that: you and your students, alone in a room, waiting for funny ideas to make themselves known and instead only being visited by the humorist's bedfellows Depression, Anxiety, and Restlessness—ha ha, very funny, right? Here's something I wish I would've known when I was a young student: Feelings of apathy, depression, and restlessness are often the best starting point for writing humor, especially satire. Once I understood that you didn't necessarily find yourself in a funny mood before writing something funny, I realized there is hope. And potential! We, the quiet or bored, the seemingly uninterested, the long faces and short attention spans, the energized and dead tired, we could have a laugh and even, sometimes, change a few things in the process. There was only one teacher who recognized that kind of hope and potential where I went to school.

Lesson Plan

On the chalkboard—a very subversive piece of media if there ever was one, in that anything you write on it can be made to disappear—write a list of three subjects and Thought Starterz™. Actually, if schools have replaced the chalkboard with lasers or holograms by now, please disregard my use of the word. I guess now that I've dated myself, I would like to say that Def Leppard's *Pyromania* rocks. Also: No Nukes. Okay, so…

List on board:

- Fake memo from authority figure (Principal? Boss?)

- Humorous version of school newsletter.

- Acceptance speech

Then go over the below with the class, hand out the handouts, and watch the comedy magic happen.

Fake Memo

The fake memo from an authority figure can be about anything. You've seen some of the memos issued in the so-called modern world. A world of semi-effective managers drunk on the combination of the illusory power of title and middling jurisdiction—they're a treasure trove of possible satire! My favorites to write are fake memos from chain-restaurant managers that I used to work for in my twenties, fake vanity emails from competitive self-absorbed peers, and fake dispatches from mayors or councilmen, etc. You might type up a "MEMO FROM THE DESK OF _____" starter sheet with an opening line for students to follow up, or use the handout on page 148. I like to open with painfully honest corporate sentiments such as "While I love Mr. Myers's comedic endeavors, as the manager of McCormley's Seafood Shanty I need to issue the reminder that I do *not* see humor in employees referring to me as Dr. Evil. During yesterday's lunch shift …" (students pick up here in the lined writing space).

Humorous Version of School Newsletter

In a perfect world, this assignment could even lead to a student's first writing job, making the school announcements more fun to read or listen to. Maybe they could staff the whole thing like another yearbook gig. To get started, take the latest edition of the school newsletter or student-body newsletter and copy it into a new Word document. Keep the original set-up portion of each item and leave space for students to finish the remainder in their own words. Here, I'll do an item from one of my old high-school's newsletters:

Attention athletes: All spring sport pictures are in the Student Store now. Please pick them up before we box them up, and remember that **you only need to do this if you're an athlete/jock. There** are no pictures of loners at the Student Store, only athletes, so freshman and sophomore misfit types can continue hanging out on the stairs and nurturing the denial that is keeping us alive and sane here at PHS. Let's not fight instinct when it attempts to preserve us, you guys. But anyway, athletes: you should pick your pictures up.

The Acceptance Speech

This is wide-open territory. The speech can be for any award a student can dream of: Oscar, Grammy, Best Human in the County, State, and Possibly Universe—you name it. All of the fun (and, I might add, bolstering of self-esteem) lies in students being assigned to dream of bigger things and then deciding who they would thank or not thank for helping them accomplish these feats, who they would admit to their kingdom of success and happiness, and who they would remind to please stop calling! You can start the speech off with a few of the stock lines from celebrity thank-you speeches we've all had to endure while figuring how much money we've made off of coworkers or loved ones in the wager pool. If you like, you can get them started with the handout on page 149.

This is great...thank you. Wow, I really ... wow ... God, okay ... I would like to thank my family--except my brother Gary--for believing in me and giving me their love and support. I would also like to remind Mr. Folley from second period Algebra to please stop calling my assistant trying to act like you and I are friends in hopes of being invited to certain events. That is simply not going to happen, Mr. Foley. It is weird that you call like this. And sad that you insist on attempting to contact me daily in hopes of finding yourself admitted to parties or festivities taking place at my summer home. Thank you everyone, except Gary. Thank you.

Good luck and lots of laughs. I'm sure there's always a kid who's going to fill in the blanks with stuff like:

Metallica rulez and this assignment totally sucks it!

But, you know, applaud even that kid. I mean, if you're anything like me something like that would make you laugh and at least that student is saying something he or she honestly feels with some degree of conviction, which is more than you can say for a lot of the so-called adults on the planet. Anyway, I don't need to tell you that these kids are our only hope. Now more than ever, if it's up to the adults, we're up a creek.

A MEMO FROM THE DESK OF _____

ACCEPTANCE SPEECH

I promised myself I wouldn't cry ... _____

_____

_____

_____

_____

_____

_____

_____

_____

_____

_____

_____

_____

_____

_____

_____

_____

_____

_____

_____

_____

_____

_____

_____

_____

_____

_____

_____

_____

HOMESTYLE: WRITING ABOUT THE PLACE WHERE YOU LIVE

by TOM MOLANPHY

2 hours

It's been our experience that all students think home is hopelessly dull. They could live in a Yemenite ziggurat, an Alaskan igloo, or Versailles, and still report that there was nothing special about it. Although routine can be comforting, it can also pound the imagination like a rubber mallet. This lesson teaches students to see home in a fresh way, to walk through doors and open windows they never noticed, and find the stories that home holds.

We begin by brainstorming on the board. The abstract notion of home can easily be taken for granted, so the first task is to rediscover why a home became home in the first place. The following questions can help unlock this answer:

- Why is home a special place?

- What makes a home memorable?

- What makes home different from everywhere else?

- What's weird about it? Exciting?

- What are its secrets?

If discussion lags, I ask what makes our school a "special" place. They usually have something to say about that.

Next, we read page one of Sandra Cisneros's *House on Mango Street* and ask how home defines us. Would you be different if, say, you'd grown up on a dude ranch? In a New York highrise? In Buckingham Palace?

Then I distribute the handout and give them their assignment: to write about home. Home can be anywhere: the house they live in, or their block, their city, or a vacation spot they especially love. Encourage small, specific locales, though; the constraints of a place force the students to consider the smallest aspects and avoid sweeping generalizations.

If there's time, I have them break into groups of two to discuss the place they call home. A one-on-one discussion with a peer can jiggle the imagination to allow a new perspective on an old place to emerge. After the discussion, the students complete the handout (page 151) and share their work in class.

Encourage specific detail throughout the process, but remind students that they're not writing an apartment listing for a newspaper. Hinting at the magic of home is the best any of us can do, and students shouldn't shy away from allowing residual mystery to linger in their descriptions. The role of the creative writer is to spark the reader's imagination, not replace it.

WRITE ABOUT THE PLACE WHERE YOU LIVE

Life's a voyage that's homeward bound.
—*Herman Melville*

Write about the place you consider home. Here are some things to think about:

- Do the people in your house make that place a home?

- What's the first thing you imagine when you hear the word "home?" Think small and specific.

- What's the most surprising thing about this home?

- How does this home make you feel?

- Pretend you're a visitor and you're seeing this home for the first time. How would you describe it to someone else?

Discuss these questions with a partner, and then write about your home below (or on a separate piece of paper). Remember that everyone has a different concept of home, and that it's up to you to deliver your unique and important concept of home.

_____

_____

_____

_____

_____

_____

_____

_____

_____

_____

_____

_____

_____

_____

_____

_____

_____

_____

_____

_____

_____

Student Work

Everything a Nineteenth-Century San Francisco Building Can Be

Eight years ago my family moved into our house. The house is large, vaguely Victorian, its exterior is a nauseatingly hideous shade of pumpkin. It is dusty, it is rotting, it is creaky, it is post-vermin inhabited, it is musty, it is creepy, it is haunted, it is everything a nineteenth-century San Francisco building can be.

The backyard was a wild mess of entangled vines and bushes. To our surprise, through all the thicket was an abandoned chicken coop. The chicken coop was damp and deteriorating and producing moss. Within it lay a pile of rotting lumber and chicken wire. The chicken coop was a breeding ground for many insects and spiders. A lot of black widows.

It struck us as sort of absurd that a chicken coop was posted in the back of our urban domain. Supposedly the insane woman who lived in the house before us would lock up her German schnauzers in it when they would do bad. This information was given to us by our nine-year-old neighbor, Julia.

We decided we wanted to do something useful with the space. We cleaned it up and gave it a paint job. I chose the colors. Being only five, the colors I chose were all very bold, bright, and obnoxious. A lot of teals, turquoises, and roses. Each wall was painted a different color.

When the paint had dried, I decided I wanted to mottle the walls with cats. I painted a bunch of blue cats on the walls. The cats all carry disturbed expressions. At the time I painted the cats, I thought they looked very joyous, and playful.

—*Phoebe Morgan, 14*

Student Work

Looney Tunes

They are the standard kind of blinds found in offices, like in *Office Space*, the movie, but his are clean. Wall-to-wall carpeting welcomes your feet as you enter; it's a bland beige, but is decorated with food stains, worn, faded stains, as if a vacuum had been run over them many times. All of the contents of the room line the walls, except for a folded futon under one window, an "Ab-Sculptor," and an exercise bicycle. There is one mirror—it's a vertical one, usually hung high on a wall, but this one is tilted up—a cheat for being able to see yourself in whole.

There is a bookcase with a collection of records on the bottom shelf. On the shelf above that is an old cigar box decorated with pictures of a young girl with a gap, and glitter. In the box is a collection of chapstick, most of it cherry flavored, the favorite of the inhabitant of this room, my dad. There are a few strawberry, but at least six cherry.

If you sit on the floor in between the mirror and the bookcase and look very closely at the wall, you can see faint stickers; little stickers formed into the initials P.A.B. They used to glow in the dark but now they're worn. There are two dressers: one is next to the mirror; on the top, there is a complete manicure set, and cards, handmade ones, with lots of glitter and color, that say "Happy Birthday" or "Happy Father's Day." On the wall above that is a collage of pictures—smiling people, two boys and a younger girl appear often in these pictures. The two boys have identical smiles, and the same dark skin and small nose; the girl has braces, lighter skin, and a larger nose. But they all look related.

On the second dresser is a lotion dispenser, Vaseline non-scented brand, always the same; next to that is a dish with keys in it. Behind that are at least four Walgreens prescription bottles. In the top drawer are at least twenty bandanas, all different colors. The man whose room this is—my dad—puts one in his pocket every morning.

Next to the "Ab-Sculptor" is a boombox. There are several programmed stations on the radio: jazz, oldies, R&B, and, much to his daughter's protests, classical. The CD player is broken. Next to that is a walk-in closet, baseball caps of teams and youth programs hang on the door, and at least twelve similarly colored khaki pants hang neatly on hangers. Then there are ties on a tie organizer. The man's daughter's favorite tie of his hangs on the top: Looney Tunes.

—Ana Lucia Billingsley, 14

PRESIDENT TAKES MARTIAN BRIDE: WRITING TABLOID FICTION

by ALVIN ORLOFF

1 hour

Sure, they'll never win a Pulitzer, but tabloids have their uses. They teach us to believe (*Elvis Lives!*), to better ourselves (*The Amazing Ice Diet!*), and to have compassion (*Bat Baby Needs Your Help!*). They can also teach us to be better writers. This lesson plan uses tabloids to explore what makes good writing good and bad writing bad—and why the latter can be much more fun.

You can start this lesson by passing around a few easily obtained supermarket tabloids, preferably with humorously salacious headlines. Then, discuss what makes a paper a "tabloid," making sure students are aware of the key elements of the tabloid:

Malicious celebrity gossip. Tabloid readers love to feel like they're invading the privacy of larger-than-life celebrities, but it's not enough to say that movie star X has been spotted canoodling with pop singer Y. There has to be an outlandish twist, preferably one that allows for a bit of *schadenfreude*—taking joy at another's misfortune. Readers love hearing about the faults, foibles, and failures of celebrities, particularly those of the obnoxiously rich and beautiful, though the just plain annoying will do. Ask students why they think people want to hear about celebrities' private lives.

Shocking, tell-all confessionals. Everybody's family is a little bit weird, we all know of a strange neighbor or two, and most of us, at some time, worry about our own normality. Tabloids make readers feel better by relating stories so lurid that everybody gets to feel well adjusted by comparison. This aspect of tabloid news has been somewhat superceded by trash television, but still persists. Ask students what makes a personal story so freakish that it becomes of interest to others.

Absurd, improbable, or supernatural events. Bigfoot, space aliens, Elvis Presley, ghosts, and suchlike all make their appearance in the tabloid world with amazing frequency. In this way the tabloids are carrying on ancient folkloric traditions, relating the sort of tales grandma used to tell in hushed tones late at night as the family huddled by the fireplace. Urban myths of the alligators-in-the-sewers variety are also a key component of the tabloid cosmology. Ask students what urban myths they've heard of and how they know they're not true.

Clichés. Authors of non-tabloid fiction go to great lengths to avoid clichés (words or phrases that have lost their effectiveness through overuse), but tabloid stories revel in them. In tabloidland, every "ordeal" must be "grueling" and no story of romance can be complete without "vixens," a "love nest," or a "two-timing hussy." Ask the class to think up as many tabloid-style clichés as possible.

Hyperbole and alliteration. Tabloids are positively addicted to the tacky tricks of alliteration (the repetition of initial letters of adjoining words) and hyperbole (deliberate and obvious exaggeration used for effect). Good writers do their best to avoid these, but tabloids thrive on them. Not much to discuss here, but students need to be aware.

Society in general, and literary people in particular, look down on tabloids, so to finish up the discussion, it might be nice to give another perspective. Realism (lifelike representation of people and the world without any idealization or fantastical invention) is only one way to tell a story. Many writers feel that just stating facts only gives readers one side of reality, one that doesn't convey the actual lived experience of the human mind. By inventing things, authors of fiction let readers see life as someone else sees it. Some genres of fiction, like magic realism and surrealism, use fantastical invention that isn't, on the face of it, that different from tabloid fiction. Plenty of general fiction, too, employs elements of the tabloid style: histrionic narrative voices, improbably or impossibly zany plot lines, and depraved celebrities. This can be done for humorous effect, with a wink and a nod to let the reader know one is appropriating tabloid style, or with complete deadpan seriousness, as in million-selling trash novels sold at supermarkets.

Discussion finished, it's time to let the students have at it! The handout on page 155 will help them create their own tabloid masterpieces.

 SUPERTEACHER BONUS ACTIVITY: *Compile all the students' articles into a tabloid authored by the whole class, and distribute it to the school at large.*

WRITE YOUR OWN PIECE OF TABLOID FICTION

Good news—tabloid fiction is supposed to be fun for the reader, and the best way to make it that way is to have fun writing it. Remember to use lots of alliteration, hyperbole, and clichés for tabloid style. Still, as with traditional or real news stories, you're going to want to quote sources and answer the basic questions of journalism: who? what? where? when? and why? Remember, enquiring minds want to know!

Here are six choices for your tabloid fiction project. Your finished story should be about a page long.

1. My Christmas with a Biker Gang

Write a first-person story about a shocking experience. You can exaggerate something that really happened to you, or make something up. Your tone can be either confessional (you're sorry for whatever you did and want to warn others not to make the same mistake) or defiant (I don't care what anyone thinks, I love my husband even if he is a space alien!).

2. Bigfoot Tries Out for the Dodgers

Write a news article about a nonexistent creature. Remember, it's the interaction of the everyday and the fantastic that captures people's attention, so make the parts of your story that don't deal with the imaginary creature as realistic as possible. Put yourself in the creature's position and try to imagine what it would say or think about things.

3. Brad Pitt and High School Senior Call It Quits after 72-Hour Marriage

Imagine a quickie Vegas wedding between you and your favorite star, and write it up as either a news story or a tell-all memoir. Remember, celebrities don't live the way regular people do. They're apt to go around bathing in champagne, flying in specialists to groom their eyebrows, and having fresh orchids delivered daily to their pet Chihuahua.

4. Egotistical Star Makes Fans Retch with Disgust

Real newspapers try to deliver stories from an objective point of view. Not so with tabloids! Write a story about a celebrity, real or imagined, in which you display an obvious bias. You could be worshipful, or mean, or (and this is particularly nasty) pretend to feel sorry for the star.

5. Great-Grandmother Wins Snowboarding Competition

Tabloids occasionally serve up heartwarming tales of triumph. These usually involve the last person you'd expect winning a contest or saving the day in some manner (rescuing a puppy from under a steamroller, raising enough money to pay a mortgage on the orphanage by knitting socks). If you make the story ridiculously sweet enough, it can even become funny.

6. Short Story

Write a short story using elements of the tabloid style. Let your imagination run wild, but remember to contrast the preposterous parts of your story (celebrities, fantastic events or beings) with the mundane. If everything in the story is unbelievable it becomes fantasy, which is another genre of writing altogether.

THE FIRST DRAFT IS MY ENEMY

by SARAH VOWELL

2 hours

When I was in high school I was enthralled with the Beats and spontaneity and things happening in the moment. I wouldn't revise or pore over a paper because that would make it fake, dry, professional. Also, I didn't have to. The teacher would mark it up and then we'd never fix it.

Now I treasure making things better, going over the nineteenth draft, making it funnier and shorter.

That only happens with patience and time and doing it again and again. In this lesson plan we learn to do exactly that.

The assignment: Take a paper you've already turned in and fix it. Picking a paper you got an A on is cheating. Choose something that needs work. Polish it up and spit-shine it into something better. The following handout has eight tips to make the project easier.

HOW TO REVISE:
SARAH VOWELL'S EIGHT BEST TIPS

Tip One: Read Your Paper Aloud

The best way to figure out what works and what doesn't is to read your paper aloud. The parts you cannot wait to get through are probably really boring. That's a red flag saying you need to make it shorter or funnier or gone. The parts that you find yourself looking forward to reading are generally okay.

Tip Two: Lose the Topic Sentence

The first sentence is really important, but it shouldn't tell what the thing is about. That's just bad poker playing. You don't want to open with a topic sentence. Topic sentences spoil the mystery. A first sentence should be a lapel grabber. Maybe it's your jerkiest sentence, or an exclamation point of an idea, or some jarring piece of dialogue.

Tip Three: Think *Behind the Music*

Your paper probably has to convey some facts. The trick is deciding which facts are relevant and interesting and which are just deadweight. Imagine you just read something and now you're telling someone about it. What would you tell this person about this topic? What were the weird things, the cool things, the things that made you mad or made you want to learn more? Include whatever facts or figures or anecdotes that make you want to phone your best friend and say, "Get *this*."

I call this the Behind the Music approach. *Behind the Music* leaves out the drudgery to focus on the juicy details, the drama, the embarrassments, the setbacks. There's something human about failure and quirks, the stuff that would never be mentioned in a eulogy or a travel brochure.

Tip Four: Outline on the Rug

In school, they always told us to do an outline, and I never, ever, did, because of course I wrote everything at the last minute. But now, what I do is use my living room rug. I get index cards and I make a note of every joke I want to tell, every anecdote I want to recount, every idea I want to get across, every fact I need to convey, and then I lay them out on the rug and move them around, sometimes for days, once or twice for weeks, trying to arrange them in some kind of logical narrative form. When you know where you're going, it's easier to get there.

Tip Five: Shenanigans

Sometimes you've got something really great, some funny joke or bizarre anecdote, and you don't know where to put it or what to do with it. I call those "shenanigans." You can't have too many of them but you have to allow yourself a few. That's part of what's fun about being a writer—throwing in some random cool thing. If you're disciplined about it, your reader will allow and enjoy the digression.

Tip Six: Cut the Clutter

Watch out for clichés and tired phrases. If "Don't even go there" appears in your essay, cut it immediately. Replace any words that are so overused they've lost all meaning, like "crazy" or "amazing."

Tip Seven: Spell Check

Even some of the best writers are some of the worst spellers. Don't be a hero. Use spell check and a dictionary.

Tip Eight: Endings are Hard

Beginnings are hard, but endings are harder. There's something sad about every ending, even happy ones, because something's over. An ending should be poetic. If you've said all you have to say, your last thought should be philosophic or poetic or pretty. There should be a graceful little moment at the end, something melancholy or reflective. It shouldn't be another person's quote if you can help it. Ending with a quote is the easy way out. Your last sentence should be your own.

If you're stuck for an ending, you may have already written it. Somewhere in the middle of your paper, maybe, you've got your best sentence or paragraph. It has a kind of wisdom and finality. Move that to the end.

BAD WRITING

by NEAL POLLACK

5 hours

There's nothing easy about teaching literature to high school students, but *writing* is even harder to teach. You can't give a student a copy of *The Great Gatsby* and say, "Go home and write something like that." Your best student could read *Crime and Punishment* six times in one weekend and still not come up with anything that remotely resembled Dostoyevsky. And she would also come back to school frustrated, saying that there's no way she could ever write that well.

On the other hand, if you sent your students home with a bodice-ripper about ancient Egypt, or some clumsy science ficion, and said, "write like this," the student might actually produce something that vaguely approximates literature. It will be bad literature, but literature nonetheless. Clichéd, melodramatic stories with clunky prose, far from being literary anathema, are actually the building blocks of all literature, and they provide an excellent writer's education.

I first was inspired to write by a turgid eight-part series of historical novels that featured lines like "'Amanda, meet Abraham Lincoln.'" From there, I graduated to the vast plains of James Michener and the like. My early inspirations weren't comic books or sitcoms or *Star Wars*. They were bad books, the kinds of books that I could see myself, with a little experience, producing. I wish someone had challenged me to create something like that.

So here's how the class should go. The entire plan can take a long time, spaced out over weeks, or could be condensed.

- Assign a photocopied reading of four or five of the purplest pages imaginable from a literary howler (preferably epic in scope) of your choice. Along with that, you assign four or five standard "analysis" questions, of the same type you'd give on a *Hamlet* quiz. Play it totally straight: "When Tanya says Jonathan's rippling muscles give her a 'special feeling that she'd never felt before,' to what is she referring? What is the author's purpose in creating this scene?"

- Discuss this passage at the next class for ten or fifteen minutes before showing your hand and telling the class that this is a lesson in "Bad Writing." Explain to them that bad writing contains nothing like the universal truths and subtle beauties you've been discussing all year. It's all clichés and warmed-over historical research written in melodramatic prose with no subtlety.

- Then ask them to turn on a dime and discuss the clichés and warmed-over historical research. Have them figure out, for themselves, the essential elements of bad writing. In some ways, Tolstoy's maxim applies here: "All good writing is alike. Every piece of bad writing is bad in its own way." So there are no universal qualities to a bad piece of writing. Just try to decide what those are in the passage you've chosen.

- Next, drop another bomb. Tell them that by the end of the lesson, you want to see a piece of bad writing from all of them. Length is up to you.

- Have a list of twenty or so "bad" novels available in the classroom. Tell them to read bits from as many of them as possible. Have discussion groups to share clichés and historical howlers. Immerse the students as fully as possible in the language and rhythm of bad fiction of any genre.

- After that, tell them to choose a "quality" piece of literature and ask them to redo it as "bad writing." Make sure to recap the list of clichés and general characteristics of bad literature, both in terms of style and content.

- Tell them to have fun with it. There's no pressure. After all, the worse the writing, the better they'll do on the assignment. By the time it's over, they should have a pretty solid idea of what separates bad writing from good.

See the handout (page 160) for a few short examples of good writing transmuted into bad writing. You can have them use it as a starting point. Good luck!

GOOD LITERATURE GONE BAD

Crime and Punishment by Fyodor Dostoyevsky

"Raskolnikov loved Russia. He loved the way it smelled in the morning after a heavy rain, and the way everything went quiet after a heavy snow, and he loved its women more than anything. 'There's no doubt in my mind,' he said to himself that fateful morning, as he ate a bowl of thin gruel that his landlady had reluctantly prepared for him, 'that Russian women are the finest in the world. This fire in my loins will never be extinguished.'"

The Sun Also Rises by Ernest Hemingway

"Jake Barnes knew he could never be the man the bullfighter was. He had no chance with Lady Brett. His war impotence hung heavy on his soul that fateful morning as he downed his third *café con leche*. How he longed for freedom, freedom of his soul from its terrible bondage of memory!"

Death Comes for the Archbishop by Willa Cather

"The Archbishop was going to die. He could feel it in his bones. But when, he thought to himself that fateful morning as he finished off his bowl of posole, which is a kind of Mexican stew. When will death come for me?"

Don Quixote by Miguel de Cervantes

"Don Quixote was not his real name, but regardless, he loved tilting at windmills. Sancho Panza felt powerless to stop him. 'What can I do?' Sancho thought to himself that fateful morning, as he fed breakfast to the donkey that doubled as the Quixote's magnificent steed. 'The man has quite an active imagination, after all, and I am just a simple peasant.'

Just then, the Quixote came running out of the house.

'Sancho!' he said. 'To arms! Hurry!'

'What is it, sire?' Sancho said.

'Dulcinea's in trouble! We must save her!'"

Macbeth by William Shakespeare

"'What's troubling you, honey?' asked Lady Macbeth of her brooding husband on that fateful morning. But Macbeth didn't answer. For he'd just killed his best friend. Nothing could help him now. Those witches had lied to him!

LOOK SMART FAST: COLLEGE APPLICATION ESSAY BOOT CAMP

by RISA NYE

3 hours

[*Risa Nye reads application essays for one of the nation's largest and most prestigious universities. Her insider tips have been invaluable to our students. In this lesson plan, she shares them with yours.*]

Since the hardest part of writing a college essay is just getting started, I like to help students get some ideas on paper right away. Here are three techniques to jump-start the writing process and generate first drafts.

Thinking Inside the Box

- Ask students to take a piece of paper and draw two lines down and one across, creating six boxes on the page. Like this, but bigger:

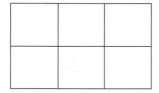

- Now ask them to label each space with some aspect of their lives: everyone can be a son or daughter, some will be a brother or a sister. From here, everyone can fill in other things: computer geek, diva, tap dancer, class clown, or cat lover.

- When all six boxes have a name, the students are then asked to come up with five story ideas about being a banjo player, a big sister, a "Trekkie," and so on, until they have a grand total of thirty possible essay topics.

- At this point, students may see how several of these ideas might be woven together into one essay. Ask for volunteers to copy one of their boxes onto the board. Students can then "pair share" their ideas and brainstorm the best combination of topics, asking some probing questions to bring out details. ("When did you take up the accordion? Why?")

- Everyone can now take ten or fifteen minutes and freewrite an essay that answers the question "Tell us about yourself" using some of their favorite story ideas.

The Keyhole Essay

Building on one of the story ideas from the box exercise, this kind of essay starts with something small, and then uses that small beginning to show the reader the larger picture—kind of like peeking through a keyhole and looking around a room.

- Students are asked to think of an object that is important to them, come up with a way to introduce it to the reader, and then use this object as a way of showing some of their qualities and characteristics. For example: "The velvet painting of Elvis is the closest thing to an heirloom my family has," or "I don't care what anyone thinks, I always wear the lucky dinosaur socks I got for my birthday when I take a test," or "I found the old bowling trophy in a thrift store, and I often wonder about the guy who won it." In each example (painting, socks, trophy), the object opens up many possibilities.

- By describing a treasure or personal ritual or things to wonder about, the writer lets the reader peek inside the keyhole too. Ask students to try this out with the first thing that comes to mind, and take ten minutes to freewrite about it. (Find good examples of this technique in a short story anthology. Students may like to hear a few before they start.)

The List That Is More Than a List

An essay may ask for a list of things you would take to a desert island, or put into your own personal time capsule—or bring to college! Students have an opportunity to highlight what is important to them, while also letting the reader see how they define their character and personality. So if you start off with "I could never choose just one book to take," the reader gets a clue that you love to read. Likewise, if your essential items include a Giants hat or a package of marshmallow Peeps or some *Star Wars* action figures, that tells a story too. The more detail you provide, the more the reader learns about you. This can work very well for essays that ask you to come up with your own question and answer it. (Example: "If you were leaving Earth to live on another planet, what would you bring? And it has to fit in the overhead compartment of your space craft!")

- Ask students to come up with a question that could be answered with a list that is more than a list—which tells something important about them as a person—and then let them go for it. (It might be fun to read a few out loud and see if the kids can guess who wrote them.)

Students will now have buckets of great essay ideas. The handout (page 163–164) will help them avoid common college essay pitfalls.

WRITING THE COLLEGE ESSAY:
SOME POSITIVE POINTERS AND A FEW MAJOR NO-NO'S

The strength of your essay may set the tone for how the rest of your application is read, so make it sparkle!

- Choose a topic you are really passionate about, whether it's making paper airplanes or collecting buttons. You can make anything sound exciting if you believe it is.

- Read the question and instructions carefully first.

- Write in your own voice, using words you don't need to look up in the dictionary.

- Tell the story *only you* can tell, by showing the reader details and observations from your unique perspective.

- Be thoughtful and reflective as you conclude your essay. If you have learned a lesson or gained an insight from the experience you have written about, the reader needs to understand how you got there.

Experienced admissions officers are familiar with the common pitfalls students inadvertently fall into when writing college essays. Most are avoidable, but if you don't know about them, you might tumble into the Cliché Crevasse or the Bottomless Pit of Banality.

Some topics just don't work on a college application. Some are simply inappropriate, while others are extremely popular topics that make admissions officers' eyes glaze over. For example:

- Your relationship with your girlfriend or your boyfriend (or how it ended)

- Your religious beliefs (unless the question asks you to write about them)

- Your political views

- Sex

- How great you are

- The importance of a college education

- Placing the blame for your academic shortcomings (if any) on others

- Big ideas that you have not given much thought to before

- "The Best Game of My Life" or another athletic incident written in glib style

- Your trip abroad, unless truly noteworthy

There are always exceptions, however, and some students can create enough context and detail that the reader comes away with a sense of knowing something important about the writer—which is the point of writing this kind of essay!

Avoid clichés like the plague

Especially:

> *"My hard work really paid off."*
>
> *"It [or he or she] made me who I am today."*
>
> Starting your first sentence with alarm clock sounds (e.g. *"Brrrrrrrrrrrring!!!"*)

Overused words: *plethora* and *epiphany*

Any word that sounds plucked out of the thesaurus should be thrown back. Use vocabulary that is in your comfort zone.

Major pitfalls

- Writing about the death of a distant relative you didn't know very well for the dramatic impact.

- Writing about a relative you did know well, without saying anything about yourself.

- Writing at a superficial level and not from the heart.

- Letting anyone else add another "voice" to your writing. (This means parents, aunts, uncles, your college-age neighbor, or your seventh-grade English teacher.) Ask for and accept feedback, but always use your own words.

- Choosing a deeply personal topic to write about (parents' divorce, coming out in high school, any kind of abuse) without getting feedback from a trusted adult. This is the hardest thing of all—knowing when a topic is just too personal and revealing, although it is of great importance to you.

- Not answering the question or following directions (very important!).

- Use of humor: Are you funny? That is, "funny ha ha"? Always run this by someone who understands the difference between funny and not funny when it comes to college essays. College folks do appreciate creativity and wit, but they also have to read an awful lot of essays so don't write backwards or in Pig Latin or use crazy fonts. If you have a natural sense of humor, though, let your writing reflect this—it's part of who you are!

- Perhaps the biggest pitfall ever is blowing off the essay because you think "No one really reads them." Not true! A good essay can make a big difference on an application that may not otherwise stand out in a field of highly qualified and competitive applicants.

WHERE STORIES COME FROM

by JULIE ORRINGER

1 hour

Materials: Photographs, newspaper clippings, poems

Most students are accustomed to having assignments; the freedom of short story writing may be overwhelming at first. This lesson can help students get words onto the page.

First, show students where other writers get their ideas. One of the best sources I've found for this is the back section of the *Best American Short Stories* (BASS) series, where writers are asked to contribute a paragraph or so describing the origins of their selected stories. I like to copy some of these brief explanations and have students read three or four of them. Here are some stories that took their inspiration from photos, magazine clippings, newspaper headlines, poems, and other forms of writing:

—*Elizabeth Graver, "The Body Shop," BASS 1991*

—*Alice Fulton, "Queen Wintergreen," BASS 1993*

—*Robert Olen Butler, "Jealous Husband Returns in Form of Parrott", BASS 1996*

—*Chris Adrian, "Every Night for a Thousand Years," BASS 1998 (picture, letter)*

—*Heidi Julavits, "Marry the One Who Gets There First," BASS 1999 (photo essay)*

—*Kathleen Hill, "The Anointed," BASS 2000 (childhood memorabilia)*

—*Stuart Dybek, "We Didn't," BASS 1994 (a poem)*

—*Rick Moody, "Boys," BASS 2001 (a sentence)*

—*Jim Shepard, "Love and Hydrogen," BASS 2002 (a children's book)*

To help students start their own stories, assemble three collections of materials:

1. Photographs: snapshots or magazine cut-outs work well. The photos can include human beings, but they don't have to. Photos of interesting settings work well too. Very old photographs are great, if you have them.

2. Newspaper clippings: general news can work; wedding announcements, obituaries, and science news are all good sources.

3. Poems: I like to use short excerpts from Berryman's *Dream Songs*, Neruda's *Residence on Earth*, Rilke's persona poems, and Gabrielle Calvocoressi's *The Last Time I Saw Amelia Earhart*, for example.

Bring the materials to class. Pass them around after the *Best American Short Stories* discussion and let students take a few minutes to choose a few pieces they find particularly compelling. After they take some time to examine the items they've chosen, have them freewrite about one item for ten to twelve minutes. Then they'll move on to another item and freewrite about that.

Before they begin writing, give them a few basic pointers:

- If you're writing from a photo of a person, write from the point of view of one of the people depicted. Try to imagine a situation around that person and his place within it. What is he worried about? What does he care about? What's immediately at issue at that particular moment? Try to imagine the person's life outside this photo. What concerns are driving him? If you're writing from a photo that doesn't depict a person, or in which the person is less interesting to you than the setting, what is it about this place that's particularly compelling? What might you imagine happening there? What objects can you see, and what activities do they suggest?

- If you're writing from a newspaper article, don't bother taking the time to read the entire article; instead, look for a line or an image or a detail that captures your attention. Then try to imagine the human situation behind this article. Who is involved? What are the main players like? Choose one of these people, and freewrite from their point of view. How did they get into this particular situation? What's at stake here?

- If you're writing from a poem, take a few minutes to read the poem completely and hold it in your mind. What images does it evoke? What kinds of characters does it suggest? What mood does the poem create? As soon as possible, put pen to paper and begin freewriting.

From their freewriting, students should begin to see stories emerging. Ask them to take the idea they find most compelling and develop it into a full-length piece.

Student Work

The Beehive

"**I**s something living in your hair?" one guy jokes.

"What? Why would anything be living in my hair?" snaps back the woman, patting her head tentatively. She knows it's just a joke and that's the price to pay when you have a foot-tall beehive on your head, but she can't help feeling miffed. She tries to enjoy herself for the rest of the party, but she can't help but feel everyone's eyes boring into her hair.

That night she sits on the edge of her bathtub, scraping the makeup that was meant to conceal her blemishes, peeling off the tights that supposedly held in her stomach, and discarding the vest that the saleswoman promised would make her three sizes smaller. She pauses at the beehive, so perfectly stacked and coiffed, a work of art in itself. She hesitates, then climbs into bed, beehive and all, closing her eyes and waiting for the security and peace that sleep brings her. But all she can hear is the overpowering and overwhelming buzzing resonating all throughout her head.

—Hannah Kingsley-Ma, 14

HOW SHORT IS SHORT?

by VENDELA VIDA

3 hours

It's not uncommon for a writer to approach a short story with a sense of trepidation: what if I spend weeks (or months) working on it, and it amounts to nothing? Sometimes the fear of time wasted gives way to stalling—or at least provides a good excuse. The goal of this class is to help students realize how much they can accomplish in short, intense bursts.

We start by reading some short short stories (loosely defined as being under five pages), such as "Snow" by Julia Alvarez and "Girl" by Jamaica Kincaid. The students are then asked to write their own stories using each of these works as a prompt. For example, after reading "Girl," which is told in the second person, the class is given twenty minutes to compose a short short story in the second person. After reading "Snow," about a girl who comes to America from the Dominican Republic and sees snow for the first time, the class is given about fifteen minutes to describe what snow or thunder or an earthquake could look like, or be mistaken for, by someone who had never seen any of these things before.

In the next class, we delve into selections from issue twelve of *McSweeney's*. For this issue of the literary journal, a number of authors were asked to write a story in twenty minutes. It's both interesting and inspiring to see how different writers approach this challenge, and the students feel encouraged that maybe they, too, can produce something publishable in a restricted period of time. For her entry, the novelist Jennifer Egan wrote an outline for a story, which, in effect, is the story. The students then try their hand at writing an outline that reveals something about the narrator—for example, a shopping list or a to-do list. As with all in-class exercises, the students share their works aloud when the allotted time period is over.

Another submission to *McSweeney's 12*, one by J. Robert Lennon (below), also serves as a great writing prompt. His story is composed entirely of subjects and verbs. After reading and briefly discussing it, the students are given twenty minutes to write a story in a similar vein. Without adjectives and adverbs, they're forced to really think about the power of verbs. It's easy to get lazy and grab the plainest, blandest verb: go, want, ask. But in the resulting students' stories, the characters stumble, pray, plead. And more.

"He noticed. He stared. She noticed. She smiled. He approached. She rebuffed. He offered. She accepted. He said, she said, he said, she said. They drank. They said. They drank. He touched. She laughed. They danced. He pressed. She kissed. They left. They did. He left. She slept.

He called. He called. He called. He begged. She refused. He called. He wrote. He visited. He called, called, called, called. She reported. He arrived, shouted, vowed, departed. He plotted. He waited. He visited. She gasped. He demanded. She refused. He grabbed. She screamed. He slapped. She ran, locked, called, waited. He panicked. He fled, hid, failed.

She accused. He denied. She described. He denied. She won, he lost. They aged. She wed, reproduced, parented, saddened, divorced. He bided, waited, hardened. Fought. Smoked. Plotted, planned. Escaped. Vanished.

They lived. She thrived, he faded. He wandered; she traveled. They encountered.

He sat, she sat, they ignored. He noticed. She noticed. He gaped. She jumped. She warned, he assured. She reminded, he admitted. She threatened, he promised. She considered. She sat. She asked. He told. He asked. She told. He smoked. She smoked. He apologized. She cried. He explained. He begged. He pleaded. She considered, resolved, refused. He stood. He clenched. He perspired. He spat. She flinched, paled.

He stopped. He slumped. He collapsed. She stood. She pitied. She left.

They lived. They forgot. They died."

—*J. Robert Lennon, March 28, 2002, 9:05—9:25 A.M., Ithaca, NY*

The "How Short Is Short?" class runs for several sessions, and the students end up with some great short pieces. Often, they're so good they want them to expand on them, so I encourage students to pick their strongest story (or two) to flesh out into a longer work. As for the exercises they're not as fond of, well, they only spent twenty minutes on them. And who knows? Maybe the prompts planted the seed for something else.

Student Work

He Opened

He opened. He dressed. He stood. He stared. He smiled. He giggled. She opened. She saw. She screamed. She ran. She told. She cried. They disowned.

He moved. He lived. He cried, lived, failed. He smoked, he smoked, he smoked. He paced, pined; he worked. He continued, he failed. He frowned, he cried.

He desired. He pined. He stared. He crossed. He opened, he dressed. He smiled. He giggled. He laughed. He danced.

He visited. He waited. He told, he listened. He comprehended. He decided. He left. He walked, walked, walked.

He visited. He operated. He recovered. He became she. She lived.

—Anna Gonick, 16

WORD KARAOKE

by MATTHUE ROTH

2 hours

Sometimes, you want to say something and you're not sure exactly how. Sometimes, there's a song or a poem that you think is better than anything you could ever write—or, maybe, there's a song or a poem that you could do better.

That's the jumping-off point for Word Karaoke, a way of getting students inspired when they say they're not. Karaoke is the ancient Japanese art of singing along with prerecorded background music. Singing along with the radio is karaoke. Singing in the shower can be karaoke. When hip-hop MCs rap over a beat— well, don't tell them, but that's karaoke too.

We start by asking the students, "What's your favorite line from a song?" Get some suggestions. Write them on the board. Offer some of your own. Encourage more general-sounding, ambiguous responses, "Oops! I Did It Again" works much better than "My name is Shaa-dy," although, for the purpose of this exercise, any suggestion is useful.

Writing, and especially music writing, is about using the listener's expectation and then turning it on its head. Using samples is a way to do this. When Eminem sings, "Stop—pajama time," he's borrowing from the briefly popular '80s rapper M.C. Hammer when *he* sang "Stop—Hammer time." Sometimes, too, songs can use samples to express an idea. When dealing with the death of a friend, P. Diddy chose to use the feeling of the old song "Every Breath You Take." He changed one word in the line "I'll be watching you," and ended up with a moving tribute called "I'll Be Missing You."

Once we've got their brains grinding (it will probably start out slow, then, as they realize what's going on, produce a maelstrom of suggestions), call for a halt—a *temporary* halt—and separate the class into pairs. Make sure each student has a pencil and paper. Then, ask every pair to write a short poem or song (one side of one page is plenty) using one of the lines on the board, or their own idea. (The handout on page 172 provides a format). Suggest that they use their original line in another context—"Oops, I spilled the paint again," or "My name is mud." Get them to understand the idea behind karaoke: that, given a line of a song, they can create or change the meaning to whatever they want. They can start their verse with the "sample," or alternate that line with their own lines, going back and forth like a call-and-response.

Afterward, as time allows, students can perform their verses together. Encourage creative methods of presentation—one person can recite the sample line and the other can recite the rest of the verse, or one can recite while the other performs an interpretive dance (be careful when offering this option to certain classes).

As an additional exercise, or for homework, students can write a new piece, either using the same verse from class with a different idea or coming up with their own. For a real twist, get students to listen to one of their parents' songs and rewrite it from their own viewpoint!

BECOME A HIP-HOP LYRICAL GENIUS

Song lyrics can come from anywhere—from things we say, things our friends say, even from having a deadline to hand in an assignment. For this exercise, we're going to take one line from an existing song and turn it into an all-new song—well, an *almost* all-new song.

Here is my sample line:

_____

_____

from the song _____ by _____
(Don't forget to give props to the masters!)

Now, use that line in a poem or song of your own. It can be the title, the line that starts your song, the line that closes it, or a chorus that the poem or song keeps coming back to. Use the back of the page if you need more space. Most importantly, try to add your own ideas to the sample—if people wanted to hear the original song, they can always just run to a record store and buy the album! Make them buy yours instead!

_____

_____

_____

_____

_____

_____

_____

_____

_____

_____

_____

_____

_____

_____

_____

_____

TALL TALES AND SHORT STORIES
by STEVE ALMOND

1 hour
Materials: Index cards, lollipops

There are two competing impulses when you're writing. One is the feeling that everything you do is awful, and when that takes over, you get writer's block. The other is the unchecked belief that everything you do is great. This exercise tries to shoot the gap between the two, by bringing things back down to earth and lowering the stakes. When you tell students to write fiction it's kind of crushing—such a grandiose mandate. This exercise turns that mandate into play. You're just trying to fool some people, not write *the* great american short story.

Start by passing out 3x5 index cards. Instruct the students to write down three strange and unusual facts about themselves. Two must be lies. One must be true.

> *"I once fell down a waterfall."*
> *"I sat on Jerry Garcia's lap."*
> *"I've seen Kevin Costner in his underwear."*

One by one, the students read their three strange facts aloud and then face an interrogation session. The class gets five minutes to ask questions, trying to figure out which of the statements is true. "How big was the waterfall? Did you get hurt?" "Where did you meet Jerry Garcia? What did he smell like?" "Boxers or tighty-whities?" Meanwhile, the student in the hot seat lies as best he can (like a good politician), trying to keep the class from spotting the fakes.

Some tips for beginning liars: You shouldn't make everything up. Pull some details from real life, from something that happened to your cousin, or that you read about in the paper. Believe it or not, this is how stories usually get started. I hear some strange true story, and I start thinking "And then what? And then what?"—trying to come up with background, imagining the scene.

To make the exercise more interesting you can keep score, having students vote for the statement they think is true, and rewarding the student who fools the most people. I usually provide suckers for the winner. (Get it?)

After a little while the students start to notice things. They see what makes a story believable and what rings false. A short story is just an elaborate improvised lie, and the way you establish its veracity is by including lots of compelling details. You have to sound very sure of them and you have to be loose enough to just riff. This game jump-starts your lying faculties.

Once we're warmed up we get down to work. For the second part of the exercise, students turn one of their statements into a short story. It can be true or false, as long as it's interesting. Hopefully, the interrogation allowed them to figure out which of their statements was most compelling. What story was the easiest to elaborate on? Which one got the biggest reaction? What made them jump out of their seats? Write about that.

WELCOME TO THE FUNHOUSE: WRITING FUNNY SCENES

by MARK O'DONNELL

12 hours

This class proves that anyone can learn to write funny scenes. Each week, we practice writing a different comedy scenario. Try these out with your students and in no time at all your class will be a regular Friars' Club. Thank you! I'll be here all week!

We get in the mood with some funny viewing and reading. We start with video clips of Daffy Duck, W.C. Fields, John Leguizamo, *The Kids in the Hall*, *Strangers with Candy*, *The Upright Citizens' Brigade*, *Monty Python and the Holy Grail*, and *Raising Arizona*.

We follow up by reading aloud from Chekhov's "The Evils of Tobacco," Robert Frost's "Grass," Philip Larkin's "This Be the Verse," W. H. Auden's "As Poets Have Mournfully Sung," Frank O'Hara's "Lana Turner Has Collapsed," Bob and Ray, Bruce McCall, and Steve Martin, and, if they're willing, the submissions of several brave and instantly popular students themselves.

Once we're warmed up we get to work writing the following scenarios.

Scenario One: The Great Made Small, the Small Made Great

You're pretty much guaranteed laughs when you make a mountain out of a molehill or vice versa. Reduce an epic! Conversely, make a big anguished deal over a triviality. Make a fairy tale repulsive. Parody anything pretentious. Imagine the royal family getting drunk; Lilliput having a military parade, or a wart in Brobdingnag; the Plumber of the Year Award ceremony; The Royal Order of Raccoons; *Star Trek's U.S.S. Enterprise* as a revolving seafood restaurant on *SNL*; a Kid in the Hall anguishing over his missing ballpoint pen; *South Park's* mayor, teachers, and Jesus; Zeus's furtive affairs; *Monsterpiece Theater*; chimpanzees reenacting *Titanic*; people fighting over a turnip.

Suggested reading: anything from *The Onion*; James Thurber's *Fables for Our Times*; Charles Portis's *Masters of Atlantis*; P.J. O'Rourke's *Give War a Chance* and *Holidays in Hell*; *Candide*; *Don Quixote*.

Assignment: Write the script for a news report that either makes a huge deal out of a little event ("Area Man Can't Decide Between Vanilla and Chocolate") or deflates a huge story ("End of World Announced: Details to Follow 11:00 Rerun of Friends").

Scenario Two: A Tale Told by an Idiot

Here, the speaker is unaware of his own awfulness or stupidity. Maybe he's a boor. Maybe she's a terrible snob. Either way, their complete lack of self-awareness makes for some great material. Think of Ring Lardner's senile teller of "The Golden Honeymoon" and the dizzy teen of "I Can't Breathe"; Charles Portis's stoic cowboy Norwood; Eudora Welty's "Why I Live at the P.O."; Twain's naïf narrator of *Huckleberry Finn*.

Suggested viewing: *Gentlemen Prefer Blondes*, *The Search for Intelligent Life in the Universe*.

Assignment: Write a scene in which a completely clueless person holds a position of power.

Scenario Three: The Wrong Person for the Job

Competence is not funny. Instead, get a load of Inspector Clouseau, Tom Sawyer, a skunk who thinks he's a great lover, well-bred gophers, a clumsy dentist, a mad psychiatrist, Monty Python's harmless Inquisitors ("The comfy chair!"). Think antiheroics and silly villains: Austin Powers; Dudley Do-Right; Don Quixote, the moronic messengers in *Dumb & Dumber*; or Gilbert and Sullivan's *Pirates of Penzance*, who are, in fact, nice.

Suggested viewing: *Take the Money and Run*, *The Pink Panther*

Assignment: Write a scene about someone who takes on a job they're completely unqualified for—an irresponsible guidance counselor, a skittish bomb squad expert, etc.

Scenario Four: Overlooking the Obvious

"Er—I don't see any elephant!" Ignoring the unignorable is usually pretty entertaining. Think Ingrid Bergman in *Gaslight*—he's clearly trying to kill her, but she doesn't notice. The new ambassador is a gorilla,

Godzilla's in the bedroom, the cat is in the goldfish bowl. Also funny: complete denial (ironing during the apocalypse, chatting as the Titanic sinks) and selfishness without self-awareness (saving the Pekinese but not the children).

Assignment: Write a scene in which somebody is missing something huge that's completely obvious to the reader.

Scenario Five: The Monkey in the Palace of Heaven

As per the Chinese folk tale, order leads to disaster. In Native American myth, Coyote messes up the gods' orderly rows of stars to create our splashy Milky Way. Things fall apart; chaos runs roughshod over stuffed shirts. Think of Eddie Murphy at an Embassy Ball, the Three Stooges in the courtroom, Bugs Bunny doing Wagner's *Ring* Cycle, Jim Carrey in *Dumb & Dumber*, The Blues Brothers destroying an entire mall, *A Connecticut Yankee in King Arthur's Court*, a dog on the table, a dull orchestra learning to swing it.

Suggested viewing: *Dumb & Dumber, Animal House, A Night at the Opera*

Assignment: Set up an important scene (wedding, formal poetry reading, surgery, etc.) and then have everything descend into chaos.

Scenario Six: Defending the Preposterous

Sticking to your guns can be very amusing when your guns are completely and obviously wrong. Best is deadpan nonsense: You say that *Bikini Beach Bingo* is the best movie every made? Satan is a sweetheart? Lassie was a human in a suit? Your neighbor is sending solar-derived brainwaves to drive you mad so he can steal your spoons? Shooting fish in a barrel is actually very difficult? People over age ninety go through a "rebel" phase? Barney is a menace to children? There are aliens in your soup? Tell us more!

Suggested reading: Robert Benchley's "Treasurer's Report," Jorge Luis Borges' *Ficciones*

Assignment: Write a scene in which a character defends a ridiculous idea (e.g., all dogs and cats are secretly married) with careful logic.

Scenario Seven: Slang and Language

This is the poetry of comedy. It can be highbrow (Bertie Wooster's "That's exerting the old cerebellum, Jeeves!") or low- (Bill and Ted's righteous, bodacious surfer-ese, *Wayne's World's* "babe-osity"). Think of beatnik slang, teen talk, hip-hop argot, workplace lingo ("Adam and Eve on a raft, wreck 'em!").

Assignment: Write a scene in which all the dialogue is slang. It can be real, or you can make it up.

Scenario Eight: Confusion, Delusion, and Mistaken Identity

We know something they don't know. The duchess is mistaken for a maid, the bum for a billionaire, the gay man for the straight, Jack Lemmon and Tony Curtis in *Some Like It Hot*. Think of *The Comedy of Errors*, *Twelfth Night*, *Much Ado About Nothing*, and just about every episode of *Three's Company*. The possibilities are endless: A vain man thinks an indifferent woman loves him. The spies are after the wrong guy. Someone isn't as smooth as he thinks he is.

Suggested viewing: *The Gods Must Be Crazy*

Assignment: Write a scene in which trouble follows when someone either misunderstands or refuses to believe what the situation really is (e.g., "I'd be scared of this burning building if it weren't a hologram!").

Scenario Nine: Things Happen Too Fast

A relationship begins, grows, and ends in the space of an elevator ride; human history happens at a lightning pace. Think of the Marx Brothers, the Keystone Kops, any farce. The action fast-forwards or jump-cuts. Allegiances change in a second if money, love, or violence enter into negotiations.

Suggested reading: Martin Amis's *Time's Arrow*

Assignment: Show a romance begin, grow, and fail in one minute; or, show us fifty years of a family epic in two minutes.

Scenario Ten: Ridiculous Ambition

Show tiny people with godlike projects. Greed and competition escalate among idiots or even geniuses. Think of *Pinky and the Brain*, *Dexter's Laboratory*, Spongebob's Plankton nemesis, *Yertle the Turtle*, the highfalutin' *poseur* brothers Niles and Frazier on *Frazier*, any game show, all money-grubbing inheritance farces. This is the small made great, the great made small again.

Suggested viewing: *The Adventures of Baron Munchausen*; *Time Bandits*; *It's a Mad, Mad, Mad, Mad World*; Blake Edwards's *The Great Race*

Assignment: Write a scene about a fool with a cosmic plan.

Scenario Eleven: Exaggeration/Grotesque

This is cartoonish comedy: caricatures, grossouts, tall tales, bad luck surpassing belief. Think of Homer Simpson's thickheadedness, or Itchy and Scratchy's horrific overkill; Monty Python; *Sunset Boulevard* and *Whatever Happened to Baby Jane*. Write hyperbolically. Characters aren't just dumb, but the dumbest people in the world; not simply poor, but so hard-up they live in a puddle, carve a pea into fifths, or eat pictures of food. Imagine the wildly fidgety man at an auction; the glutton who literally explodes in *Monty Python's Meaning of Life*; a really, really dense cowpoke in the city; an impossibly prudish aunt.

Suggested viewing: *Strangers with Candy*

Assignment: Write a scene about the dirtiest, or the cleanest, or the weirdest, or the richest, or the unluckiest, or the sweetest, people on earth.

Scenario Twelve: Try a Little Tenderness

Comedy can also be delivered with tenderness and strong, true emotion. Think Woody Allen's *Annie Hall*, *Radio Days*, and *Manhattan*; *Diner*, *When Harry Met Sally*, *Raising Arizona*, *My Life as a Dog*, *The Rules of the Game*, *The Truth About Cats and Dogs*; *Much Ado about Nothing*, *Twelfth Night*, *As You Like It*, and all of Chekhov.

Suggested reading: Frank O'Hara's *Lunch Poems*

Assignment: Write a tender and loving reminiscence about something dumb you did when you were younger, but survived.

LOOK, KIDS!
FREE BONUS SUGGESTIONS!

Parody

The best way to start. Write a parody of your favorite TV show, movie, novel, or play. The fastest short-cut to originality is imitation.

Kwik 'n' E-Z

Write a commercial, a game show, or a foolish trailer for a nonexistent movie.

Quirks and Annoying Habits

Write a scene about the world's worst guest, the nut on the subway, the compulsive liar, the giggling spinster.

Old Habits Die Hard

Nature will out; beasts will be beasts. Write a scene about the impatient man (Yosemite Sam, say) trying to hold his temper, the lady on the Titanic lifeboat wondering when the Funny Hats contest will resume, the gentleman being dainty while the cannibals cook him.

An Idiot Con Man

He wants to cheat you, but his ploy, disguise and alibi are all obvious and lousy. Think *Dirty Rotten Scoundrels*. Write a scene in which he gets his just desserts.

Look Down on Everyone

Write a scene in which everyone is bad, or even the virtuous are stupid and ridiculous.

The Dopey-of-the-Seven-Dwarves Syndrome

Include one character who just doesn't get it: the out-of-sync dancer, the hungry fool at the philosophers' salon, the high-strung guy in Shangri La, the drunk who doesn't notice the earthquake. Think Penny in John Waters's *Hairspray*: "I got a nosebleed!" "I missed the bus!"

APPENDIX

WRITERS' PROOFS

A few years ago, 826 Valencia asked dozens of professional writers if they would loan us original proofs from their work. The idea was to show young writers how much effort goes into any given story or book or poem, to make clear how much revision even the most seasoned writers require. Many writers responded, sending us proofs full of their own handwritten marks and those of their editors, which are now framed and hanging on the walls of our writing lab. We invite you to stop by to view the full collection. In the meantime, we've included a few samples for you here. Share them with your students, and tell them that the next time they get a marked-up paper back, they can feel like real writers. They are!

Chabon--Kavalier & Clay

1

Among the dreams of escape engendered by the German occupation was a plan

to send the Golem of Prague into the safety of exile. The coming of the Nazis was

attended by rumors of confiscation, expropriation and plunder, in particular of Jewish

artifacts and sacred objects. The great fear of its secret keepers was that the Golem

would be packed up and shipped off to ornament some Institut or private collection in

Berlin or Munich. Already a pair of soft-spoken, keen-eyed young Germans, carrying

notebooks had spent the better part of two days nosing around the Old-New

Synagogue, in whose eaves legend had secreted the long-slumbering champion of the

ghetto. The men had claimed to be merely interested scholars without official ties to

the Reichsprotektorat, but this was disbelieved. Rumor had it that certain high-ranking

party members in Berlin were avid students of theosophy and the so-called occult. It

seemed only a matter of time before the Golem was discovered, in its giant pine casket,

in its dreamless sleep, and seized.

There was, in the circle of its keepers, a certain amount of resistance to the idea

of sending the Golem abroad, even for its own protection. Some argued that since it

had originally been formed of the mud of the River Moldau, it might well suffer physical

degradation when removed from its native climate and element. Those of a historical

bent--who like historians everywhere prided themselves on a level-headed sense of

perspective--reasoned that the Golem had already survived many centuries of invasion,

calamity, war and pogrom without being exposed or dislodged, and they counseled

Michael Chabon

Chabon is the Berkeley-based author of many books, including Werewolves in Their Youth *and* Wonder Boys. *This is from* The Amazing Adventures of Kavalier and Clay, *which won the Pulitzer Prize.*

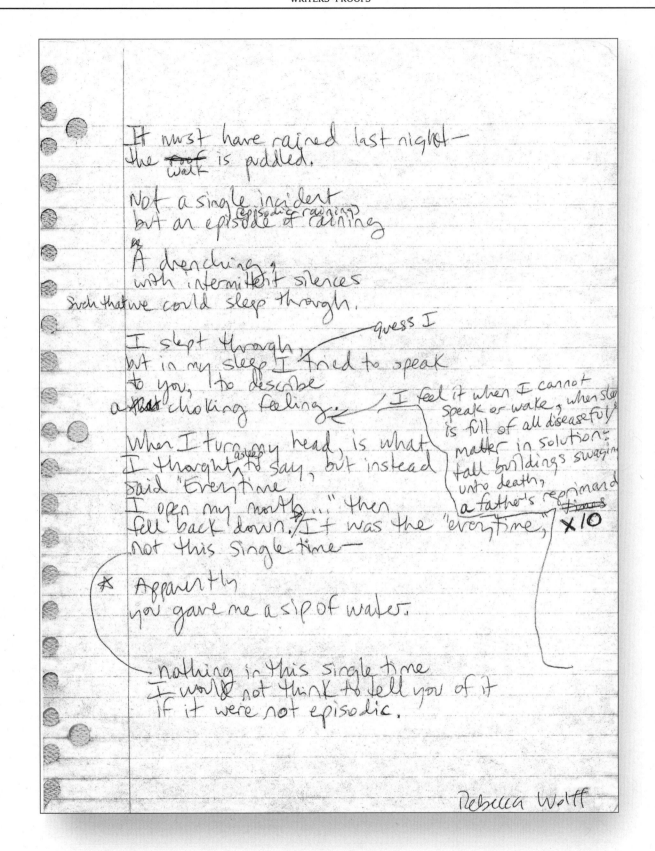

Rebecca Wolff

Wolff is the editor of Fence, *a literary quarterly magazine, and also a poet. Her collection,* Manderley: Poems *was published in 2001. This is a handwritten (duh) first draft.*

Waldman—MANDATORY 303

"Yes, and before. I'll write tomorrow," Elaine answered, doing her best to imitate her

daughter's measured tones.

"Okay." Olivia reached her free arm around her mother's waist and hugged her. Then she kissed her on the cheek. She kissed Arthur, too, and then held Luna out at arm's length.

"Mama's going bye bye, baby girl," she said. Luna kicked and smiled. "I will think of you every minute of every day. And I'll be back for you. Do you understand me? My darling baby, I will be back for you." Tears rolled down Olivia's face but her voice was firm and soft. She hugged the baby to her, and nestled her face in Luna's fat little skin. She inhaled deeply and pushed her lips into her yielding cheek, burying her mouth in her silken neck. Then, she handed Luna to Elaine, and turned to the door that the guard held open for her.

"Goodbye," Olivia said. She stepped through the door and it closed behind her with a final, permanent thud.

* * *

The week before Olivia's last day of freedom, Elaine had bought a plane ticket on Aeromexico for Leon, a city not too distant from San Miguel, the town in which Jorge's

Ayelet Waldman
Waldman has written a number of mysteries that mix intrigue and humor. This is a page from Waldman's novel.
The Mandatory Minimum, *about the absurdities of federal prosecution of first-time drug offenders.*

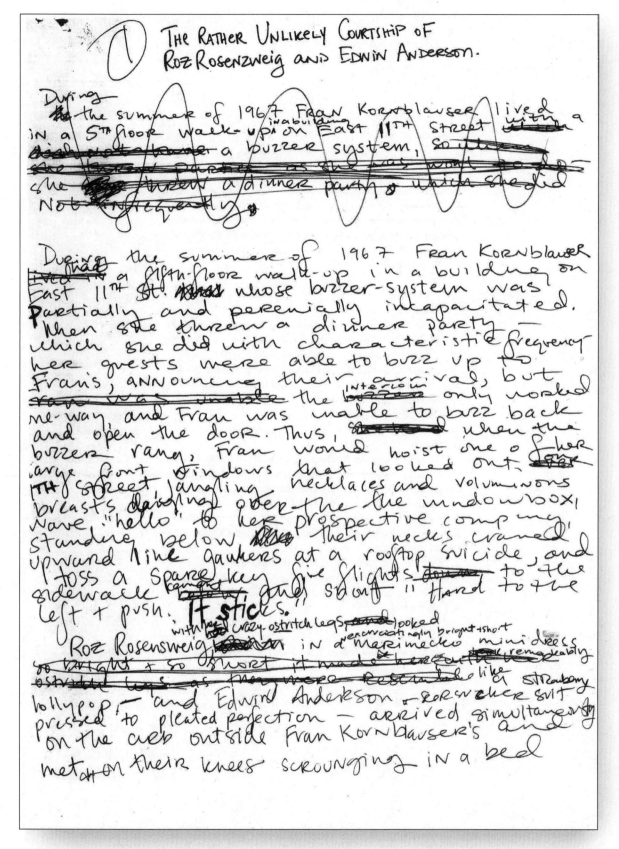

The Rather Unlikely Courtship of Roz Rosenzweig and Edwin Anderson.

During the summer of 1967 Fran Kornblauser lived in a building in a 5th floor walk-up on East 11th Street a buzzer system, so she threw a dinner party which she did not infrequently.

During the summer of 1967 Fran Kornblauser had a fifth-floor walk-up in a building on East 11th St. whose buzzer-system was partially and perenially incapacitated. When she threw a dinner party — which she did with characteristic frequency — her guests were able to buzz up to Fran's, announcing their arrival, but the interior buzzer only worked one-way and Fran was unable to buzz back and open the door. Thus, when the buzzer rang, Fran would hoist one of her large front windows that looked out, 11TH street, jangling necklaces and voluminous breasts dangling over the the windowbox, wave "hello" to her prospective company, standing below their necks craned upward like gawkers at a rooftop suicide, and toss a spare key five flights down to the sidewalk and shout "Hard to the left + push. It sticks."

Roz Rosensweig with her crazy ostrich legs looked excruciatingly bright + short in a marimecko mini dress so bright + so short it made her remarkably ostrich legs as they were like a strawberry lollypop — and Edwin Anderson + seersucker suit pressed to pleated perfection — arrived simultaneously on the curb outside Fran Kornblauser's and met on their knees scrounging in a bed

Thisbe Nissen

Nissen is the young author of The Great People of New York, *published in 2001. This is a hand-written first draft of a story called "The Rather Unlikely Courtship of Roz Rosenzweig and Edwin Anderson."*

short novel.2 1/31/02 3:11 AM Page 6

in Saskatechewan and just go from there. This decision felt good. ~~We'd been on the wrong track and now we were righted. We'd start in Africa and go from there. Or from Greenland. Greenland would make the most sense. Then, once there, we'd see what was~~ flying out, ideally somewhere warm, and then on from there.

"Visas," Hand said.

"What?"

"Visas."

"~~Back.~~"

Half the destinations were thrown out. Saskatchewan was fine but Rwanda and Yemen required visas. Mongolia needed one. Qatar, in a ludicrous show of hubris for a country the shape of a thumb, wanted a visa that would take a week to process. We were only a few days away from the week Hand had taken off work. He called. "Greenland doesn't want a visa."

"Okay. That's where we start."

"~~Good.~~"

"~~Good.~~"

The tickets were deadly cheap, about $400 each from O'Hare. Winter rates, ~~said the woman from GreenlandAir.~~ We signed on and got ready. Hand would drive down from Milwaukee and meet me in Chicago on the 16th, we'd hit the airport on the 17th together for the flight, which stopped first in Ottawa, then at Iqaluit (on Baffin Island), then Kangerlussuaq (no idea) sometime around midnight.

We'd decided ~~mutually~~ to limit the baggage to one each— nothing checked, nothing awaited or lost. It was good to think of only one bag, a small one, a standard backpack. We'd wear most of what we had.

"Coats?" asked Hand.

"No," I said. "Layers."

It was freezing in Chicago so we'd head to the airport in everything we brought and ~~just~~ lose it all if we ever made it

6

Dave Eggers

Eggers is the Bay Area author of A Heartbreaking Work of Staggering Genius *and* How We Are Hungry, *a collection of short stories. This is a proof from his novel* You Shall Know Our Velocity.

ELEMENTARY SCHOOL EVALUATION RUBRIC

	STRUCTURE		STYLE	GRAMMAR & USAGE
	Nonfiction	**Fiction**		
GREAT	• Clearly expresses a main idea • Points are well supported • Shows evidence of strong research • Points flow logically from paragraph to paragraph • Has a strong conclusion	• Setting, characters and plot are vibrant, rounded, and connected • Story has strong imaginative fictional elements • Action flows logically or naturally • Dialogue is strong • Ending is effective and fitting	• Includes lots of descriptive detail • Writing reflects a unique voice • Word choice is inventive and appropriate	• Uses advanced punctuation, like semicolons and dashes • Harder words are spelled and used correctly • Sentences are complete and don't run on
GOOD	• Expresses a main idea, but occasionally wanders off • Points are sometimes supported • Shows evidence of some research • Uses paragraphs, though transitions may be rough • Has a definite conclusion, but may end on a weak note	• Setting, characters, and plot are fairly well rounded but underdeveloped or disconnected at points • Story has some imaginative fictional elements • Dialogue is present and fairly strong • Ending is present but may feel somewhat sudden or disjointed	• Includes some descriptive detail • Words are well chosen	• Uses advanced punctuation, like semicolons and dashes • Harder words are spelled and used correctly • Sentences are complete and don't run on
BASIC	• Doesn't express a main idea • Statements lack development or support • Shows no evidence of research • No paragraphs • Conclusion is weak or missing	• Story features characters, setting and a plot but they may not be developed or connected • Story lacks imaginative elements • Little or no dialogue • Ending is missing or very abrupt	• Includes little descriptive detail • Word choice is basic	• Many words are spelled or used incorrectly • Lacks punctuation or capitalization • Sentences may be fragmented • Writing is hard to read

MIDDLE SCHOOL EVALUATION RUBRIC

	STRUCTURE		STYLE	GRAMMAR & USAGE
	Nonfiction	**Fiction**		
GREAT	• Sticks closely to topic • Topic is inventive and original • Organization is strong and apparent • Ideas are well supported • Ideas flow logically from paragraph to paragraph • Has a strong conclusion	• Setting, characters, and plot are fully fleshed out, vibrant, and connected • Action flows logically or naturally • Dialogue is effective and believable • Ending is effective and fitting	• Includes lots of descriptive detail • Writing reflects a unique, consistent personal voice • Word choice is inventive and appropriate	• Uses advanced punctuation, like semicolons and dashes • Advanced words are spelled correctly • Sentence structure is varied
GOOD	• Has a fairly strong thesis and sticks to it somewhat • Organization is apparent and generally strong, with some weaker points • Uses paragraphs, though transitions may be rough • Has a definite conclusion, but may end on a weak note	• Setting, characters, and plot are fairly well rounded but underdeveloped or disconnected at points • Dialogue is generally strong with some weak spots • Ending is fairly strong but may feel somewhat sudden or disjointed	• Includes some descriptive detail • Writing may reflect a personal voice but it may not be consistent • Word choice is occasionally inventive	• Uses correct punctuation • Most words are spelled correctly • Sentences are complete
BASIC	• Lacks a strong thesis • Organization is weak • Expresses feelings and ideas, but may not have development or support • Little or no use of paragraphs • Conclusion is weak or missing	• Story features characters, setting and a plot but they may not be developed or connected • Dialogue is lacking or unrealistic • Ending is missing or very abrupt	• Includes little descriptive detail • Personal voice is weak or inconsistent • Word choice is flat or stale	• Many words are used or spelled incorrectly • Lacking punctuation in places • Sentences may be fragmented

HIGH SCHOOL EVALUATION RUBRIC

	STRUCTURE		STYLE	GRAMMAR & USAGE
	Nonfiction	**Fiction**		
GREAT	• Has a strong thesis and sticks closely to it • Topic is inventive and original • Organization is strong and apparent • Ideas are well supported and researched • Ideas flow logically from paragraph to paragraph • Has a strong conclusion	• Setting, characters, and plot are fully fleshed out, vibrant and connected • Action flows logically or naturally • May have multiple subplots • May use symbolism or subtext • Dialogue is effective and believable • Ending is effective and fitting	• Includes lots of descriptive detail • Writing reflects a unique, consistent personal voice • May experiment successfully with different styles, like stream-of-consciousness or magic realism • Word choice is inventive and appropriate	• Uses advanced punctuation, like semicolons and dashes • Advanced words are spelled correctly • Sentence structure is varied and complex
GOOD	• Has a thesis and sticks to it most of the time • Organization is apparent and generally strong, • Ideas are sometimes supported and researched • Uses paragraphs, though transitions may be rough • Has a definite conclusion, but may end on a weak note	• Setting, characters and plot are fairly well rounded but underdeveloped or disconnected at points • May have a subplot • Dialogue is generally strong with some weak spots • Ending may feel sudden or disjointed	• Includes some descriptive detail • Writing may reflect a personal voice that is strong at times • Word choice is occasionally inventive	• Uses correct punctuation • Most words are spelled correctly • Sentences are complete
BASIC	• Has a topic, though may wander off • Organization is weak • Expresses feelings and ideas, but may not have development or support • Little or no use of paragraphs • Conclusion is weak or missing	• Story features characters, setting, and a plot but they may not be developed or connected • Dialogue may sound unnatural • Ending is missing or very abrupt	• Includes little descriptive detail • Personal voice is weak or inconsistent • Word choice is flat or stale	• Words are frequently misspelled • Punctuation is occasionally misused • Sentences may be fragmented

ELEMENTARY SCHOOL
SELF-ASSESSMENT CHECKLIST

☐ I showed that I know a lot about my topic.

☐ I expressed what I think and feel.

☐ My paper has a main idea.

☐ My ideas are supported.

☐ My paper has paragraphs that flow from one idea to the next.

☐ My paper has a beginning, middle, and end.

☐ I spelled words correctly. When I didn't know how to spell a word, I looked it up.

☐ I used punctuation correctly.

☐ My sentences are complete.

☐ I capitalized words correctly.

☐ I included descriptive details.

☐ I used colorful, energetic, meaningful words instead of bland words like *nice*.

☐ I had fun writing it!

MIDDLE SCHOOL
SELF-ASSESSMENT CHECKLIST
NONFICTION

☐ My paper has an inventive, original topic.

☐ My paper sticks closely to the topic idea.

☐ My introduction draws the reader in.

☐ My paper is well organized.

☐ My ideas are well supported.

☐ I show the reader that I know a lot about my topic.

☐ My ideas flow logically from paragraph to paragraph.

☐ I included a lot of descriptive detail.

☐ I used colorful, energetic words, instead of bland words like *nice*.

☐ I edited out hesitant words like *sort of* and *seems to*.

☐ I wrote in a unique personal voice.

☐ I used correct punctuation.

☐ I used some advanced punctuation, like semicolons and dashes.

☐ I spelled all the words correctly. When I didn't know how to spell something, I looked it up.

☐ There are no run-on sentences.

☐ My sentence structure is sometimes complex and varied.

☐ My paper has a strong conclusion.

☐ I proofread my paper.

MIDDLE SCHOOL
SELF-ASSESSMENT CHECKLIST
FICTION

☐ My introduction draws the reader in.

☐ My plot is well thought out and includes an introduction, climax, and conclusion .

☐ My characters are well rounded, believable, and interesting.

☐ The setting, characters, and plot are well integrated.

☐ The action flows logically or naturally.

☐ The dialogue is effective and believable.

☐ I included a lot of descriptive detail.

☐ I used colorful, energetic words, instead of bland words like *nice*.

☐ I used strong, active language instead of hesitant words like *sort of* and *seems to*.

☐ I wrote in a unique personal voice.

☐ I used correct punctuation.

☐ I used some advanced punctuation, like semicolons and dashes.

☐ I spelled all the words correctly. When I didn't know how to spell something, I looked it up.

☐ There are no run-on sentences.

☐ My sentence structure is sometimes complex and varied.

☐ My ending is strong and fitting.

☐ I proofread my story.

HIGH SCHOOL
SELF-ASSESSMENT CHECKLIST
NONFICTION

- ☐ My paper has a strong, original thesis.

- ☐ My paper sticks closely to my thesis.

- ☐ My introduction draws the reader in.

- ☐ My paper is well organized.

- ☐ My ideas are well supported.

- ☐ I show the reader that I researched my topic well.

- ☐ My ideas flow logically from paragraph to paragraph.

- ☐ I included a lot of descriptive detail.

- ☐ My word choice is inventive and appropriate.

- ☐ I used strong, active language instead of hesitant phrases like *sort of* and *seems to*.

- ☐ I wrote in a unique personal voice.

- ☐ I used correct punctuation.

- ☐ I used some advanced punctuation, like semicolons and dashes.

- ☐ I checked my spelling.

- ☐ There are no run-on sentences.

- ☐ My sentence structure is complex and varied.

- ☐ My paper has a strong conclusion that gives the reader something to think about.

- ☐ I proofread my paper.

HIGH SCHOOL
SELF-ASSESSMENT CHECKLIST
FICTION

- ☐ My introduction draws the reader in.

- ☐ My plot is well thought out and includes an introduction, climax, and conclusion .

- ☐ My characters are well rounded, believable, and interesting.

- ☐ The setting, characters and plot are well integrated.

- ☐ The action flows logically or naturally.

- ☐ My story may have multiple subplots.

- ☐ My story may use symbolism or subtext.

- ☐ The dialogue is effective and believable.

- ☐ My story might experiment with different techniques, like magic realism or stream-of-consciousness.

- ☐ I included a lot of descriptive detail.

- ☐ My word choice is inventive and appropriate. I avoid bland words like *nice*.

- ☐ I used strong, active language instead of hesitant phrases like *sort of* and *seems to*.

- ☐ I wrote in a unique personal voice.

- ☐ I used correct punctuation.

- ☐ I used some advanced punctuation, like semicolons and dashes.

- ☐ I checked my spelling.

- ☐ There are no run-on sentences.

- ☐ My sentence structure is complex and varied.

- ☐ The ending is effective and fitting.

- ☐ I proofread my story.

STANDARDS FOR THE ENGLISH LANGUAGE ARTS
SPONSORED BY THE NATIONAL COUNCIL OF TEACHERS OF ENGLISH
& THE INTERNATIONAL READING ASSOCIATION

The vision guiding these standards is that all students must have the opportunities and resources to develop the language skills they need to pursue life's goals and to participate fully as informed, productive members of society. These standards assume that literacy growth begins before children enter school as they experience and experiment with literacy activities—reading and writing, and associating spoken words with their graphic representations. Recognizing this fact, these standards encourage the development of curriculum and instruction that make productive use of the emerging literacy abilities that children bring to school. Furthermore, the standards provide ample room for the innovation and creativity essential to teaching and learning. They are not prescriptions for particular curriculum or instruction. Although we present these standards as a list, we want to emphasize that they are not distinct and separable; they are, in fact, interrelated and should be considered as a whole.

1. Students read a wide range of print and non-print texts to build an understanding of texts, of themselves, and of the cultures of the United States and the world; to acquire new information; to respond to the needs and demands of society and the workplace; and for personal fulfillment. Among these texts are fiction and nonfiction, classic and contemporary works.

2. Students read a wide range of literature from many periods in many genres to build an understanding of the many dimensions (e.g., philosophical, ethical, aesthetic) of human experience.

3. Students apply a wide range of strategies to comprehend, interpret, evaluate, and appreciate texts. They draw on their prior experience, their interactions with other readers and writers, their knowledge of word meaning and of other texts, their word identification strategies, and their understanding of textual features (e.g., sound-letter correspondence, sentence structure, context, graphics).

4. Students adjust their use of spoken, written, and visual language (e.g., conventions, style, vocabulary) to communicate effectively with a variety of audiences and for different purposes.

5. Students employ a wide range of strategies as they write and use different writing process elements appropriately to communicate with different audiences for a variety of purposes.

6. Students apply knowledge of language structure, language conventions (e.g., spelling and punctuation), media techniques, figurative language, and genre to create, critique, and discuss print and non-print texts.

7. Students conduct research on issues and interests by generating ideas and questions, and by posing problems. They gather, evaluate, and synthesize data from a variety of sources (e.g., print and non-print texts, artifacts, people) to communicate their discoveries in ways that suit their purpose and audience.

8. Students use a variety of technological and information resources (e.g., libraries, databases, computer networks, video) to gather and synthesize information and to create and communicate knowledge.

9. Students develop an understanding of and respect for diversity in language use, patterns, and dialects across cultures, ethnic groups, geographic regions, and social roles.

10. Students whose first language is not English make use of their first language to develop competency in the English language arts and to develop understanding of content across the curriculum.

11. Students participate as knowledgeable, reflective, creative, and critical members of a variety of literacy communities.

12. Students use spoken, written, and visual language to accomplish their own purposes (e.g., for learning, enjoyment, persuasion, and the exchange of information).

Standards for the English Language Arts, by the International Reading Association and the National Council of Teachers of English, copyright 1996 by the International Reading Association and the National Council of Teachers of English. Reprinted with permission

Elementary School Standards	Students adjust their use of spoken, written, and visual language (e.g., conventions, style, vocabulary) to communicate effectively with a variety of audiences and for different purposes.	Students employ a wide range of strategies as they write and use different writing process elements appropriately to communicate with different audiences for a variety of purposes.	Students apply knowledge of language structure, language conventions (e.g., spelling and punctuation), media techniques, figurative language, and genre to create, critique, and discuss print and non-print texts.	Students conduct research on issues and interests by generating ideas and questions, and by posing problems. They gather, evaluate, and synthesize data from a variety of sources (e.g., print and non-print texts, artifacts, people) to communicate their discoveries in ways that suit their purpose and audience.
Writing for Pets	●	●	●	
How to Be a Detective	●	●	●	●
Message in a Bottle	●	●	●	
Best Imaginary Vacation Ever!			●	
A Thousand Words	●	●	●	●
How to Write a Comic	●	●	●	●
Make-Believe Science	●	●	●	●
Everyone's a Comedian	●	●	●	
If I Were a King or Queen	●	●	●	●
Word Portraiture	●	●	●	●
Oh, You Shouldn't Have, Really…			●	●
Body Language	●	●	●	●
Kid Café			●	●
Spy School	●	●	●	●

	Students use a variety of technological and information resources (e.g., libraries, databases, computer networks, video) to gather and synthesize information and to create and communicate knowledge.	Students develop an understanding of and respect for diversity in language use, patterns, and dialects across cultures, ethnic groups, geographic regions, and social roles.	Students participate as knowledgeable, reflective, creative, and critical members of a variety of literacy communities.	Students use spoken, written, and visual language to accomplish their own purposes (e.g., for learning, enjoyment, persuasion, and the exchange of information).
Writing for Pets			●	●
How to Be a Detective	●		●	●
Message in a Bottle			●	●
Best Imaginary Vacation Ever!		●	●	●
A Thousand Words	●		●	●
How to Write a Comic		●	●	●
Make-Believe Science			●	●
Everyone's a Comedian			●	●
If I Were a King or Queen	●	●	●	●
Word Portraiture			●	●
Oh, You Shouldn't Have, Really…			●	●
Body Language		●	●	●
Kid Café			●	●
Spy School	●		●	●

Middle School Standards	Students adjust their use of spoken, written, and visual language (e.g., conventions, style, vocabulary) to communicate effectively with a variety of audiences and for different purposes.	Students employ a wide range of strategies as they write and use different writing process elements appropriately to communicate with different audiences for a variety of purposes.	Students apply knowledge of language structure, language conventions (e.g., spelling and punctuation), media techniques, figurative language, and genre to create, critique, and discuss print and non-print texts.	Students conduct research on issues and interests by generating ideas and questions, and by posing problems. They gather, evaluate, and synthesize data from a variety of sources (e.g., print and non-print texts, artifacts, people) to communicate their discoveries in ways that suit their purpose and audience.
Whining Effectively	●	●	●	●
Eat This Essay: Food Writing	●	●	●	●
Meet Your Protagonist!	●	●	●	●
Get Your Haiku On	●	●	●	●
Tiny Tales	●	●	●	●
How to Turn Lies into Literature	●	●	●	
Stories from the Year 3005	●	●	●	
Recess for Your Brain			●	●
I Wrote a Guidebook	●	●	●	●
Grammarama			●	●
Found Poetry	●	●	●	●
Laugh Your Headline Off	●	●	●	●
My Boring Life	●	●	●	●
How to Write a Mystery	●	●	●	●
Fightin' Words	●	●	●	●
Writing Through the Senses	●	●	●	●
The Story of Me	●	●	●	●
All Witnesses Die Eventually	●	●	●	●
In the Press Room	●	●	●	

	Students use a variety of technological and information resources (e.g., libraries, databases, computer networks, video) to gather and synthesize information and to create and communicate knowledge.	Students develop an understanding of and respect for diversity in language use, patterns, and dialects across cultures, ethnic groups, geographic regions, and social roles.	Students participate as knowledgeable, reflective, creative, and critical members of a variety of literacy communities.	Students use spoken, written, and visual language to accomplish their own purposes (e.g., for learning, enjoyment, persuasion, and the exchange of information).
Whining Effectively	●	●	●	●
Eat This Essay: Food Writing		●	●	●
Meet Your Protagonist!			●	●
Get Your Haiku On	●	●	●	●
Tiny Tales		●	●	●
How to Turn Lies into Literature			●	●
Stories from the Year 3005			●	●
Recess for Your Brain			●	●
I Wrote a Guidebook	●	●	●	●
Grammarama			●	●
Found Poetry		●	●	●
Laugh Your Headline Off	●	●	●	●
My Boring Life		●	●	●
How to Write a Mystery			●	●
Fightin' Words	●		●	●
Writing Through the Senses			●	●
The Story of Me		●	●	●
All Witnesses Die Eventually		●	●	●
In the Press Room				●

High School Standards	Students adjust their use of spoken, written, and visual language (e.g., conventions, style, vocabulary) to communicate effectively with a variety of audiences and for different purposes.	Students employ a wide range of strategies as they write and use different writing process elements appropriately to communicate with different audiences for a variety of purposes.	Students apply knowledge of language structure, language conventions (e.g., spelling and punctuation), media techniques, figurative language, and genre to create, critique, and discuss print and non-print texts.	Students conduct research on issues and interests by generating ideas and questions, and by posing problems. They gather, evaluate, and synthesize data from a variety of sources (e.g., print and non-print texts, artifacts, people) to communicate their discoveries in ways that suit their purpose and audience.
Details, Character, and Setting	●	●	●	●
Wicked Style & How to Get It	●	●	●	●
This Class Sucks	●	●	●	●
The Essay	●	●	●	●
Screenwriting	●	●	●	●
Magic Realism	●	●	●	●
Writing from Experience	●	●	●	●
826 Unplugged	●	●	●	●
Creating Characters	●	●	●	●
Sportswriting	●	●	●	●
Humor Writing	●	●	●	●
Homestyle	●	●	●	●
President Takes Martian Bride	●	●	●	●
The First Draft is My Enemy	●	●	●	●
Bad Writing	●	●	●	●
Look Smart Fast	●	●	●	●
Where Stories Come From	●	●	●	●
How Short is Short?	●	●	●	●
Word Karaoke	●	●	●	●
Tall Tales and Short Stories	●	●	●	●
Welcome to the Funhouse	●	●	●	●

	Students use a variety of technological and information resources (e.g., libraries, databases, computer networks, video) to gather and synthesize information and to create and communicate knowledge.	Students develop an understanding of and respect for diversity in language use, patterns, and dialects across cultures, ethnic groups, geographic regions, and social roles.	Students participate as knowledgeable, reflective, creative, and critical members of a variety of literacy communities.	Students use spoken, written, and visual language to accomplish their own purposes (e.g., for learning, enjoyment, persuasion, and the exchange of information).
Details, Character, and Setting	●		●	●
Wicked Style & How to Get It	●	●	●	●
This Class Sucks	●		●	●
The Essay			●	●
Screenwriting	●	●	●	●
Magic Realism			●	●
Writing from Experience		●	●	●
826 Unplugged	●	●	●	●
Creating Characters		●	●	●
Sportswriting	●		●	●
Humor Writing			●	●
Homestyle		●	●	●
President Takes Martian Bride	●	●	●	●
The First Draft is My Enemy	●		●	●
Bad Writing			●	●
Look Smart Fast		●	●	●
Where Stories Come From	●	●	●	●
How Short is Short?			●	●
Word Karaoke	●	●	●	●
Tall Tales and Short Stories		●	●	●
Welcome to the Funhouse	●	●	●	●

CONTRIBUTORS

Steve Almond is the author of two story collections, *My Life in Heavy Metal* and *The Evil B.B. Chow*, and the nonfiction book *Candyfreak*. He lives in Somerville and teaches at Boston College.

Jonathan Ames is the author of the novels *I Pass Like Night*, *The Extra Man*, and *Wake Up, Sir!*, and the essay collections *What's Not to Love?* and *My Less Than Secret Life*. He is the editor of *Sexual Metamorphosis: An Anthology of Transsexual Memoirs*. A new book of essays, *I Love You More Than You Know*, will be published in 2006. He is the winner of a Guggenheim Fellowship and is a former columnist for *New York Press*.

Christina Amini lives in the Bay Area and is an associate editor at Chronicle Books. She has written for *Salon*, *Bust*, *ReadyMade*, and the *Marin Independent Journal*. Her current favorite projects include working for a San Francisco–based Pep Talk Squad and co-publishing *Before the Mortgage*, a 'zine for those who aren't ready to settle.

Aimee Bender is the author of *The Girl in the Flammable Skirt*, *An Invisible Sign of my Own*, and the upcoming collection *Willful Creatures*. Her short fiction has been published in *GQ*, *The Paris Review*, *Tin House*, *McSweeney's*, and elsewhere, and she has been teaching various forms of creative writing for the past thirteen years to students aged four to seventy-five.

Brenna Burns is a writer, an artist, and an 826 Valencia speed-illustrator. Her writing can be found in *Inkpot*, *Bailliwik*, and a forthcoming issue of the *GW Review*. She holds an MFA from Cranbrook Academy of Art. Always a realist, she dreams about running away to join the postal service.

Nínive Calegari is the founding Executive Director of 826 Valencia. A classroom teacher for ten years, she is a graduate of the Harvard Graduate School of Education. She's the recipient of a NEH grant and the co-author of *Teachers Have It Easy: The Big Sacrifices and Small Salaries of America's Teachers*.

Meghan Daum is the author of the novel *The Quality of Life Report* and the essay collection *My Misspent Youth*. She has contributed to National Public Radio's *Morning Edition* and Public Radio International's *This American Life* and has written for numerous publications, including *The New Yorker*, *Harper's*, *GQ*, *Vogue*, *Self*, *New York*, *Radar*, *Black Book*, *Harper's Bazaar*, *The Village Voice*, and *The New York Times Book Review*. Meghan is a graduate of Vassar College and the MFA writing program at Columbia University's School of the Arts. She has taught at the California Institute for the Arts, and currently lives in Los Angeles.

Dave Eggers is the founder of 826 Valencia and *McSweeney's*. He is the author of *A Heartbreaking Work of Staggering Genius*, *You Shall Know Our Velocity!*, and *How We Are Hungry*, and co-author of *Teachers Have It Easy: The Big Sacrifices and Small Salaries of America's Teachers*.

Sophie Fels lives in Brooklyn. She does Bonnie Schiff-Glenn's bidding on all projects involving ice cream.

Nadia Gordon is the author of the Sunny McCoskey Napa Valley mystery series, including *Sharpshooter*, *Death by the Glass*, and *Murder Alfresco*, all published by Chronicle Books. Gordon lives in the San Francisco Bay Area, where she is currently at work on book four in the series.

Daphne Gottlieb is a San Francisco–based performance poet who stitches together the ivory tower and the gutter using just her tongue. She is the author of *Final Girl*, *Why Things Burn*, and *Pelt*, and the editor of *Homewrecker*. She is currently at work on *Jokes and the Unconscious*, a graphic novel with illustrator Diane DiMassa, and her fourth book of poetry.

Ryan Harty grew up in Arizona and northern California and graduated from UC Berkeley and the Iowa Writers' Workshop. His stories have appeared in numerous magazines and have been anthologized in *The Pushcart Prize* and *The Best American Short Stories*. He is a former Stegner Fellow and Jones Lecturer at Stanford University and the recipient of the Henfield-Transatlantic Review Award. His collection, *Bring Me Your Saddest Arizona*, won the 2004 John Simmons Short Fiction Award. He lives in San Francisco.

Noah Hawley is the author of the novels *A Conspiracy of Tall Men* and *Other People's Weddings*. He has published short fiction in *The Paris Review*. He wrote and directed the film *Being Vincent*. Another of his screenplays, *The Alibi*, will be released this year.

Angela Hernandez holds a B.A. from UC Berkeley and an M.A. from SUNY Buffalo. Currently pursuing another M.A. in education, Angela teaches severely emotionally disturbed teenagers. She's also been known to lead a kickboxing class or two.

Abigail Jacobs is a Bay Area native and has been a volunteer with 826 Valencia since the lab opened its doors in 2002. When she's not at 826, she is a public relations manager for Williams-Sonoma, Inc. She has co-taught the College Essay Writing workshop at 826 Valencia for the past three years and is the lead tutor on Sundays during drop-in sessions. In addition, she assists on the grant-writing committee.

Taylor Jacobson is a Bay Area native with a B.A. in creative writing. After several years of working in the restaurant industry and dabbling in graphic design, she and a friend started a silkscreen T-shirt line for women (www.mielefresca.com). She enjoys reading, food, film, and tutoring at 826 Valencia.

Emily Katz recently graduated from Bard College and is now living in San Francisco, writing and teaching writing to talented young students.

Dan Kennedy edits ReallySmallTalk.com, is the author of the book *Loser Goes First* (Random House/ Crown), and writes a column at *McSweeney's* in which he attempts to solve your problems with paper and paper-related products. Please send your classroom success stories or demands to cease and desist to dskmail@earthlink.net.

Susie Kramer is a fiction writer and teacher. Sometimes she writes about food for *The Oakland Tribune*, and she's working on a novel. Currently she teaches narrative storytelling at the Academy of Art College in San Francisco, where she lives with her husband.

Victoria Q. Legg is an abstract painter, writer of nonfiction and short fiction, and editor of a quarterly parent education newsletter. She thoroughly enjoys her work because of its marvelous blend of analytic and imaginative skill.

Hilary Liftin is the author of *Candy and Me: A Girl's Tale of Life, Love and Sugar* and the co-author of *Dear Exile: The True Story of Two Friends Separated (for a Year) by an Ocean*. She has also ghostwritten several books. She lives in Los Angeles with her husband, Chris Harris.

Erika Lopez is an art chick who wishes she had a scrap book of some of her favorite teachers—like the one who let her sew a life-sized doll when she was ten, and the other who insisted she was black. Erika had a few years there where she tried to catch up on her black history and was mad at her white mama for oppressing everyone.

Margaret Mason is a writer and editor living in San Francisco. Her work has appeared in the *New York Times*, the *Sacramento Bee*, and the *Dallas Morning News*. She publishes MightyGirl.com, her personal blog, and MightyGoods.com, a shopping blog, each of which draw several thousand readers a day. She is also a lifestyle columnist for *The Morning News*, a web magazine based in New York. Margaret has been a tutor at 826 Valencia since it opened.

Molly Meng is an 826 volunteer as well as a freelance artist and designer. She has created her own line of greeting cards, which she distributes under the name of 8mm ideas. Her work was included in the 2005 Artspan Benefit Auction and she has also sold her work through 12 Galaxies Gallery and several other independent boutiques in San Francisco.

Tony Millionaire's grandparents taught him to love and draw comics in the seaside town of Gloucester, Massachusetts. His comic strip *MAAKIES* appears weekly in *The Village Voice, The LA Weekly, The Chicago Reader, The Seattle Stranger* and many other newspapers. He has won numerous Eisner and Harvey Awards, including Best Syndicated Strip in 2004. He now lives in Pasadena, California with his wife and two daughters.

Tom Molanphy is English coordinator for the Academy of Art University in San Francisco. His fiction has been published by Colorado College Press, and his memoir of his two years in Belize teaching Mayans, *Following Mateo*, is available at www.followingmateo. com. He went to an all-boys Catholic prep school run by Hungarian monks in Texas for eight years, an experience he tried to forget by attending college in New Orleans. He received his MFA in creative writing from the University of Montana.

Lisa Morehouse began her career in education with Teach For America, first teaching middle school in rural Georgia and then opening the organization's Arizona office. This is her tenth year teaching English at San Francisco's Balboa High School.

Bita Nazarian is the assistant principal at James Lick Middle School in San Francisco. Prior to that, she was the instructional reform facilitator at Everett Middle School.

Erin Neeley is 826 Valencia's Program Director. Erin is an English and theater teacher. She has also served as an educational programs director for elders, and was once a semi-professional wrestler.

Amie E. Nenninger loves reading, writing, and problem solving, and she puts these skills to use daily as an educational and developmental tutor and 826 volunteer. After graduating from the University of Illinois, she taught with AmeriCorps in north-central Washington and was fortunate to attend graduate school in Sydney, Australia, through a Rotary Ambassadorial Scholarship. She enjoys fact-checking for *The Believer* magazine because it makes her feel a bit like a private investigator.

Risa Nye is a college counselor, writer, and Bay Area native. She is the author of *Road Scholar: An Investigative Journal for the College-Bound Student*, available through No Flak Press.

Mark O'Donnell received the 2003 Tony Award for *Hairspray*. His other plays include *That's It, Folks!*; *Fables for Friends*; *The Nice and the Nasty*; *Strangers on Earth*; *Vertigo Park*; and the book and lyrics for the musical *Tots in Tinseltown*. His books include *Elementary Education* and *Vertigo Park and Other Tall Tales*, as well as two novels, *Getting Over Homer* and *Let Nothing You Dismay* (both in Vintage paperback). His humor has appeared in *The New Yorker*, *The New York Times*, *The Atlantic*, and *Spy*, among others. He has received a Guggenheim Fellowship, the Lecomte du Nuoy Prize, and the George S. Kaufman Award.

Alvin Orloff began writing in 1978 as a lyricist for his best friend's punk band, the Blowdryers. Since then he has put out numerous zines and published two novels, *I Married an Earthling* and *Gutter Boys*, both from Manic D Press. He lives in San Francisco and is currently working on his third novel.

Kate Pavao is a freelance writer living in San Francisco with her husband, daughter, and two fluffy cats. She mostly writes for and about teens, though she hasn't been a teenager herself for a long time. Her poor eyesight would make her a very bad spy.

Chris Perdue has drawn on his experience teaching piano, guitar, and bass lessons for over five years to conduct songwriting workshops for 826 Valencia. When he's not busy teaching music or doling out his web design services to myriad arts and education organizations, this astute singer/songwriter can be found performing the dark and dreamy venues that define San Francisco's independent music scene.

Micah Pilkington is very proud to be a part of 826 Valencia. She works professionally in theater (as an actor and writer), film (as a minion), and the exciting world of copywriting and editing. Her work is being published this fall in *Defenestration*, a glamorous new journal.

Todd Pound fell into a string of fortunate collaborations with extremely talented people following his graduation from UCLA in 1993. At the animation studio Protozoa, he art-directed the (animated) presidential campaign for Garry Trudeau's *Doonesbury* character Uncle Duke. Todd has directed, designed, and storyboarded a variety of storytelling experiments, including many beautiful failures. He is currently developing two comic stories. When not drawing, he's watching his son giggle, his wife paint, and his dog shed.

Melissa Price began her literary career as a lowly editorial assistant for the legendary (and now defunct) *Partisan Review*. After weathering several New England winters, Price moved to partly sunny San Francisco, where she skyrocketed to obscurity working a series of thankless yet unrewarding administrative jobs. She lucked out and became reviews and then features editor for Sonicnet.com, which was eventually gobbled up by MTV. Her work has appeared on Salon; Soundbitten.com; CommonAssets.org; the late, great Suck.com; and on her own site, Slanted.com. She currently reviews books for the *San Francisco Chronicle* and is working on a book called *Advice for the Foodlorn*.

Kazz Regelman has written, and lived, all over. After graduating from Princeton University, she was a Fulbright scholar in Taiwan, the Tokyo correspondent for Variety, a scuba instructor in the Philippines, and a cook on Maui. Her first professional reviews were of films, published in *Variety*, but her earliest criticism was of her mother's cooking (dreadful, and even her mother admits it). Her work has appeared in the *Hollywood Reporter*, the *Boston Globe*, *Boys' Life*, the *San Francisco Bay Guardian*, and other publications. With thirty-six countries, five continents, five languages, four food-poisoning incidents, and one overseas hospital visit under her belt, she now lives and writes in San Francisco.

Jason Roberts is the author of the upcoming *The Gentleman in The Distance* (HarperCollins), an examination of the life of James Holman (1786-1857), the blind man who became history's greatest traveler. His previous publications include three books on technology and one that was, at least in part, about shaving and campfires.

Matthue Roth is a performance poet and novelist. His first book, *Never Mind the Goldbergs*, was just published by Scholastic. It's about an Orthodox Jewish punk-rock girl who moves to Hollywood to star on a TV sitcom. He keeps a secret online journal at www.matthue.com.

Bonnie Schiff-Glenn is a volunteer at 826NYC. She teaches first grade in Brooklyn Heights, and is currently pursuing a masters degree at Bank Street College of Education. In the past, she has been an editor and a rock musician. She thinks that first graders have a lot in common with writers and rock stars.

Jon Scieszka is the author of numerous children's books including *The True Story of the Three Little Pigs*, *The Stinky Cheese Man*, *Math Curse*, *Baloney*, and *Sam Samurai*. He lives in Brooklyn.

Laura Scholes is a freelance writer and editor in San Francisco. She has an MFA in fiction from the University of Montana and has recently completed her first novel. She makes a mean French toast.

J. Ryan Stradal holds a B.S. from Northwestern University. He used to work for VH1, MTV News, and various ABC programs. He's now working on a novel and volunteering/blogging for 826LA. He made his first fictional country at age twelve and continued drawing weird maps well into his adult life.

Maureen Sullivan teaches fourth and fifth grade in the Dual Immersion Program at Fairmount Elementary. An ex-ballerina, she is also a Bay Area Writer's Project teacher consultant and loves pirates.

Jenny Traig has a Ph.D. in English from Brandeis. She is the author of *Devil in the Details* as well as *Judaikitsch* and the Crafty Girl series.

Jason Turbow works for *The San Francisco Chronicle* and follows the San Francisco Giants with avid glee in his spare time.

Vendela Vida is the author of the novel *And Now You Can Go* and the nonfiction book *Girls on the Verge*, a journalistic study of female initiation rituals in America. She is co-editor of *The Believer* magazine and a founding board member and tutor at 826 Valencia.

Alvaro Villanueva is the in-house graphic designer and publishing director of 826 Valencia, production manager for *The Believer* magazine, and backup type consultant for *McSweeney's*. (He is a font nerd, basically.) He is forever grateful for the various twists of fate that have led him to be a publisher of children's writing.

Sarah Vowell is the author of *Assassination Vacation*, *The Partly Cloudy Patriot*, *Take the Cannoli*, and *Radio On*. She is also the voice of teenage superhero Violet Parr in Pixar Animation Studio's *The Incredibles*. She lives in New York City.

Doug Wilkins, professional goof-off, was the debate coach at Clovis High School when they won the California State Championship. He reads voraciously and writes occasionally. He currently operates the Sanchez Grotto Annex in the Castro District of San Francisco, where his office is the old laundry porch. His little dog Higgons keeps him company as he writes.

Marcy Zipke, a grad student in educational psychology, dabbles in dissertation writing, teaching, and freelance editing. Whole days go by in which she talks to no one older than eight years old. She teaches at Brooklyn College and works for Writing Across the Curriculum at Medgar Evers College. She lives with her husband in Brooklyn.

826 CENTERS & STAFF

826 VALENCIA

www.826valencia.org
Nínive Calegari, executive director
Leigh Lehman, programs director
Erin Neeley, programs director
Jory John, programs assistant
Tracy Barreiro, finance manager
Marta Martínez, national coordinator
Anna Ura, retail and special events director
Alvaro Villanueva, design and publishing director

826LA

www.826la.org
Pilar Perez, executive director
Amber Early, educational programs director
Claire Smith, volunteer coordinator
Mac Barnett, programs assistant

826NYC

www.826nyc.org
Scott Seeley, executive director
Joan Kim, director of education
Miriam Siddiq, program coordinator
Ted Thompson, events and publishing director
Julia White, education associate

826 CHICAGO

www.826chi.org
Leah Guenther, executive director
Mara O'brien, educational programs director

826 MICHIGAN

www.826michigan.org
Erin Bennett, executive director
Amy Sumerton, program director
John Snyder, volunteer coordinator

826 SEATTLE

www.826seattle.org
Teri Hein, executive director
Heidi Broadhead, operations manager

DROP US A LINE!

We'd love to hear from you. Use this form to send us your tips, anecdotes, suggestions, or just a howdy.

What's on your mind?

_____

_____

_____

_____

_____

_____

_____

_____

_____

_____

_____

_____

_____

_____

_____

_____

_____

_____

Also, please feel free to send us samples of student work created in response to these lesson plans.

If you have a favorite writing lesson plan you know belongs in this book, please send it to us; we would love include your great ideas in our 2007 edition of *Don't Forget to Write*. If we do publish your lesson, we'll make sure to send you a book.

Thanks for getting in touch!

Name:

Subject taught/Grade level/School:

Address:

E-mail:

826 VALENCIA
Don't Forget to Write
826 Valencia Street
San Francisco, California 94110